WEBSTER'S
Vocabulary Skill Builder

Created in Cooperation with the Editors of

MERRIAM-WEBSTER

FEDERAL
STREET
PRESS

A Division of Merriam-Webster, Incorporated

Springfield, Massachusetts

Printed in Canada

This 2017 edition published by
Federal Street Press,
a Division of Merriam-Webster, Incorporated
P.O. Box 281
Springfield, MA 01102

Federal Street Press books are available for
bulk purchase for sales promotions and premium use.
For details write the manager of special sales,
Federal Street Press, P.O. Box 281, Springfield, MA 01102

ISBN: 978-1-59695-173-0

1st Printing   Webcom, Toronto, ON   5/2017   PDPS

INTRODUCTION

Webster's Vocabulary Skill Builder is designed to achieve two goals: (1) to add a large number of words to your permanent working vocabulary, and (2) to teach the most useful of the classical word-building roots to help you continue expanding your vocabulary in the future.

To achieve these goals, *Webster's Vocabulary Skill Builder* employs an original approach that takes into account how people learn and remember. Some vocabulary builders simply present their words in alphabetical order; some provide little or no discussion of the words and how to use them; and a few even fail to show the kinds of sentences in which the words usually appear. But memorizing a series of random and unrelated things can be difficult and time-consuming. The fact is that we tend to remember words easily and naturally when they appear in some meaningful context, when they've been shown to be useful and therefore worth remembering, and when they've been properly explained to us. Knowing precisely how to use a word is just as important as knowing what it means.

Greek and Latin have been the sources of most of the words in the English language (the third principal source being the family of Germanic languages). All these words were added to the language long after the fall of the Roman empire, and more continue to be added to this day, with most new words—especially those in the sciences—still making use of Greek and Latin roots. A knowledge of Greek and Latin roots will not only help you remember the meanings of the words in this book but will help you guess at the meanings of new words that you run into elsewhere. Remember what a root means and you'll have at least a fighting chance of understanding a word in which it appears.

The roots in this book are only a fraction of those that exist, but they include almost all the roots that have produced the largest number of common English words. All these roots (sometimes called *stems*) formed parts of Greek and Latin words. Some are shown in more than one form (for example, CURR/CURS), which means that they changed form in the original language, just as *buy* and *bought* are forms of the same English word.

Each of the roots in this book is followed by four words based on the root. Each group of eight words (two roots) is followed by two quizzes. Every fifth group of words is a special eight-word section which may contain words based on classical mythology or history, words borrowed directly from Greek or Latin, or other special categories of terms. Each set of 40 words makes up a unit. In addition, the brief paragraphs discussing each word include in italics many words closely related to the main words. So mastering a single word (for example, *compel*) can increase your vocabulary by several words (in this case, *compelling*, *compulsion*, and *compulsive*).

The words presented here aren't all on the same level of difficulty—some are quite simple and some are truly challenging— but the great majority are words that could be encountered on the SAT and similar standardized tests. Most of them are in the vocabularies of well-educated Americans, including professionals such as scientists, lawyers, professors, and doctors. Even the words you feel familiar with may only have a place in your *recognition* vocabulary—that is, the words you recognize when you see or hear them but don't actually use in your own speech and writing.

Each main word is followed by its most common pronunciation. Any pronunciation symbols unfamiliar to you can be learned easily by referring to the Pronunciation Symbols table on page vii.

The definition comes next. We've tried to provide only the most common senses or meanings of each word, in simple and straightforward language, and no more than two definitions of any word are given. (A more complete range of definitions can be found in a college dictionary such as *Merriam-Webster's Collegiate Dictionary*.)

An example sentence marked with a bullet (•) follows the definition. This sentence by itself can indicate a great deal about the word, including the kind of sentence in which it often appears. It can also serve as a memory aid; when you meet the word in the future, you may recall the example sentence more easily than the definition.

An explanatory paragraph rounds out each entry. The paragraph may do a number of things: It may tell you what else you need to know in order to use the word intelligently and correctly, when the definition and example sentence aren't enough. It may tell you more about the word's roots and its history. It may discuss additional meanings or provide additional example sentences. It may demonstrate the use of closely related words. And it may provide an informative or entertaining glimpse into a subject related to the word. The intention is to make you as comfortable as possible with each word in turn and to enable you to start using it immediately, without fear of embarrassment.

The quizzes following each eight-word group, along with the review quizzes at the end of each unit, will test your memory. Many of them ask you to fill in a blank in a sentence. Others require you to identify *synonyms* (words with the same or very similar meaning) or *antonyms* (words with the opposite meaning). Perhaps most difficult are the *analogies*, which ask that you choose the word that will make the relationship between the last two words the same as the relationship between the first two. Thus, you may be asked to complete the analogy "calculate : count :: expend : _____" (which can be read as "*Calculate* is to *count* as *expend* is to _____") by choosing one of four words: *stretch*, *speculate*, *pay*, and *explode*. Since *calculate* and *count* are nearly synonyms, you will choose a near synonym for *expend,* so the correct answer is *pay*.

Studies have shown that the only way a new word will remain alive in your vocabulary is if it's regularly reinforced through use and through reading. Learn the word here and look and listen for it elsewhere; you'll probably find yourself running into it frequently, just as when you've bought a new car you soon realize how many other people own the same model.

Carry this book in your shoulder bag or leave it on your night table. Whenever you find yourself with a few minutes to spare, open it to the beginning of a brief root group. (There's no real need to read the units in any particular order, since each unit is entirely self-contained. However, studying the book straight through from the beginning will ensure that you make maximum use of it.) Pick a single word or a four-word group or an eight-word section; study it, test yourself, and then try making up new sentences for each word. Be sure to pronounce every new word aloud at least once, along with its definition.

Start using the words immediately. As soon as you feel confident with a word, start trying to work it into your writing wherever appropriate—your papers and reports, your diary and your poetry. An old saying goes, "Use it three times and it's yours." That may be, but don't stop at three. Make the words part of your *working* vocabulary, the words that you can not only recognize when you see or hear them but that you can comfortably call on whenever you need them. Astonish your friends, amaze your relatives, astound *yourself* (while trying not to be too much of a show-off)—and have fun!

Acknowledgments: The first edition of this book, written by Mary Wood Cornog, also benefited from the contributions of numerous members of the Merriam-Webster staff, including Michael G. Belanger, Brett P. Palmer, Stephen J. Perrault, and Mark A. Stevens. This new edition was edited by Mark A. Stevens, with assistance from C. Roger Davis.

PRONUNCIATION SYMBOLS

ə — banana, collide, abut

'ə, ˌə — humdrum, abut

ᵊ — immediately preceding \l\, \n\, \m\, \ŋ\, as in battle, mitten, eaten, and sometimes open \'ō-pᵊm\, lock and key \-ᵊŋ-\

ər — further, merger, bird

a — mat, map, mad, gag, snap, patch

ā — day, fade, date, aorta, drape, cape

ä — bother, cot

är — car, heart, bazaar, bizarre

aů — now, loud, out

b — baby, rib

ch — chin, nature \'nā-chər\

d — did, adder

e — bet, bed, peck

er — bare, fair, wear, millionaire

ē — easy, mealy

f — fifty, cuff

g — go, big, gift

h — hat, ahead

i — tip, banish, active

ir — near, deer, mere, pier

ī — site, side, buy, tripe

j — job, gem, edge, join, judge

k — kin, cook, ache

l — lily, pool

m — murmur, dim, nymph

n — no, own

ⁿ — indicates that a preceding vowel or diphthong is pronounced with the nasal passages open, as in French un bon vin blanc \œ̃ⁿ-bōⁿ-vaⁿ-bläⁿ\

ŋ — sing \'siŋ\, singer \'siŋ-ər\, finger \'fiŋ-gər\, ink\'iŋk\

ō — bone, know, beau

ȯ — saw, all, gnaw, caught

ȯi — coin, destroy

ȯr — boar, port, door, shore

p — pepper, lip

r — red, rarity

s — source, less

sh — as in shy, mission, machine, special

t — tie, attack, late, later, latter

th — as in thin, ether

th — then, either, this

ü — rule, youth, union \'yün-yən\, few \'fyü\

ů — pull, wood, book

ůr — boor, tour, insure

v — vivid, give

w — we, away

y — yard, young, cue \'kyü\, mute\ 'myüt\, union \'yün-yən\

z — zone, raise

zh — as in vision, azure \ 'a-zhər\

\ — backslash used in pairs to mark the beginning and end of a transcription: \'pen\

' — mark preceding a syllable with primary (strongest) stress: \'pen-mən-ˌship\

ˌ — mark preceding a syllable with secondary (medium) stress: \'pen-mən-ˌship\

- — mark of syllable division

UNIT

1

BENE is Latin for "well." A *benefit* is a good result or effect. Something *beneficial* produces good results or effects. The Latin root can be heard in other languages as well: "Good!" or "Fine!" in Spanish is "Bueno!"; in French, it's "Bon!"; and in Italian, just say "Bene!"

benediction \ˌbe-nə-ˈdik-shən\ A prayer that asks for God's blessing, especially a prayer that concludes a worship service.

• The moment the bishop had finished his benediction, she squeezed quickly out of her row and darted out the cathedral's side entrance.

In *benediction*, the *bene* root is joined by another Latin root, *dictio*, "speaking" (see DICT, p. 272), so the word's meaning becomes something like "well-wishing." Perhaps the best-known benediction is the so-called Aaronic Benediction from the Bible, which begins, "May the Lord bless you and keep you." An important section of the Catholic Mass was traditionally known as the *Benedictus*, after its first word (meaning "blessed"). It was St. *Benedict* who organized the first Christian monasteries; many Christians have been baptized Benedict in his honor, and 16 popes have taken it as their papal name.

benefactor \ˈbe-nə-ˌfak-tər\ Someone who helps another person or group, especially by giving money.

- An anonymous benefactor had given $15 million to establish an ecological institute at the university.

A benefactor may be involved in almost any field. One may endow a scholarship fund; another may give money to expand a library; still another may leave a generous sum to a hospital in her will. The famous *benefactions* of John D. Rockefeller included the gifts that established the University of Chicago, the Rockefeller Foundation, and Rockefeller University. Many benefactors have reported that giving away their money turned out to be the most rewarding thing they ever did.

beneficiary \ˌbe-nə-ˈfi-shē-ˌer-ē\ A person or organization that benefits or is expected to benefit from something, especially one that receives money or property when someone dies.

- Living in a trailer in near-poverty, she received word in the mail that her father had died, naming her as the sole beneficiary of his life-insurance policy.

Beneficiary is often used in connection with life insurance, but it shows up in many other contexts as well. A college may be the beneficiary of a private donation. Your uncle's will may make a church his sole beneficiary, in which case all his money and property will go to it when he dies. A "third-party beneficiary" of a contract is a person (often a child) who the people signing the contract (which is usually an insurance policy or an employee-benefit plan) want to benefit from it. In a more general way, a small business may be a beneficiary of changes to the tax code, or a restaurant may be the beneficiary when the one across the street closes down and its whole lunch crowd starts coming in.

benevolence \bə-ˈnev-ləns\ Kindness, generosity.

- In those financially desperate years, the young couple was saved only by the benevolence of her elderly great-uncle.

Part of *benevolence* comes from the Latin root meaning "wish." The novels of Charles Dickens often include a *benevolent* figure who rescues the main characters at some point—Mr. Brownlow in *Oliver Twist*, Abel Magwitch in *David Copperfield*, Mr. Jarndyce in Bleak House, Ebenezer Scrooge in *A Christmas Carol*. To be benevolent, it helps to have money, but it's not necessary; kind assistance of a non-financial sort may turn out to be lifesaving benevolence as well.

AM comes from the Latin *amare*, "to love." The Roman god of love was known by two different names, Cupid and *Amor*. *Amiable* means "friendly or good-natured," and *amigo* is Spanish for "friend."

amicable \\ˈa-mi-kə-bəl\\ Friendly, peaceful.

• Their relations with their in-laws were generally amicable, despite some bickering during the holidays.

Amicable often describes relations between two groups, or especially two nations—for example, the United States and Canada, which are proud of sharing the longest unguarded border in the world. So we often speak of an amicable meeting or an amicable settlement. When *amicable* describes more personal relations, it may indicate a rather formal friendliness. But it's always nice when two friends who've been quarreling manage to have an amicable conversation and to say amicable good-byes at the end.

enamored \\i-ˈna-mərd\\ Charmed or fascinated; inflamed with love.

• Rebecca quickly became enamored of the town's rustic surroundings, its slow pace, and its eccentric characters.

Computer hackers are always enamored of their new programs and games. Millions of readers have found themselves enamored with Jane Austen's novels. And Romeo and Juliet were, of course, utterly enamored of each other. But we also often use the word in negative contexts: A friend at work may complain that she's not enamored of the new boss, and when you start talking about how you're not enamored with the neighbors it may be time to move. (Note that both *of* and *with* are commonly used after *enamored*.)

amorous \\ˈa-mə-rəs\\ Having or showing strong feelings of attraction or love.

• It turned out that the amorous Congressman had gotten his girlfriend a good job and was paying for her apartment.

A couple smooching on a park bench could be called amorous, or a young married couple who are always hugging and kissing. But the word is often used a bit sarcastically, as when a tabloid newspaper gets hold of some scandalous photos and calls the participants "the amorous pair." In such cases, we may be encouraged to think the attraction is more physical than emotional.

paramour \\'per-ə-ˌmu̇r\ A lover, often secret, not allowed by law or custom.

- He had been coming to the house for two years before her brothers realized that he was actually the paramour of their shy and withdrawn sister.

Paramour came to English from French (a language based on Latin), though the modern French don't use the word. Since *par amour* meant "through love," it implies a relationship based solely on love, often physical love, rather than on social custom or ceremony. So today it tends to refer to the lover of a married man or woman, but may be used for any lover who isn't obeying the social rules.

Quizzes

A. Choose the closest synonym:

1. beneficiary   a. benefit   b. prayer   c. recipient
   d. contributor
2. amorous   a. friendly   b. sympathetic   c. loving   d. kind
3. benediction   a. blessing   b. gift   c. saint   d. favor
4. amicable   a. difficult   b. friendly   c. curious   d. lazy
5. enamored   a. strengthened   b. engaged   c. fond   d. free
6. benefactor   a. supporter   b. priest   c. donation
   d. kindness
7. paramour   a. lover   b. husband   c. heaven   d. affection
8. benevolence   a. value   b. kindness   c. luck   d. approval

B. Complete the analogy:

1. charming : enchanting :: amorous : _____
   a. sublime   b. pleasant   c. likeable   d. passionate
2. greeting : farewell :: benediction : _____
   a. motto   b. speech   c. curse   d. saying
3. lender : borrower :: benefactor : _____
   a. giver   b. beneficiary   c. participant   d. partner
4. gentle : tender :: enamored : _____
   a. lively   b. charmed   c. cozy   d. enraged
5. liking : appreciation :: benevolence : _____
   a. opinion   b. sentimentality   c. interest   d. generosity

6. frozen : boiling :: amicable : _____
    a. calm b. comfortable c. shy d. unfriendly
7. patient : doctor :: beneficiary : _____
    a. tycoon b. investor c. lover d. benefactor
8. friend : companion :: paramour : _____
    a. lover b. theater c. mother d. wife

BELL comes from the Latin word meaning "war." *Bellona* was the little-known Roman goddess of war; her husband, Mars, was the god of war.

---

antebellum \ˌan-ti-ˈbe-ləm\ Existing before a war, especially before the American Civil War (1861–65).

*   When World War I was over, the French nobility found it impossible to return to their extravagant antebellum way of life.

Even countries that win a war often end up worse off than they had been before, and the losers almost always do. So *antebellum* often summons up images of ease, elegance, and entertainment that disappeared in the postwar years. In the American South, the antebellum way of life depended on a social structure, based on slavery, that collapsed after the Civil War; Margaret Mitchell's *Gone with the Wind* shows the nostalgia and bitterness felt by wealthy Southerners after the war more than the relief and anticipation experienced by those released from slavery. In Europe, World War I shattered the grand life of the upper classes, even in victorious France and Britain, and changed society hugely in the space of just four years.

bellicose \ˈbe-li-ˌkōs\ Warlike, aggressive, quarrelsome.

*   The more bellicose party always got elected whenever there was tension along the border and the public believed that military action would lead to security.

Since *bellicose* describes an attitude that hopes for actual war, the word is generally applied to nations and their leaders. In the 20th century, it was commonly used to describe such figures as Germany's Kaiser Wilhelm, Italy's Benito Mussolini, and Japan's General Tojo, leaders who believed their countries had everything to gain by starting wars. The international relations of a nation with a bellicose foreign policy tend to be stormy and difficult, and *bellicosity* usually makes the rest of the world very uneasy.

belligerence \bə-ˈli-jə-rəns\ Aggressiveness, combativeness.

• The belligerence in Turner's voice told them that the warning was a serious threat.

Unlike *bellicose* and *bellicosity*, the word *belligerence* can be used at every level from the personal to the global. The belligerence of Marlon Brando's performances as the violent Stanley Kowalski in *A Streetcar Named Desire* electrified the country in the 1940s and '50s. At the same time, *belligerent* speeches by leaders of the Soviet Union and the United States throughout the Cold War were keeping the world on edge. *Belligerent* is even a noun; the terrible war in the Congo in recent years, for example, has involved seven nations as belligerents.

rebellion \ri-ˈbel-yən\ Open defiance and opposition, sometimes armed, to a person or thing in authority.

• A student rebellion that afternoon in Room 13 resulted in the new substitute teacher racing out of the building in tears.

Plenty of teenagers *rebel* against their parents in all kinds of ways. But a rebellion usually involves a group. Armed rebellions are usually put down by a country's armed forces, or at least kept from expanding beyond a small area. The American War of Independence was first viewed by the British as a minor rebellion that would soon run its course, but this particular rebellion led to a full-fledged revolution—that is, the overthrow of a government. Rebellion, armed or otherwise, has often alerted those in power that those they control are very unhappy.

PAC is related to the Latin words for "agree" and "peace." The *Pacific Ocean*—that is, the "Peaceful Ocean"—was named by Ferdinand Magellan because it seemed so calm after he had sailed through the storms near Cape Horn. (Magellan obviously had never witnessed a Pacific typhoon.)

---

pacify \ˈpa-sə-ˌfī\ (1) To soothe anger or agitation. (2) To subdue by armed action.

• It took the police hours to pacify the angry demonstrators.

Someone stirred up by a strong emotion can usually be pacified by some kind words and the removal of its causes. Unhappy babies are often given a rubber *pacifier* for sucking to make them stop crying. During the Vietnam War, *pacification* of an area meant using armed force to drive out the enemy, which might be followed by bringing the local people over to our side by building schools and providing social services. But an army can often bring "peace" by pure force, without soothing anyone's emotions.

pacifist \\'pa-sə-fist\\ A person opposed to war or violence, especially someone who refuses to bear arms or to fight, on moral or religious grounds.

• Her grandfather had fought in the Marines in World War II, but in his later years he had become almost a pacifist, opposing every war for one reason or another.

The Quakers and the Jehovah's Witnesses are *pacifist* religious groups, and Henry David Thoreau and Martin Luther King are probably the most famous American pacifists. Like these groups and individuals, pacifists haven't always met with sympathy or understanding. Refusing to fight ever, for any reason, calls for strong faith in one's own moral or religious convictions, since *pacifism* during wartime has often gotten people persecuted and even thrown in prison.

pact \\'pakt\\ An agreement between two or more people or groups; a treaty or formal agreement between nations to deal with a problem or to resolve a dispute.

• The girls made a pact never to reveal what had happened on that terrifying night in the abandoned house.

Pact has "peace" at its root because a pact often ends a period of unfriendly relations. The word is generally used in the field of international relations, where diplomats may speak of an "arms pact," a "trade pact," or a "fishing-rights pact." But it may also be used for any solemn agreement or promise between two people; after all, whenever two parties shake hands on a deal, they're not about to go to war with each other.

pace \\'pā-sē\\ Contrary to the opinion of.

• She had only three husbands, *pace* some Hollywood historians who claim she had as many as six.

This word looks like another that is much more familiar, but notice how it's pronounced. It is used only by intellectuals, and often printed in italics so that the reader doesn't mistake it for the other word. Writers use it when correcting an opinion that many people believe; for example, "The costs of the program, *pace* some commentators, will not be significant." So what does *pace* have to do with peace? Because it says "Peace to them (that is, to the people I'm mentioning)—I don't want to start an argument; I just want to correct the facts."

Quizzes

A. Match the word on the left to the correct definition on the right:

1.	antebellum	a.	quarrelsome
2.	*pace*	b.	solemn agreement
3.	rebellion	c.	to make peaceful
4.	pacify	d.	before the war
5.	pacifist	e.	aggressiveness
6.	belligerence	f.	opposition to authority
7.	pact	g.	contrary to the opinion of
8.	bellicose	h.	one who opposes war

B. Fill in each blank with the correct letter:

a.	antebellum	e.	rebellion
b.	pacifist	f.	bellicose
c.	pact	g.	pacify
d.	*pace*	h.	belligerence

1. The native _____ began at midnight, when a gang of youths massacred the Newton family and set the house afire.
2. The grand _____ mansion has hardly been altered since it was built in 1841.
3. The Senate Republicans, outraged by their treatment, were in a _____ mood.
4. _____ some of the younger scholars, no good evidence has been found that Japan was involved in the incident.
5. The cease-fire _____ that had been reached with such effort was shattered by the news of the slaughter.

6. Their relations during the divorce proceedings had been mostly friendly, so his _____ in the judge's chambers surprised her.

7. The world watched in amazement as the gentle _____ Gandhi won India its independence with almost no bloodshed.

8. Her soft lullabies could always _____ the unhappy infant.

CRIM comes from the Latin words for "fault or crime" or "accusation." It's obvious where the root shows up most commonly in English. A *crime* is an act forbidden by the government, which the government itself will punish you for, and for which you may be branded a *criminal*. A crime is usually more serious than a *tort* (see TORT, p. 488), a "civil wrong" for which the wronged person must himself sue if he wants to get repaid in some way.

---

criminology \ˌkri-mə-'nä-lə-jē\ The study of crime, criminals, law enforcement, and punishment.

• His growing interest in criminology led him to become a probation officer.

Criminology includes the study of all aspects of crime and law enforcement—criminal psychology, the social setting of crime, prohibition and prevention, investigation and detection, capture and punishment. Thus, many of the people involved—legislators, social workers, probation officers, judges, etc.—could possibly be considered *criminologists,* though the word usually refers only to scholars and researchers.

decriminalize \dē-'kri-mə-nə-ˌlīz\ To remove or reduce the criminal status of.

• An angry debate over decriminalizing doctor-assisted suicide raged all day in the statehouse.

Decriminalization of various "victimless crimes"—crimes that don't directly harm others, such as private gambling and drug-taking—has been recommended by conservatives as well as liberals, who often claim that it would ease the burden on the legal system, decrease the amount of money flowing to criminals, and increase personal liberty. Decriminalization is not the same as legalization; decriminalization may still call for a small fine (like a traffic ticket), and may apply only to use or possession of something, leaving the actual sale of goods or services illegal.

incriminate \in-ˈkri-mə-ˌnāt\ To show evidence of involvement in a crime or a fault.

• The muddy tracks leading to and from the cookie jar were enough to incriminate them.

Testimony may incriminate a suspect by placing him at the scene of a crime, and *incriminating* evidence is the kind that strongly links him to it. But the word doesn't always refer to an actual crime. We can say, for instance, that a virus has been incriminated as the cause of a type of cancer, or that video games have been incriminated in the decline in study skills among young people.

recrimination \rē-ˌkri-mə-ˈnā-shən\ (1) An accusation in answer to an accusation made against oneself. (2) The making of such an accusation.

• Their failure to find help led to endless and pointless recriminations over responsibility for the accident.

Defending oneself from a verbal attack by means of a counter-attack is as natural as physical self-defense. So a disaster often brings recriminations among those connected with it, and divorces and child-custody battles usually involve recriminations between husband and wife. An actual crime isn't generally involved, but it may be; when two suspects start exchanging angry recriminations after they've been picked up, it often leads to one of them turning against the other in court.

PROB comes from the Latin words for "prove or proof" and "honesty or integrity." A *probe*, whether it's a little object for testing electrical circuits or a spacecraft headed for Mars, is basically something that's looking for evidence or proof. And *probable* originally described something that wasn't certain but might be "provable."

---

approbation \ˌa-prə-ˈbā-shən\ A formal or official act of approving; praise, usually given with pleasure or enthusiasm.

- The senate signaled its approbation of the new plan by voting for it unanimously.

Approbation is a noun form of *approve*, but approbation is usually stronger than mere *approval*. An official commendation for bravery is an example of approbation; getting reelected to office by a wide margin indicates public approbation; and the social approbation received by a star quarterback in high school usually makes all the pain worthwhile.

probate \\'prō-,bāt\\ The process of proving in court that the will of someone who has died is valid, and of administering the estate of a dead person.

- When her father died, she thought she would be able to avoid probate, but she wasn't that lucky.

Ever since people have written wills, those wills have had to be proven genuine by a judge. Without a probate process, greedy acquaintances or relatives could write up a fake will stating that all the person's wealth belonged to them. To establish a will as genuine, it must generally be witnessed and stamped by someone officially licensed to do so (though wills have sometimes been approved even when they were just written on a piece of scrap paper, with no witnesses). Today we use *probate* more broadly to mean everything that's handled in *probate court*, a special court that oversees the handling of estates (the money and property left when someone dies), making sure that everyone eventually receives what is properly theirs.

probity \\'prō-bə-tē\\ Absolute honesty and uprightness.

- Her unquestioned probity helped win her the respect of her fellow judges.

Probity is a quality the public generally hopes for in its elected officials but doesn't always get. Bankers, for example, have traditionally been careful to project an air of probity, even though banking scandals and bailouts have made this harder than ever. An aura of probity surrounds such public figures as Warren Buffett and Bill Moyers, men to whom many Americans would entrust their children and their finances.

reprobate \\'re-prə-,bāt\\ A person of thoroughly bad character.

- His wife finally left him, claiming he was a reprobate who would disappear for weeks at a time, gambling and drinking away all his money.

The related verb of *reprobate* is *reprove*, which originally, as the opposite of *approve*, meant "to condemn." Thus, a reprobate, as the word was used in Biblical translations, was someone condemned to hell. But for many years *reprobate* has been said in a tone of joshing affection, usually to describe someone of doubtful morals but good humor. Shakespeare's great character Falstaff—a lazy, lying, boastful, sponging drunkard—is the model of a reprobate, but still everyone's favorite Shakespeare character.

Quizzes

A. Indicate whether the following pairs of words have the same or different meanings:

1. decriminalize / tolerate   same ___ / different ___
2. probity / fraud   same ___ / different ___
3. criminology / murder   same ___ / different ___
4. incriminate / acquit   same ___ / different ___
5. probate / trial   same ___ / different ___
6. recrimination / faultfinding   same ___ / different ___
7. reprobate / scoundrel   same ___ / different ___
8. approbation / criticism   same ___ / different ___

B. Match the definition on the left to the correct word on the right:

1.	utter honesty	a.	approbation
2.	approval	b.	reprobate
3.	rascal	c.	recrimination
4.	legal process for wills	d.	criminology
5.	study of illegal behavior	e.	probity
6.	accuse	f.	probate
7.	reduce penalty for	g.	decriminalize
8.	counterattack	h.	incriminate

GRAV comes from the Latin word meaning "heavy, weighty, serious." *Gravity* is, of course, what makes things heavy, and without it there wouldn't be any life on earth, since nothing would stay *on* earth at all. This doesn't stop us from yelling in outrage when the familiar laws of gravity cause something to drop to the floor and break.

grave \\'grāv\\ (1) Requiring serious thought or concern. (2) Serious and formal in appearance or manner.

* We realized that the situation was grave and that the slightest incident could spark all-out war.

Gravity has a familiar physical meaning but also a nonphysical meaning—basically "seriousness." Thus, something *grave* possesses gravity. You can refer to the gravity of a person's manner, though public figures today seem to have a lot less gravity than they used to have. Or you can talk about a grave situation, as in the example sentence. But even though Shakespeare makes a pun on *grave* when a dying character talks about being buried the next day ("Ask for me tomorrow and you shall find me a grave man"), the word meaning "hole for burying a body" isn't actually related.

gravitas \\'gra-və-ˌtäs\\ Great or very dignified seriousness.

* The head of the committee never failed to carry herself with the gravitas she felt was appropriate to her office.

This word comes to us straight from Latin. Among the Romans, gravitas was thought to be essential to the character and functions of any adult (male) in authority. Even the head of a household or a low-level official would strive for this important quality. We use *gravitas* today to identify the same solemn dignity in men and women, but it seems to come easier in those who are over 60, slow-moving—and a bit overweight.

gravitate \\'gra-və-ˌtāt\\ To move or be drawn toward something, especially by natural tendency or as if by an invisible force.

* On hot evenings, the town's social life gravitated toward the lakefront, where you could stroll the long piers eating ice cream or dance at the old Casino.

To gravitate is to respond, almost unconsciously, to a force that works like *gravity* to draw things steadily to it as if by their own weight. Thus, young people gravitate toward a role model, moths gravitate to a flame, a conversation might gravitate toward politics, and everyone at a party often gravitates to the bar.

aggravate \\'a-grə-ˌvāt\\ (1) To make (an injury, problem, etc.) more serious or severe. (2) To annoy or bother.

• She went back to the soccer team before the knee was completely healed, which naturally aggravated the injury.

Since the *grav-* root means basically "weighty or serious," the original meaning of *aggravate* was "to make more serious." A bad relationship with your parents can be aggravated by marrying someone who nobody likes, for example, or a touchy trade relationship between two countries can be aggravated by their inability to agree on climate-change issues. Depression can be aggravated by insomnia—and insomnia can be aggravated by depression. But when most people use *aggravate* today, they employ its "annoy" sense, as in "What really aggravates my dad is having to listen to that TV all day long."

LEV comes from the Latin adjective *levis,* meaning "light," and the verb *levare,* meaning "to raise or lighten." So a *lever* is a bar used to lift something, by means of *leverage.* And *levitation* is the magician's trick in which a body seems to rise into the air by itself.

---

alleviate \\ə-'lē-vē-ˌāt\\ To lighten, lessen, or relieve, especially physical or mental suffering.

• Cold compresses alleviated the pain of the physical injury, but only time could alleviate the effect of the insult.

Physical pain or emotional anguish, or a water shortage or traffic congestion, can all be alleviated by providing the appropriate remedy. But some pain or anguish or shortage or congestion will remain: to alleviate is not to cure.

elevation \\ˌe-lə-'vā-shən\\ (1) The height of a place. (2) The act or result of lifting or raising someone or something.

• Her doctor is concerned about the elevation of her blood pressure since her last visit.

When you're hiking, you may be interested in knowing the highest elevation you'll be reaching. Psychologists use the term "mood elevation" to mean improvement in a patient's depression, and some leg ailments require elevation of the limb, usually so that it's higher than the heart for part of each day. *Elevation* can also mean "promotion"; thus, a vice president may be *elevated* to president, or a captain may be elevated to admiral.

cantilever \\'kan-tə-ˌlē-vər\\ A long piece of wood, metal, etc., that sticks out from a wall to support something above it.

* The house's deck, supported by cantilevers, jutted out dramatically over the rocky slope, and looking over the edge made him dizzy.

Cantilevers hold up a surface or room without themselves being supported at their outer end. Many outdoor balconies are *cantilevered*, and theater balconies may be as well. A cantilevered bridge may have a huge span (as long as 1,800 feet) built out on either side of a single large foundation pier. Architects sometimes use cantilevered construction to produce dramatic effects; Frank Lloyd Wright's "Fallingwater" house, which extends out over a rocky river, is a famous example. But the Grand Canyon's "Skywalk" has become perhaps the best-known piece of cantilevered construction in America.

levity \\'le-və-tē\\ Lack of appropriate seriousness.

* The Puritan elders tried to ban levity of all sorts from the community's meetings, but found it increasingly difficult to control the younger generation.

Levity originally was thought to be a physical force exactly like gravity but pulling in the opposite direction, like the helium in a balloon. As recently as the 19th century, scientists were still arguing about its existence. Today *levity* refers only to lightness in manner. To stern believers of some religious faiths, levity is often regarded as almost sinful. But the word, like its synonym *frivolity*, now has an old-fashioned ring to it and is usually used only half-seriously.

Quizzes

A. Fill in each blank with the correct letter:

a. grave   e. alleviate
b. gravitate   f. cantilever
c. gravitas   g. levity
d. aggravate   h. elevation

1. Even the smallest motion would _____ the pain in his shoulder.
2. She hesitated to step onto the balcony, which was supported by a single _____.
3. At their father's funeral they showed the same solemn _____ at which they had often laughed during his lifetime.
4. To relieve the swelling, the doctor recommended _____ of her legs several times a day.
5. Attracted magically by the music, all animals and natural objects would _____ toward the sound of Orpheus's lyre.
6. With the two armies moving toward the border, they knew the situation was _____.
7. The neighboring nations organized an airlift of supplies to _____ the suffering caused by the drought.
8. The board meeting ended in an unusual mood of _____ when a man in a gorilla suit burst in.

B. Match the word on the left to the correct definition on the right:

1. levity   a. solemn dignity
2. gravitas   b. relieve
3. grave   c. raising
4. alleviate   d. support beam
5. elevation   e. move toward as if drawn
6. aggravate   f. lack of seriousness
7. cantilever   g. serious
8. gravitate   h. worsen

Words from Mythology and History

cicerone \ˌsi-sə-ˈrō-nē\ A guide, especially one who takes tourists to museums, monuments, or architectural sites and explains what is being seen.

• On Crete they sought out a highly recommended cicerone, hoping to receive the best possible introduction to the noteworthy historical sites.

The Roman statesman and orator Cicero was renowned for his elegant style and great knowledge (and occasional long-windedness). So 18th-century Italians seem to have given the name *cicerone* to the guides who would show well-educated foreigners around the great cultural sites of the ancient Roman empire—guides who sought to be as eloquent and informed as Cicero in explaining the world in which he lived.

hector \ˈhek-tər\ To bully or harass by bluster or personal pressure.

• He would swagger around the apartment entrance with his friends and hector the terrified inhabitants going in and out.

In Homer's great *Iliad,* Hector was the leader of the Trojan forces, and the very model of nobility and honor. In the Greek war against Troy, he killed several great warriors before being slain by Achilles. His name began to take on its current meaning only after gangs of bullying young rowdies, many of them armed soldiers recently released from service following the end of the English Civil War, began terrorizing the residents of late-17th-century London. The gangs took such names as the Roysters, the Blades, the Bucks, and the Bloods, but the best-known of them was called the Hectors. The names Blades and Hectors may have seemed appropriate because, like Hector and Achilles, they often fought with swords.

hedonism \ˈhē-də-ˌni-zəm\ An attitude or way of life based on the idea that pleasure or happiness should be the chief goal.

• In her new spirit of hedonism, she went out for a massage, picked up champagne and chocolate truffles, and made a date that evening with an old boyfriend.

Derived from the Greek word for "pleasure," hedonism over the ages has provided the basis for several philosophies. The ancient

Epicureans and the 19th-century Utilitarians both taught and pursued *hedonistic* principles. But although we generally use the word today when talking about immediate pleasures for the senses, philosophers who talk about hedonism are usually talking about quiet pleasures that aren't pursued in a selfish way.

nestor \\'nes-₁tȯr\\ A senior figure or leader in one's field.

- The guest of honor was a nestor among journalists, and after dinner he shared some of his wisdom with the audience.

Nestor was another character from the *Iliad,* the eldest of the Greek leaders in the Trojan War. A great warrior as a young man, he was now noted for his wisdom and his talkativeness, both of which increased as he aged. These days, a nestor is not necessarily long-winded, but merely wise and generous with his advice.

spartan \\'spär-tən\\ Marked by simplicity, avoidance of luxury, and often strict self-discipline or self-denial.

- When he was single, he had lived a spartan life in a tiny, undecorated apartment with one chair, a table, and a bed.

In ancient times, the Greek city-state of Sparta had a reputation for the severe and highly disciplined way of life it enforced among its citizens, so as to keep them ready for war at any time. Physical training was required for both men and women. A boy would begin his military training at 7 and would live in army barracks for much of his life, even after he was married. Today, when a cargo ship or a remote beach resort offers "spartan accommodations," some tourists jump at the chance for a refreshing change from the luxuries they've been used to—and no one worries that they'll be forced out of bed at dawn to participate in war games.

stentorian \\sten-'tȯr-ē-ən\\ Extremely loud, often with especially deep richness of sound.

- Even without a microphone, his stentorian voice was clearly audible in the last rows of the auditorium.

Stentor, like Hector, was a warrior in the *Iliad,* but on the Greek side. His unusually powerful voice (Homer calls him "brazen-voiced"—that is, with a voice like a brass instrument) made him the natural choice for delivering announcements and proclamations to the assembled Greek army, in an era when there was no way of artificially increasing the volume of a voice.

stoic \\'stō-ik\\ Seemingly indifferent to pleasure or pain.

- She bore the pain of her broken leg with such stoic patience that most of us had no idea she was suffering.

The *Stoics* were members of a philosophical movement that first appeared in ancient Greece and lasted well into the Roman era. *Stoicism* taught that humans should seek to free themselves from joy, grief, and passions of all kinds in order to attain wisdom; its teachings thus have much in common with Buddhism. The great Stoics include the statesman Cicero, the playwright Seneca, and the emperor Marcus Aurelius, whose *Meditations* is the most famous book of Stoic philosophy. Today we admire the kind of stoicism that enables some people (who may never have even heard of Marcus Aurelius) to endure both mental and physical pain without complaint.

sybaritic \\‚si-bə-'ri-tik\\ Marked by a luxurious or sensual way of life.

- When I knew them they were living a sybaritic existence—hopping from resort to resort, each more splendid than the last—but a year later the money ran out.

The ancient city of Sybaris (near modern Terranova di Sibari), founded by the Greeks on the toe of Italy's "boot," was famous for the wealth and luxury of its citizens in the 6th century B.C. But the *Sybarites'* wealth made them overconfident, and when they went to war with a nearby city, they were defeated by a much smaller army. After the victory, their enemies diverted the course of the river running through Sybaris so that it destroyed the whole city forever.

Quiz

Choose the closest definition:

1. hedonism   a. preference for males   b. habit of gift-giving   c. tendency to conceal feelings   d. love of pleasure

2. hector   a. encourage b. harass c. deceive d. swear
3. cicerone   a. guide b. cartoon character c. orator
   d. lawyer
4. spartan   a. cheap b. Greek c. severe d. luxurious
5. nestor   a. journalist b. long-winded elder c. domestic
   hen d. judge
6. stoic   a. pleasure-seeking b. bullying c. repressed
   d. unaffected by pain
7. sybaritic   a. pleasure-seeking b. free of luxury
   c. sisterly d. ice-cold
8. stentorian   a. obnoxious b. muffled c. loud d. dictated

Review Quizzes

A. Fill in each blank with the correct letter:

a. bellicose   h. benevolence
b. stentorian   i. incriminate
c. *pace*   j. gravitate
d. sybaritic   k. hector
e. grave   l. enamored
f. alleviate   m. stoic
g. belligerence   n. pacify

1. Her grandfather had a _____ manner, moved slowly,
   and never laughed.
2. The mood at the resort was _____, and the drinking
   and dancing continued long into the night.
3. To rattle the other team, they usually _____ them
   constantly.
4. The judge was known for issuing all his rulings in a
   _____ voice.
5. He wouldn't even have a place to live if it weren't for
   the _____ of his wealthy godfather.
6. Thoroughly _____ of the splendid Victorian house,
   they began to plan their move.
7. She attempted to _____ his anxiety by convincing him
   he wasn't to blame.
8. Whenever she entered a bar alone, the lonely men would
   always _____ toward her.

9. Their refusal to cease work on nuclear weapons was seen as a _____ act by the neighboring countries.
10. _____ my many critics, I have never had reason to change my views on the subject.
11. Unable to calm the growing crowd, he finally ordered the police to _____ the area by force.
12. Whenever her boyfriend saw anyone looking at her, his _____ was alarming.
13. He bore all his financial losses with the same _____ calm.
14. Who would have guessed that it would take the killer's own daughter to _____ him.

B. Choose the closest definition:

1. hedonism   a. fear of heights b. hatred of crowds
    c. liking for children d. love of pleasure
2. levity   a. lightness b. policy c. leverage d. literacy
3. aggravate   a. lessen b. decorate c. intensify d. lighten
4. reprobate   a. researcher b. commissioner
    c. scoundrel d. reformer
5. bellicose   a. fun-loving b. warlike c. impatient
    d. jolly
6. decriminalize   a. discriminate b. legalize
    c. legislate d. decree
7. antebellum   a. preventive b. unlikely c. impossible
    d. prewar
8. benediction   a. slogan b. prayer c. greeting
    d. expression
9. pact   a. bundle b. form c. agreement d. presentation
10. amicable   a. technical b. sensitive c. friendly
    d. scenic
11. criminology   a. crime history b. crime book c. crime
    study d. crime story
12. approbation   a. approval b. resolution c. reputation
    d. substitution

C. Match the definition on the left to the correct word on the right:

1. secret lover   a. elevation
2. estate process   b. gravitas
3. accusation   c. probate
4. integrity   d. probity

5.	gift receiver	e.	recrimination
6.	giver	f.	paramour
7.	peace lover	g.	benefactor
8.	promotion	h.	beneficiary
9.	dignity	i.	rebellion
10.	revolt	j.	pacifist

UNIT

2

MANIA in Latin means "madness," and the meaning passed over into English unchanged. Our word *mania* can mean a mental illness, or at least an excessive enthusiasm. We might call someone a *maniac* who was wild, violent, and mentally ill—or maybe just really enthusiastic about something. Too much caffeine might make you a bit *manic*. But the intense mood swings once known as *manic-depressive illness* are now usually called *bipolar disorder* instead.

kleptomania \ˌklep-tə-ˈmā-nē-ə\ A mental illness in which a person has a strong desire to steal things.

• Kleptomania leads its sufferers to steal items of little value that they don't need anyway.

Klepto- comes from the Greek word *kleptein*, "to steal." Even though kleptomania is often the butt of jokes, it's actually a serious mental illness, often associated with mood disorders, anxiety disorders, eating disorders, and substance abuse. Kleptomaniacs tend to be depressed, and many live lives of secret shame because they're afraid to seek treatment.

dipsomaniac \ˌdip-sə-ˈmā-nē-ˌak\ A person with an extreme and uncontrollable desire for alcohol.

• She didn't like the word *alcoholic* being applied to her, and liked *dipsomaniac* even less.

Dipsomaniac comes from the Greek noun *dipsa*, "thirst," but thirst usually has nothing to do with it. Some experts distinguish between an alcoholic and a dipsomaniac, reserving *dipsomaniac* for someone involved in frequent episodes of binge drinking and blackouts. In any case, there are plenty of less respectful words for a person of similar habits: *sot, lush, wino, souse, boozer, guzzler, tippler, tosspot, drunkard, boozehound*—the list goes on and on and on.

megalomaniac \ˌme-gə-lō-ˈmā-nē-ˌak\ A mental disorder marked by feelings of great personal power and importance.

• When the governor started calling for arming his National Guard with nuclear weapons, the voters finally realized they had elected a megalomaniac.

Since the Greek root *megalo-* means "large," someone who is *megalomaniacal* has a mental disorder marked by feelings of personal grandeur. *Megalomania* has probably afflicted many rulers throughout history: The Roman emperor Caligula insisted that he be worshipped as a living god. Joseph Stalin suffered from the paranoia that often accompanies megalomania, and had thousands of his countrymen executed as a result. J.-B. Bokassa, dictator of a small and extremely poor African nation, proclaimed himself emperor of the country he renamed the Central African Empire. And even democratically elected leaders have often acquired huge egos as a result of public acclaim. But *megalomaniac* is generally thrown around as an insult and rarely refers to real mental illness.

egomaniac \ˌē-gō-ˈmā-nē-ˌak\ Someone who is extremely self-centered and ignores the problems and concerns of others.

• He's a completely unimpressive person, but that doesn't keep him from being an egomaniac.

Ego is Latin for "I," and in English *ego* usually means "sense of self-worth." Most people's egos stay at a healthy level, but some become exaggerated. Egomaniacs may display a grandiose sense of self-importance, with fantasies about their own brilliance or beauty, intense envy of others, a lack of sympathy, and a need to be adored or feared. But, like *megalomaniac*, the word *egomaniac* is thrown around by lots of people who don't mean much more by it than *blowhard* or *know-it-all*.

PSYCH comes from the Greek word *psyche*, meaning "breath, life, soul." *Psychology* is the science of mind and behavior, and a *psychologist* treats or studies the mental problems of individuals and groups. *Psychiatry* is a branch of medicine that deals with mental and emotional disorders, and a *psychiatrist* (like any other doctor) may prescribe drugs to treat them.

psyche \\'sī-kē\ Soul, personality, mind.

• Analysts are constantly trying to understand the nation's psyche and why the U.S. often behaves so differently from other countries.

Sometime back in the 16th century, we borrowed the word *psyche* directly from Greek into English. In Greek mythology, Psyche was a beautiful princess who fell in love with Eros (Cupid), god of love, and went through terrible trials before being allowed to marry him. The story is often understood to be about the soul redeeming itself through love. (To the Greeks, *psyche* also meant "butterfly," which suggests how they imagined the soul.) In English, *psyche* often sounds less spiritual than *soul*, less intellectual than *mind*, and more private than *personality*.

psychedelic \\,sī-kə-'de-lik\ (1) Of or relating to a drug (such as LSD) that produces abnormal and often extreme mental effects such as hallucinations. (2) Imitating the effects of psychedelic drugs.

• In her only psychedelic experience, back in 1970, she had watched with horror as the walls began crawling with bizarrely colored creatures.

The most famous—or notorious—of the psychedelic drugs is LSD, a compound that can be obtained from various mushrooms and other fungi but is usually created in the lab. The other well-known *psychedelics* are psilocybin (likewise obtained from fungi) and mescaline (obtained from peyote cactus). How psychedelics produce their effects is still fairly mysterious, partly because research ceased for almost 20 years because of their reputation, but scientists are determined to find the answers and much research is now under way. Psychedelics are now used to treat anxiety in patients with cancer, and are being tested in the treatment of such serious conditions as severe depression, alcoholism, and drug addiction.

psychosomatic \ˌsī-kō-sə-ˈma-tik\ Caused by mental or emotional problems rather than by physical illness.

• Her doctor assumed her stomach problems were psychosomatic but gave her some harmless medication anyway.

Since the Greek word *soma* means "body," *psychosomatic* suggests the link between mind and body. Since one's mental state may have an important effect on one's physical state, research on new medicines always involves giving some patients in the experiment a placebo (fake medicine), and some who receive the sugar pills will seem to improve. You may hear someone say of someone else's symptoms, "Oh, it's probably just psychosomatic," implying that the physical pain or illness is imaginary—maybe just an attempt to get sympathy—and that the person could will it away if he or she wanted to. But this can be harsh and unfair, since, whatever the cause is, the pain is usually real.

psychotherapist \ˌsī-kō-ˈther-ə-pist\ One who treats mental or emotional disorder or related bodily ills by psychological means.

• He's getting medication from a psychiatrist, but it's his sessions with the psychotherapist that he really values.

Many psychologists offer psychological counseling, and psychological counseling can usually be called *psychotherapy*, so many psychologists can be called psychotherapists. The most intense form of psychotherapy, called *psychoanalysis*, usually requires several visits a week. A competing type of therapy known as *behavior therapy* focuses on changing a person's behavior (often some individual habit such as stuttering, tics, or phobias) without looking very deeply into his or her mental state.

Quizzes

A. Fill in each blank with the correct letter:

a.	psychedelic	e.	megalomaniac
b.	kleptomania	f.	psychosomatic
c.	psyche	g.	dipsomaniac
d.	egomaniac	h.	psychotherapist

1. Her boss was an _____ who always needed someone around telling him how brilliant he was.
2. Testing _____ drugs on cancer patients was difficult because of their unpredictable mental effects.
3. By now the dictator had begun to strike some observers as a possibly dangerous _____.
4. His fear of AIDS was so intense that he'd been developing _____ symptoms, which his doctor hardly bothered to check out anymore.
5. After finding several of her missing things in the other closet, she began wondering if her roommate was an ordinary thief or actually suffering from _____.
6. They'd only been together two weeks, but already she suspected there was a lot hidden in the depths of her boyfriend's _____.
7. A medical report from 1910 had identified her great-grandfather as a _____, and ten years later his alcoholism would kill him.
8. He hated the thought of drugs but knew he needed someone to talk to, so his brother recommended a local _____.

B. Match each word on the left to the best definition on the right:

1. psyche
2. egomaniac
3. psychotherapist
4. psychosomatic
5. dipsomaniac
6. megalomaniac
7. kleptomania
8. psychedelic

a. alcoholic
b. caused by the mind
c. person deluded by thoughts of grandeur
d. producing hallucinations
e. compulsive thieving
f. mind
g. extremely self-centered person
h. "talk" doctor

CEPT comes from the Latin verb meaning "take, seize." *Capture,* which is what a *captor* has done to a *captive,* has the same meaning. *Captivate* once meant literally "capture," but now means only to capture mentally through charm or appeal. But in some other English words this root produces, such as those below, its meaning is harder to find.

reception \ri-ˈsep-shən\ (1) The act of receiving. (2) A social gathering where guests are formally welcomed.

• Although the reception of her plan by the board of directors was enthusiastic, it was months before anything was done about it.

Reception is the noun form of *receive*. So at a formal reception, guests are received or welcomed or "taken in." A bad TV reception means the signal isn't being received well. When a new novel receives good reviews, we say it has met with a good critical reception. If it gets a poor reception, on the other hand, that's the same as saying that it wasn't *well-received*.

intercept \ˌin-tər-ˈsept\ To stop, seize, or interrupt (something or someone) before arrival.

• The explosives had been intercepted by police just before being loaded onto the jet.

Since the prefix *inter* means "between" (see INTER, p. 653), it's not hard to see how *intercept* was created. Arms shipments coming to a country are sometimes intercepted, but such *interceptions* can sometimes be understood as acts of war. In football, soccer, and basketball, players try to intercept the ball as it's being passed by the other team. In years gone by, letters and documents being carried between officers or officials were sometimes intercepted when the carrier was caught; today, when these communications are generally electronic, an intercepted e-mail isn't actually stopped, but simply read secretly by a third party.

perceptible \pər-ˈsep-tə-bəl\ Noticeable or able to be felt by the senses.

• Her change in attitude toward him was barely perceptible, and he couldn't be sure he wasn't just imagining it.

Perceptible includes the prefix *per-*, meaning "through," so the word refers to whatever can be taken in through the senses. A *perceptive* person picks up minor changes, small clues, or hints and shades of meaning that others can't *perceive,* so one person's *perception*—a tiny sound, a slight change in the weather, a different tone of voice— often won't be perceptible to another.

susceptible \sə-ˈsep-tə-bəl\ (1) Open to some influence; responsive. (2) Able to be submitted to an action or process.

- She impressed everyone immediately with her intelligence, so they're now highly susceptible to her influence and usually go along with anything she proposes.

With its prefix *sus-,* "up," *susceptible* refers to something or someone that "takes up" or absorbs like a sponge. A sickly child may be susceptible to colds, and an unlucky adult may be susceptible to back problems. A lonely elderly person may be susceptible to what a con man tells him or her on the phone. And students are usually susceptible to the teaching of an imaginative professor—that is, likely to enjoy and learn from it.

FIN comes from the Latin word for "end" or "boundary." *Final* describes last things, and a *finale* or a *finish* is an ending. (And at the end of a French film, you may just see the word "Fin.") But its meaning is harder to trace in some of the other English words derived from it.

---

confine \kən-ˈfīn\ (1) To keep (someone or something) within limits. (2) To hold (someone) in a location.

- He had heard the bad news from the CEO, but when he spoke to his employees he confined his remarks to a few hints that sales had slipped.

Confine means basically to keep someone or something within borders. Artist Frida Kahlo taught herself to paint when she was confined to bed after a serious bus accident. A person under "house arrest" is confined to his or her house by the government. The discussion at a meeting may be confined to a single topic. A town may keep industrial development confined to one area by means of zoning. And when potholes are being repaired, traffic on a two-way road may be confined to a single lane.

definitive \di-ˈfi-nə-tiv\ (1) Authoritative and final. (2) Specifying perfectly or precisely.

- The team's brilliant research provided a definitive description of the virus and its strange mutation patterns.

Something definitive is complete and final. A definitive example is the perfect example. A definitive answer is usually a strong yes or no. A definitive biography contains everything we'll ever need to know about someone. Ella Fitzgerald's famous 1950s recordings of

American songs have even been called definitive—but no one ever wanted them to be the last.

finite \\'fī-ˌnīt\\ Having definite limits.

• Her ambitions were infinite, but her wealth was finite.

It has come as a shock to many of us to realize that resources such as oil—and the atmosphere's ability to absorb greenhouse gases— are finite rather than unlimited. The debate continues as to whether the universe is finite or *infinite* and, if it's finite, how to think about what lies beyond it. Religion has always concerned itself with the question of the finite (that is, human life on earth) versus the infinite (God, eternity, and infinity). But *finite* is mostly used in scientific writing, often with the meaning "definitely measurable."

infinitesimal \\ˌin-ˌfi-nə-'te-sə-məl\\ Extremely or immeasurably small.

• Looking more closely at the research data, he now saw an odd pattern of changes so infinitesimal that they hadn't been noticed before.

Just as *infinite* describes something immeasurable ("without limit"), *infinitesimal* describes something endlessly small. When Antonie van Leeuwenhoek invented the microscope in the 17th century, he was able to see organisms that had been thought too *infinitesimally* small to exist. But today's electron microscope allows us to see infinitesimal aspects of matter that even Leeuwenhoek could not have imagined.

Quizzes

A. Fill in each blank with the correct letter:

a. confine	e. finite
b. susceptible	f. intercept
c. definitive	g. infinitesimal
d. reception	h. perceptible

1. By the fall there had been a _____ change in the mood of the students.

2. An _____ speck of dust on the lens can keep a CD player from functioning.

3. They waited weeks to hear about the board's _____ of their proposal.

4. Let's _____ this discussion to just the first part of the proposal.

5. Small children are often _____ to nightmares after hearing ghost stories in the dark.

6. He was at the post office the next morning, hoping to _____ the foolish letter he had sent yesterday.

7. We have a _____ number of choices, in fact maybe only three or four.

8. This may be the best book on the subject so far, but I wouldn't call it _____.

B. Match the word on the left to the correct definition on the right:

1.	confine	a.	noticeable
2.	susceptible	b.	ultimate
3.	definitive	c.	seize
4.	reception	d.	easily influenced
5.	finite	e.	tiny
6.	intercept	f.	limit
7.	infinitesimal	g.	receiving
8.	perceptible	h.	limited

JECT comes from *jacere,* the Latin verb meaning "throw" or "hurl." To *reject* something is to throw (or push) it back; to *eject* something is to throw (or drive) it out; and to *inject* something is to throw (or squirt) it into something else.

---

interject \\ˌin-tər-ˈjekt\\ To interrupt a conversation with a comment or remark.

• His anger was growing as he listened to the conversation, and every so often he would interject a crude comment.

According to its Latin roots, *interject* ought to mean literally "throw between." For most of the word's history, however, the only things that have been interjected have been comments dropped suddenly into a conversation. *Interjections* are often humorous, and sometimes even insulting, and the best interjections are so quick that the conversation isn't even interrupted.

conjecture \kən-ˈjek-chər\ To guess.

- He was last heard of in Bogotá, and they conjectured that he had met his end in the Andes at the hands of the guerrillas.

Formed with the prefix *con-*, "together," *conjecture* means literally "to throw together"—that is, to produce a theory by putting together a number of facts. So, for example, Columbus conjectured from his calculations that he would reach Asia if he sailed westward, and his later *conjecture* that there was a "Northwest Passage" by sea from the Atlantic to the Pacific over the North American continent was proved correct centuries later.

projection \prə-ˈjek-shən\ An estimate of what might happen in the future based on what is happening now.

- The president has been hearing different deficit projections all week from the members of his economic team.

Projection has various meanings, but what they all have in common is that something is sent out or forward. A movie is *projected* onto a screen; a skilled actress projects her voice out into a large theater without seeming to shout; and something sticking out from a wall can be called a projection. But the meaning we focus on here is the one used by businesses and governments. Most projections of this kind are estimates of a company's sales or profits—or of the finances of a town, state, or country—sometime in the future.

trajectory \trə-ˈjek-tə-rē\ The curved path that an object makes in space, or that a thrown object follows as it rises and falls to earth.

- Considering the likely range, trajectory, and accuracy of a bullet fired from a cheap handgun at 100 yards, the murder seemed incredible.

Formed with part of the prefix *trans-*, "across," *trajectory* means a "hurling across." By calculating the effect of gravity and other forces, the trajectory of an object launched into space at a known speed can be computed precisely. Missiles stand a chance of hitting their target only if their trajectory has been plotted accurately. The word is used most often in physics and engineering, but not always; we can also say, for example, that the trajectory of a whole life may be set in a person's youth, or that a new book traces the long trajectory of the French empire.

TRACT comes from *trahere,* the Latin verb meaning "drag or draw." Something *attractive* draws us toward it. Something *distracting* pulls your attention away. And when you *extract* something from behind the sofa, you drag it out.

---

traction \\'trak-shən\\ The friction that allows a moving thing to move over a surface without slipping.

• The spinning wheels were getting no traction on the ice, and we began to slip backward down the hill.

A *tractor* is something that pulls something else. We usually use the word for a piece of farm machinery, but it's also the name of the part of a big truck that includes the engine and the cab. Tractors get terrific traction, because of their powerful engines and the deep ridges on their huge wheels. A cross-country skier needs traction to kick herself forward, but doesn't want it to slow her down when she's gliding, so the bottom of the skis may have a "fish-scale" surface that permits both of these at the same time.

retract \\ri-'trakt\\ (1) To pull back (something) into something larger. (2) To take back (something said or written).

• She was forced to retract her comment about her opponent after it was condemned in the press.

The prefix *re-* ("back") gives *retract* the meaning of "draw back." Just as a cat retracts its claws into its paws when they aren't being used, a public figure may issue a *retraction* in order to say that he or she no longer wants to say something that has just been said. But it's sometimes hard to know what a retraction means: Was the original statement an error or an outright lie? Sometimes a politician even has to retract something that everyone actually assumes is the truth. Thousands of citizens were forced to publicly *retract* their "wrong" ideas by the Soviet government in the 1930s, though few of them had actually changed their minds. Someone wrongly accused may demand a retraction from his accuser—though today it seems more likely that he'll just go ahead and sue.

protracted \prō-ˈtrak-təd\ Drawn out, continued, or extended.

• No one was looking forward to a protracted struggle for custody of the baby.

With its prefix *pro-*, "forward," *protracted* usually applies to something drawn out forward in time. A protracted strike may cripple a company; a protracted rainy spell may rot the roots of vegetables; and a protracted lawsuit occasionally outlives the parties involved. Before the invention of the polio vaccines, polio's many victims had no choice but to suffer a protracted illness and its aftereffects.

intractable \ˌin-ˈtrak-tə-bəl\ Not easily handled, led, taught, or controlled.

• Corruption in the army was the country's intractable problem, and for many years all foreign aid had ended up in the colonels' pockets.

Intractable simply means "untreatable," and even comes from the same root. The word may describe both people and conditions. A cancer patient may suffer intractable pain that doctors are unable to treat. An intractable alcoholic goes back to the bottle immediately after "drying out." Homelessness, though it hardly existed thirty years ago, is now sometimes regarded as an intractable problem.

Quizzes

A. Choose the odd word:
1. conjecture   a. suppose b. assume c. guess d. know
2. protracted   a. lengthened b. continued c. circular
    d. extended
3. projection   a. survey b. forecast c. report d. history
4. traction   a. grip b. drive c. pulling force d. steering
5. trajectory   a. curve b. path c. arc d. target
6. retract   a. unsay b. withdraw c. force d. take back
7. interject   a. insert b. grab c. add d. stick in
8. intractable   a. unbelievable b. uncontrollable
    c. stubborn d. difficult

B. **Match each definition on the left to the correct word on the right:**

1. pulling force   a. protracted
2. assume   b. interject
3. expectation   c. trajectory
4. difficult   d. traction
5. unsay   e. conjecture
6. drawn out   f. intractable
7. curved path   g. retract
8. interrupt with   h. projection

DUC/DUCT, from the Latin verb *ducere,* "to lead," shows up regularly in English. *Duke* means basically "leader." The Italian dictator Mussolini was known simply as *Il Duce,* "the leader." But such words as *produce* and *reduce* also contain the root, even though their meanings show it less clearly.

---

conducive \kən-ˈdü-siv\ Tending to promote, encourage, or assist; helpful.

• She found the atmosphere in the quiet café conducive to study and even to creative thinking.

Something conducive "leads to" a desirable result. A cozy living room may be conducive to relaxed conversation, just as a boardroom may be conducive to more intense discussions. Particular tax policies are often conducive to savings and investment, whereas others are conducive to consumer spending. Notice that *conducive* is almost always followed by *to*.

deduction \dē-ˈdək-shən\ (1) Subtraction. (2) The reaching of a conclusion by reasoning.

• Foretelling the future by deduction based on a political or economic theory has proved to be extremely difficult.

To *deduct* is simply to subtract. A tax deduction is a subtraction from your taxable income allowed by the government for certain expenses, which will result in your paying lower taxes. Your insurance *deductible* is the amount of a medical bill that the insurance company makes you subtract before it starts to pay—in other words, the amount that will come out of your own pocket. But *deduction* also means "reasoning," and particularly reasoning based on general principles to produce specific findings. Mathematical reasoning is almost always deduction, for instance, since it is based on general rules. But when Dr. Watson exclaims "Brilliant deduction, my dear Holmes!" he simply means "brilliant reasoning," since Sherlock Holmes's solutions are based on specific details he has noticed rather than on general principles.

induce \in-ˈdüs\ (1) Persuade, influence. (2) Bring about.

• To induce him to make the call we had to promise we wouldn't do it again.

Inducing is usually gentle persuasion; you may, for instance, induce a friend to go to a concert, or induce a child to stop crying. An *inducement* is something that might lure you to do something, though inducements are occasionally a bit menacing, like the Godfather's offer that you can't refuse. *Induce* also sometimes means "produce"; thus, doctors must at times induce labor in a pregnant woman. Notice that *induct* and *induction* are somewhat different from *induce* and *inducement*, though they come from the identical roots.

seduction \si-ˈdək-shən\ (1) Temptation to sin, especially temptation to sexual intercourse. (2) Attraction or charm.

• The company began its campaign of seduction of the smaller firm by inviting its top management to a series of weekends at expensive resorts.

Seduction, with its prefix *se-,* "aside," means basically "lead aside or astray." In Hawthorne's novel *The Scarlet Letter,* Hester Prynne is forced to wear a large scarlet A, for "adulteress," after it is revealed that she's been *seduced* by the Reverend Dimmesdale. Seduction also takes less physical forms. Advertisements constantly try to seduce us (often using sex as a temptation) into buying products we hadn't even known existed.

SEQU comes from the Latin verb *sequi,* meaning "to follow." A *sequel* follows the original novel, film, or television show.

sequential \si-ˈkwen-shəl\ (1) Arranged in order or in a series. (2) Following in a series.

- In writing the history of the revolution, his challenge was to put all the events of those fateful days in proper sequential order.

Things in *sequence,* or regular order, are arranged *sequentially.* Most novels and films move sequentially, but some use techniques such as flashbacks that interrupt the movement forward in time. Sequential courses in college must follow each other in the proper order, just like sequential tasks or steps.

subsequent \\'səb-si-kwənt\\ Following in time, order, or place; later.

- Through all her subsequent love affairs, she never stopped thinking about the man who got away.

The prefix *sub-* normally means "below," and the *sub-* in *subsequent* seems to imply that everything after the first is somehow inferior. As the definition states, *subsequent* can refer to time ("All our subsequent attempts to contact her failed"), order ("The subsequent houses on the list looked even worse"), or place ("The subsequent villages on the river heading east become steadily more primitive"). But *subsequently*, as in "I subsequently learned the real story," simply means "later."

consequential \\ˌkän-sə-'kwen-shəl\\ (1) Resulting. (2) Important.

- None of our discussions thus far has been very consequential; next week's meeting will be the important one.

Something consequential follows or comes along with something else. The "resulting" meaning of *consequential* is usually seen in legal writing. For example, "consequential losses" are losses that supposedly resulted from some improper behavior, about which the lawyer's client is suing. But normally *consequential* means "significant" or "important," and it's especially used for events that will produce large *consequences*, or results.

non sequitur \\'nän-'se-kwə-tər\\ A statement that does not follow logically from anything previously said.

- Rattled by the question, his mind went blank, and he blurted out a non sequitur that fetched a few laughs from members of the audience.

Non sequitur is actually a complete sentence in Latin, meaning "It does not follow"—that is, something said or written doesn't logically follow what came before it. It was Aristotle who identified the non sequitur as one of the basic fallacies of logic—that is, one of the ways in which a person's reasoning may go wrong. For Aristotle, the non sequitur is usually a conclusion that doesn't actually result from the reasoning and evidence presented. Sometime when you're listening to politicians answering questions, see how many non sequiturs you can spot.

Quizzes

A. **Match the definition on the left to the correct word on the right:**

1.	out-of-place statement	a.	deduction
2.	persuade	b.	non sequitur
3.	temptation	c.	induce
4.	subtraction	d.	subsequent
5.	helpful	e.	seduction
6.	ordered	f.	consequential
7.	following	g.	conducive
8.	significant	h.	sequential

B. **Fill in each blank with the correct letter:**

a.	conducive	e.	consequential
b.	deduction	f.	subsequent
c.	induce	g.	non sequitur
d.	seduction	h.	sequential

1. The detectives insisted on a detailed and _____ account of the evening's events.
2. She fended off all his clumsy attempts at _____.
3. Conditions on the noisy hallway were not at all _____ to sleep.
4. There were a few arguments that first day, but all the _____ meetings went smoothly.
5. He sometimes thought that missing that plane had been the most _____ event of his life.
6. They arrived at the correct conclusion by simple _____.

7. He's hopeless at conversation, since practically everything he says is a _____.
8. He had tried to _____ sleep by all his usual methods, with no success.

Words from Mythology

Apollonian \ˌa-pə-ˈlō-nē-ən\ Harmonious, ordered, rational, calm.

* After a century of Romantic emotion, some composers adopted a more Apollonian style, producing clearly patterned pieces that avoided extremes of all kinds.

In Greek mythology, Apollo was the god of the sun, light, prophecy, and music, and the most revered of all the gods. Partly because of the writings of Nietzsche, we now often think of Apollo (in contrast to the god Dionysus) as a model of calm reason, and we may call anything with those qualities *Apollonian*. This isn't the whole story about Apollo, however; he had a terrible temper and could be viciously cruel when he felt like it.

bacchanalian \ˌba-kə-ˈnāl-yən\ Frenzied, orgiastic.

* The bacchanalian partying on graduation night resulted in three wrecked cars, two lawsuits by unamused parents, and more new experiences than most of the participants could remember the next day.

The Roman god of drama, wine, and ecstasy, Bacchus was the focus of a widespread celebration, the *Bacchanalia*. The festivities were originally secret, and only initiated members could participate. There was wine in abundance, and participants were expected to cut loose from normal restraints and give in to all sorts of wild desires. Eventually the Bacchanalia became more public and uncontrolled, finally getting so out of hand that in 186 B.C. the Roman authorities had it banned. Much the same bacchanalian spirit fills tropical carnivals every year, including New Orleans' Mardi Gras.

delphic \ˈdel-fik\ Unclear, ambiguous, or confusing.

- All she could get from the strange old woman were a few delphic comments that left her more confused than ever about the missing documents.

Delphi in Greece was the site of a temple to Apollo at which there resided an oracle, a woman through whom Apollo would speak, foretelling the future. The Greeks consulted the oracle frequently on matters both private and public. The prophecies were given in difficult poetry that had to be interpreted by priests, and even the interpretations could be hard to understand. When Croesus, king of Lydia, asked what would happen if he attacked the Persians, the oracle announced that he would destroy a great empire; what she didn't say was that the empire destroyed would be his own. Modern-day descendants of the oracle include some political commentators, who utter words of delphic complexity every week.

Dionysian \ˌdī-ə-ˈni-zhē-ən\ Frenzied, delirious.

- Only in the tropics did such festivals become truly Dionysian, he said, which was why he was booking his flight to Rio.

Dionysus was the Greek forerunner of Bacchus. He was the inventor of wine, which he gave to the human race. For that gift and for all the wild behavior that it led to, Dionysus became immensely popular, and he appears in a great many myths. He is often shown holding a wine goblet, with his hair full of vine leaves, and attended by a band of goat-footed satyrs and wild female spirits called maenads. In the 19th century, scholars such as Nietzsche claimed that the ancient world could be understood as a continuing conflict between the attitudes represented by Apollo (see *Apollonian* above) and Dionysus—that is, between order and disorder, between moderation and excess, between the controlled and the ecstatic.

jovial \ˈjō-vē-əl\ Jolly, good-natured.

- Their grandfather was as jovial and sociable as their grandmother was quiet and withdrawn.

Jove, or Jupiter, was the Roman counterpart of the Greek's Zeus, and like Zeus was regarded as chief among the gods. When the Romans were naming the planets, they gave the name Jupiter to the one that, as they may have already known, was the largest of all (though only the second-brightest to the naked eye). When the practice of astrology reached the Roman empire from the East, astrologers declared that those "born under Jupiter" were destined to be merry and generous, and many centuries later this would result in the words *jovial* and *joviality*.

mercurial \mər-'kyûr-ē-əl\ Having rapid and unpredictable changes of mood.

* His mother's always mercurial temper became even more unpredictable, to the point where the slightest thing would trigger a violent fit.

The god Mercury, with his winged cap and sandals, was the very symbol of speed, and the planet Mercury was named for him by the Romans because it is the fastest-moving of the planets. His name was also given to the liquid silver metal that skitters around on a surface so quickly and unpredictably. And the word *mercurial* seems to have come from the metal, rather than directly from the god (or an astrologer's view of the planet's influence). Mercurial people are usually bright but impulsive and changeable (and sometimes a bit unstable).

Olympian \ō-'lim-pē-ən\ Lofty, superior, and detached.

* Now 77, he moved slowly and spoke to the younger lawyers in Olympian tones, but his college friends could remember when he was a brash, crazy risk-taker.

The Greek gods lived high atop Mt. Olympus, which allowed them to watch what went on in the human realm below and intervene as they saw fit. They insisted on being properly worshipped by humans, but otherwise tended to treat the affairs of these weak and short-lived creatures almost like a sport. So *Olympian* describes someone who seems "lofty" and "above it all," as if surveying a scene in which other people appear the size of ants. The Olympic Games were first celebrated in the 8th century B.C., at the religious site called Olympia (far from Mt. Olympus), and *Olympian* today actually most often refers to Olympic athletes.

venereal \və-'nir-ē-əl\ Having to do with sexual intercourse or diseases transmitted by it.

* In the 19th century syphilis especially was often fatal, and venereal diseases killed some of the greatest figures of the time.

Venus was the Roman goddess of love, the equivalent of the Greek Aphrodite. Since she governed all aspects of love and desire, a word derived from her name was given to the diseases acquired through sexual contact. Most of these venereal diseases have been around for many centuries, but only in the 20th century did doctors devise tests to identify them or medicines to cure them. Today the official term is *sexually transmitted disease,* or STD; but even this name turns out to be ambiguous, since some of these diseases can be contracted in other ways as well.

Quiz

Choose the correct synonym and the correct antonym:

1. Dionysian   a. frenzied b. angry c. calm d. fatal
2. apollonian   a. fruity b. irrational c. single
     d. harmonious
3. mercurial   a. stable b. changeable c. sociable
     d. depressed
4. jovial   a. youthful b. mean-spirited c. merry
     d. magical
5. olympian   a. involved b. lame c. detached d. everyday
6. venereal   a. sensual b. intellectual c. diseased
     d. arthritic
7. bacchanalian   a. restrained b. dynamic c. frenzied
     d. forthright
8. delphic   a. clear b. dark c. stormy d. ambiguous

Review Quizzes

A.   Choose the closest definition:

1. reprobate   a. prosecution b. scoundrel c. trial
     d. refund
2. intercept   a. throw b. seize c. arrest d. close
3. confine   a. erect b. restrict c. ignore d. lock out
4. deduction   a. addition b. flirtation c. total
     d. reasoning
5. subsequent   a. unimportant b. early c. first d. later

6. sequential   a. important   b. noticeable
    c. in order   d. distant
7. non sequitur   a. distrust   b. refusal   c. odd statement
    d. denial
8. conjecture   a. ask   b. state   c. guess   d. exclaim
9. perceptible   a. noticeable   b. capable   c. readable
    d. thinkable
10. finite   a. vast   b. finished   c. nearby   d. limited

B. Match the definition on the left to the correct word on the right:

1. guess   a. olympian
2. soul   b. perceptible
3. lengthy   c. conjecture
4. godlike   d. definitive
5. ordered   e. protracted
6. clear-cut   f. psyche
7. noticeable   g. susceptible
8. sensitive   h. jovial
9. significant   i. sequential
10. jolly   j. consequential

C. Fill in each blank with the correct letter:

a. mercurial   f. seduction
b. induce   g. bacchanalian
c. intractable   h. traction
d. amicable   i. retract
e. interject   j. trajectory

1. The public isn't aware of the company's _____ of Congress through its huge contributions over many years.
2. The truck was getting almost no _____ on the snowy road.
3. The prison situation is _____, and likely to get worse.
4. He tried to _____ his statement the next day, but the damage had been done.
5. Surprisingly, her first and second husbands actually have a completely _____ relationship.
6. The argument had gotten fierce, but he somehow managed to _____ a remark about how they were both wrong.

7. The disappointing _____ of his career often puzzled his friends.

8. She again told her family that nothing could _____ her to marry him.

9. By 2:00 a.m. the party was a scene of _____ frenzy.

10. Her only excuse for her behavior was her well-known _____ temper.

UNIT

3

AMBI means "on both sides" or "around"; *ambi-* comes from Latin. Most of us are either right-handed or left-handed, but *ambidextrous* people can use their right and left hand equally well.

ambiguous \am-'bi-gyù-wəs\ (1) Doubtful or uncertain especially from being obscure or indistinct. (2) Unclear in meaning because of being understandable in more than one way.

- Successful politicians are good at giving ambiguous answers to questions on difficult issues.

Ambiguous comes from the Latin verb *ambigere,* "to be undecided." When we say someone's eyes are an ambiguous color, we mean we cannot decide which color they are—blue or green? The *ambiguity* of the Mona Lisa's smile makes us wonder what she's thinking about. An ambiguous order is one that can be taken in at least two ways; on the other hand, the order "Shut up!" may be rude but at least it's *unambiguous.*

ambient \'am-bē-ənt\ Existing or present on all sides.

- The ambient lighting in the restaurant was low, and there was a bright candle at each table.

Ambient light is the light that fills an area or surrounds something that's being viewed, like a television screen or a painting. Scientists sometimes refer to the ambient temperature, the temperature of the surrounding air. "Ambient music" is the term used today for "atmospheric" background music usually intended for relaxation or meditation. The candlelit restaurant in the example sentence is probably trying for a romantic *ambience,* or "atmosphere."

ambivalent \am-'bi-və-lənt\ (1) Holding opposite feelings and attitudes at the same time toward someone or something. (2) Continually wavering between opposites or alternative courses of action.

- He was ambivalent about the trip: he badly wanted to travel but hated to miss the summer activities at home.

Ambivalent is a fairly new word, less than a hundred years old, and, not surprisingly, it was first used by psychologists. Since being ambivalent means simply having mixed feelings about some question or issue, some of us spend most of our lives in a state of *ambivalence.* We might feel ambivalence about accepting a high-paying job that requires us to work long hours, about lending money to someone we like but don't know well—or about ordering a Tutti-Frutti Chocolate Banana Sundae El Supremo after we've been starving on a strict diet for weeks.

ambit \'am-bət\ The range or limit covered by something (such as a law).

- The treatment of farm animals generally falls outside the ambit of animal-cruelty laws in the U.S.

Ambit is a rather formal term, often used by lawyers, as in, "With this new legislation, tobacco now falls within the ambit of FDA regulation." It almost always refers to something abstract rather than an actual physical range. So, for example, an immigrant might live completely within the ambit of her immigrant community until she started college, where she might find herself in a much broader social ambit. Most of the Latin American colonies were established by Spain, but in the 19th century, as the U.S. became stronger and Spain became weaker, they began to enter the ambit of U.S. power.

EPI is a Greek prefix that may mean various things, but usually "on, over" or "attached to." So an earthquake's *epicenter* is the ground right over the center of the quake. And your *epidermis* is the outer layer of your skin, on top of the inner *dermis.*

epilogue \\'e-pə-₁lòg\ The final section after the main part of a book or play.

• Her editor told her the book really needed an epilogue, to tell where each member of the family is today.

From its Greek roots, *epilogue* means basically "words attached (at the end)." An epilogue often somehow wraps up a story's action, as in the one for a famous Shakespeare play that ends, "For never was a story of more woe / Than this of Juliet and her Romeo." In nonfiction books, we now often use the term *afterword* instead of *epilogue*, just as we now generally use *foreword* instead of *prologue* (see LOG, p. 203). Movies also often have a kind of epilogue—maybe a scene after the exciting climax when the surviving lovers meet in a café to talk about their future. The epilogue of a musical composition, after all the drama is over, is called the *coda* (Italian for "tail").

epiphyte \\'e-pi-₁fīt\ A plant that obtains its nutrients from the air and the rain and usually grows on another plant for support.

• The strangler fig begins life as an epiphyte on a tree branch, drops its tendrils to take root in the ground around the trunk, and slowly covers and strangles the tree to death.

Epiphytic plants are sometimes known as "air plants" because they seemingly survive on thin air. They rely on their host plants merely for physical support, not nourishment. Tropical epiphytes include orchids, ferns, and members of the pineapple family. To a newcomer in the tropical rain forest, the first sight of a great tree with large epiphytes hanging from every level can be eerie and astonishing. Familiar epiphytes of the temperate zone include lichens, mosses, and algae, which may grow on rocks or water without touching the soil.

epitaph \\'e-pi-₁taf\ An inscription on a grave or tomb in memory of the one buried there.

• The great architect Christopher Wren designed London's majestic St. Paul's Cathedral, the site of his tomb and epitaph: "Si monumentum requiris, circumspice" ("If you seek my monument, look around you").

Epitaph includes the root from the Greek word *taphos,* "tomb" or "funeral." Traditionally, *epitaph* refers to a tombstone inscription, but it can also refer to brief memorial statements that resemble such inscriptions. One of the most famous is Henry Lee's epitaph for George Washington: "First in war, first in peace, and first in the hearts of his countrymen."

epithet \\'e-pi-ˌthet\\ (1) A descriptive word or phrase occurring with or in place of the name of a person or thing. (2) An insulting or demeaning word or phrase.

• King Richard I of England earned the epithet "Lionhearted," while his brother, King John, was given the epithet "Lackland."

From its Greek roots, *epithet* would mean something "put on," or added. Sometimes the added name follows a given name, as in Erik the Red or Billy the Kid. In other cases, the epithet precedes the personal name, as in Mahatma ("Great-souled") Gandhi. In still others, it's used in place of the actual name, as in El Greco ("The Greek") or El Cid ("The Lord"). In its other common meaning, an *epithet* is a mocking or insulting name (like "Lackland" in the example sentence). When enemies are said to be "hurling epithets" at each other, it means they're exchanging angry insults.

Quizzes

A. Fill in each blank with the correct letter:

a. ambiguous	e. epithet
b. epiphyte	f. ambivalent
c. ambient	g. epilogue
d. epitaph	h. ambit

1. An _____ seems to live on air and water alone.
2. When the _____ light is low, photographers use a flash.
3. She felt _____ about the invitation, and couldn't decide whether to accept or decline.
4. Is any _____ inscribed on Grant's Tomb?
5. Andrew Jackson's _____, describing his lean toughness, was "Old Hickory."
6. Lord Raglan's _____ order confused the commander of the Light Brigade and led to its disastrous charge.
7. Her visit in the spring was a kind of _____ to our relationship, which had really ended two months earlier.

8. The subject really falls within the _____ of economics rather than sociology.

B. **Match each word on the left with its correct definition on the right:**

1. ambivalent
2. epithet
3. ambit
4. epiphyte
5. ambiguous
6. epitaph
7. ambient
8. epilogue

a. having more than one meaning
b. surrounding
c. wavering
d. grave inscription
e. range
f. descriptive nickname
g. ending
h. non-parasitic plant growing on another

HYP/HYPO is a Greek prefix meaning "below, under." Many *hypo-* words are medical. A *hypodermic* needle injects medication under the skin. *Hypotension*, or low blood pressure, can be just as unhealthy as the better-known *hypertension*, or high blood pressure.

hypochondriac \ˌhī-pō-ˈkän-drē-ˌak\ A person overly concerned with his or her own health who often suffers from delusions of physical disease.

• Hercule Poirot, the detective hero of the Agatha Christie mysteries, is a notorious hypochondriac, always trying to protect himself from drafts.

One disease a hypochondriac really does suffer from is *hypochondria,* the anxiety and depression that come from worrying too much about one's own health. Even though it's easy to joke about hypochondriacs, hypochondria is no joking matter for the sufferer. Somewhat surprisingly, the second part of *hypochondria* derives from *chondros,* the Greek word for "cartilage." The cartilage in question is that of the sternum, or breastbone. From ancient times, doctors believed that certain internal organs or regions were the seat of various diseases, both physical and mental, and the area under the breastbone was thought to be the source of hypochondria.

hypoglycemia \ˌhī-pō-glī-ˈsē-mē-ə\ Abnormal decrease of sugar in the blood.

• She had been controlling her hypoglycemia through diet and vitamins, but she now realized she needed to add daily exercise as well.

The root *glyk-* means "sweet" in Greek, so *glyc* shows up in the names of various terms referring to a sugar as a chemical ingredient, such as *glycerine* and *monoglyceride*. People with diabetes have difficulty controlling the sugar in their blood. Too little can be dangerous; its early symptoms may be as minor as nervousness, shaking, and sweating, but it can lead to seizures and unconsciousness. Luckily, it can be taken care of easily by eating or drinking something high in carbohydrates. Its opposite, *hyperglycemia* (see HYPER, p. 457), is the main symptom of diabetes, and usually requires an injection of insulin, which the sufferer usually gives himself. Today many people—though not doctors—use *hypoglycemia* to mean a completely different condition, with some of the same milder symptoms, that doesn't involve low blood sugar.

hypothermia \ˌhī-pō-ˈthər-mē-ə\ Subnormal temperature of the body.

• By the time rescuers were able to pull the boy from the pond's icy waters, hypothermia had reached a life-threatening stage.

Hypothermia, which usually results from submersion in icy water or prolonged exposure to cold, may constitute a grave medical emergency. It begins to be a concern when body temperature dips below 95°F, and the pulse, breathing, and blood pressure start to decline. Below 90°, the point at which the normal reaction of shivering ceases, emergency treatment is called for.

hypothetical \ˌhī-pə-ˈthe-tə-kəl\ (1) Involving an assumption made for the sake of argument or for further study or investigation. (2) Imagined for purposes of example.

• The candidate refused to say what she would do if faced with a hypothetical military crisis.

The noun *hypothesis* comes straight from the Greek word meaning "foundation" or "base"—that is something "put under" something else. So a hypothesis is something you assume to be true in order that you can use it as the base or basis for a line of reasoning—and any such assumption can be called hypothetical. So, for example, the theory that the dinosaurs became extinct because of a giant meteor that struck the earth near the Yucatán Peninsula involves the hypothesis that such a collision would have had such terrible effects on the earth's climate that the great reptiles would have been doomed. Once a hypothesis has been thoroughly studied and researched without being proved wrong, it generally comes to be called a *theory* instead.

THERM/THERMO comes from the Greek word meaning "warm." A *thermometer* measures the amount of warmth in a body, the air, or an oven. A *thermostat* makes sure the temperature stays at the same level. And it's easy to see why the German manufacturers of a vacuum-insulated bottle back in 1904 gave it the name Thermos.

---

thermal \ˈthər-məl\ (1) Of, relating to, or caused by heat. (2) Designed to insulate in order to retain body heat.

• A special weave called thermal weave traps insulating air in little pockets to increase the warmth of long underwear and blankets.

In days gone by, much of the male population of the northern states in the cold months would wear a garment of thermal underwear covering the entire body, called a union suit. Union suits kept sodbusters, cowboys, and townsfolk alike not only warm but also itchy and a little on the smelly side (back when bathing once a week was considered the height of cleanliness). Thermal imaging is photography that captures "heat pictures"—rather than ordinary light pictures—of objects. And thermal pollution occurs when industrial water use ends up warming a river in a damaging way. Small-plane pilots use *thermal* as a noun for a warm updraft, often over a plowed field or desert, that lifts their wings, just as it enables hawks to soar upward without moving their wings.

thermodynamics \ˌthər-mō-dī-ˈna-miks\ Physics that deals with the mechanical actions or relations of heat.

• With his college major in electrical engineering, he assumed it would be an easy step to a graduate-school concentration in thermodynamics.

Thermodynamics (see DYNAM, p. 389) is based on the fact that all forms of energy, including heat and mechanical energy, are basically the same. Thus, it deals with the ways in which one form of energy is converted into another, when one of the forms is heat. The study of thermodynamics dates from before the invention of the first practical steam engine—an engine that uses steam to produce physical power—in the 18th century. Today most of the world's electrical power is actually produced by steam engines, and the principal use of thermodynamics is in power production.

thermonuclear \ˌthər-mō-ˈnü-klē-ər\ Of or relating to the changes in the nucleus of atoms with low atomic weight, such as hydrogen, that require a very high temperature to begin.

• In the 1950s and '60s, anxious American families built thousands of underground "fallout shelters" to protect themselves from the radiation of a thermonuclear blast.

Nuclear is the adjective for *nucleus*, the main central part of an atom. The original nuclear explosives, detonated in 1945, were so-called *fission* bombs, since they relied on the fission, or splitting, of the nuclei of uranium atoms. But an even greater source of destructive power lay in nuclear *fusion*, the forcing together of atomic nuclei. The light and heat given off by stars such as the sun come from a sustained fusion—or thermonuclear—reaction deep within it. On earth, such thermonuclear reactions were used to develop the hydrogen bomb, a bomb based on a fusion reaction that merged hydrogen atoms to become helium atoms. The thermonuclear era, which began in 1952, produced bombs hundreds of times more powerful than those exploded at the end of World War II. Why the *thermo-* in *thermonuclear*? Because great heat is required to trigger the fusion process, and the trigger used is actually a fission bomb.

British thermal unit The quantity of heat required to raise the temperature of one pound of water one degree Fahrenheit at a specified temperature.

• Wood-stove manufacturers compete with each other in their claims of how many British thermal units of heat output their stoves can produce.

Despite its name, the British thermal unit, or BTU, may be more widely used in North America than in Britain. Air conditioners, furnaces, and stoves are generally rated by BTUs. (Though "BTUs" is often short for "BTUs per hour"; in air-conditioner ratings, for instance, "BTUs" really means "BTUs of cooling capacity per hour.") Fuels such as natural gas and propane are also compared using BTUs. The BTU first appeared in 1876 and isn't part of the metric system—the metric unit of energy is the much smaller *joule*—so it isn't much used by scientists, but its practicality keeps it popular for consumer goods and fuels. A better-known heat unit is the *calorie*; a BTU is equal to about 252 calories. (Since the familiar food calorie is actually a *kilocalorie*, a BTU equals only about a quarter of a food calorie.)

Quizzes

A. Choose the closest definition:

1. hypothermia   a. excitability b. subnormal temperature c. external temperature d. warmth
2. thermodynamics   a. science of motion b. nuclear science c. science of explosives d. science of heat energy
3. hypoglycemia   a. extreme heat b. low blood sugar c. low energy d. high blood pressure
4. thermal   a. boiling b. heat-related c. scorching d. cooked
5. hypothetical   a. typical b. substandard c. sympathetic d. assumed
6. hypochondriac   a. person with imaginary visions b. person with heart congestion c. person with imaginary ailments d. person with imaginary relatives
7. British thermal unit   a. unit of electricity b. heat unit c. ocean current unit d. altitude unit
8. thermonuclear   a. nuclear reaction requiring high heat b. chemical reaction requiring a vacuum c. biological reaction producing bright light d. nuclear reaction based on distance from the sun

B. Indicate whether the following pairs of words have the same or different meanings:

1. British thermal unit / calorie   same ___ / different ___
2. hypochondriac / wise man   same ___ / different ___
3. thermal / insulating   same ___ / different ___
4. thermonuclear / destructive   same ___ / different ___

5. hypoglycemia / high blood
   sugar   same ___ / different ___
6. hypothetical / supposed   same ___ / different ___
7. thermodynamics / explosives   same ___ / different ___
8. hypothermia / low blood sugar same ___ / different ___

POLY comes from *polys,* the Greek word for "many." A *polytechnic* institute offers instruction in many technical fields. *Polygamy* is marriage in which one has many spouses, or at least more than the legal limit of one. And *polysyllabic* words are words of many syllables—of which there are quite a few in this book.

polyp \\'pä-ləp\\ (1) A sea invertebrate that has a mouth opening at one end surrounded by stinging tentacles. (2) A growth projecting from a mucous membrane, as on the colon or vocal cords.

• She had had a polyp removed from her throat, and for two weeks afterward she could only whisper.

This term comes from *polypous,* a Greek word for "octopus," which meant literally "many-footed." To the untrained eye, the invertebrate known as the polyp may likewise appear to be many-footed, though it never walks anywhere since its "feet" are tentacles, used for stinging tiny organisms which the polyp then devours. The types of tumor known as polyps got their name because some seem to be attached to the surface by branching "foot"-like roots, even though most do not. Polyps of the nose or vocal cords are usually only inconvenient, causing breathing difficulty or hoarseness, and can be removed easily; however, polyps in the intestines can sometimes turn cancerous.

polyglot \\'pä-lē-₁glät\\ (1) One who can speak or write several languages. (2) Having or using several languages.

• As trade between countries increases, there is more need for polyglots who can act as negotiators.

Polyglot contains the root *glot,* meaning "language." It is used both as a noun and as an adjective. Thus, we could say that an international airport is bound to be *polyglot,* with people from all over the world speaking their native languages. One of history's more interesting polyglots was the Holy Roman Emperor Charles V, who claimed that he addressed his horse only in German, conversed with women in Italian and with men in French, but reserved Spanish (his original language) for his talks with God.

polymer \\'pä-lə-mər\ A chemical compound formed by a reaction in which two or more molecules combine to form larger molecules with repeating structural units.

• Nylon, a polymer commercially introduced in 1938, can be spun and woven into fabrics or cast as tough, elastic blocks.

There are many natural polymers, including shellac, cellulose, and rubber. But synthetic polymers only came into being around 1870 with Celluloid, known especially for its use in photographic film. After many decades of development, the *polymeric* compounds now include *polypropylene,* used in milk crates, luggage, and hinges; *polyurethane,* used in paints, adhesives, molded items, rubbers, and foams; and *polyvinyl chloride* (PVC), used to make pipes that won't rust. And let's not forget *polyester*, which gave us a lot of uncool clothing in the 1970s but whose strength and resistance to corrosion have ensured that it remains an extremely useful material for all kinds of goods.

polygraph \\'pä-lē-ˌgraf\ An instrument for recording changes in several bodily functions (such as blood pressure and rate of breathing) at the same time; lie detector.

• My brother-in-law is completely law-abiding, but he's such a nervous type that he's failed two polygraph tests at job interviews.

With its *graph-* root (see GRAPH, p. 277), *polygraph* indicates that it writes out several different results. A polygraph's output consists of a set of squiggly lines on a computer screen, each indicating one function being tested. The functions most commonly measured are blood pressure, breathing rate, pulse, and perspiration, all of which tend to increase when you lie. Polygraphs have been in use since 1924, and have gotten more sensitive over the years, though many experts still believe that they're unreliable and that a prepared liar can fool the machine. They're used not only for law enforcement but perhaps more often by employers—often the police department itself!—who don't want to hire someone who has broken the law in the past but won't admit to it.

PRIM comes from *primus,* the Latin word for "first." Something *primary* is first in time, rank, or importance. Something *primitive* is in its first stage of development. And something *primeval* had its origin in the first period of world or human history.

primal \ˈprī-məl\ Basic or primitive.

• There was always a primal pleasure in listening to the rain beat on the roof at night and dropping off to sleep in front of the fire.

Primal generally describes something powerful and almost instinctual. So when we speak of the primal innocence of youth or the primal intensity of someone's devotion, we're suggesting that the emotions or conditions being described are basic to our animal nature. Sitting around a campfire may feel like a primal experience, in which we share the emotions of our cave-dwelling ancestors. Intense fear of snakes or spiders may have primal roots, owing to the poison that some species carry. In "primal scream" therapy, popular in the 1970s, patients relive painful childhood experiences and express their frustration and anger through uncontrolled screaming and even violence.

primer \ˈpri-mər\ (1) A small book for teaching children to read. (2) A small introductory book on a subject.

• She announced that she'd be passing out a primer on mutual funds at the end of the talk.

Primers were once a standard part of every child's education. The first primer printed in North America, *The New England Primer* (ca. 1690), was typical; it contained many quotations from the Bible and many moral lessons, and the text was accompanied by numerous woodcut illustrations. We no longer use the word in early education, but it's widely used in everyday speech. Notice how *primer* is pronounced; don't mix it up with the kind of paint that's pronounced with a long *i* sound.

primate \ˈprī-ˌmāt\ Any member of the group of animals that includes human beings, apes, and monkeys.

• Dr. Leakey sent three young women to work with individual primates: Jane Goodall with the chimpanzees, Dian Fossey with the gorillas, and Birute Galdakis with the orangutans.

It was the great biologist Carolus Linnaeus who gave the primates their name, to indicate that animals of this order were the most advanced of all. Linnaeus listed human beings with the apes a hundred years before Charles Darwin would publish his famous work on evolution. When people told him that our close relationship to the apes and monkeys was impossible because it disagreed with the Bible, he responded that, from the biological evidence, he simply couldn't come to a different conclusion. Among the mammals, the primates are distinguished by their large brains, weak sense of smell, lack of claws, long pregnancies, and long childhoods, among other things. Along with the apes and monkey, the Primate order includes such interesting animals as the lemurs, tarsiers, galagos, and lorises.

primordial \prī-'mȯr-dē-əl\ (1) First created or developed. (2) Existing in or from the very beginning.

• Many astronomers think the universe is continuing to evolve from a primordial cloud of gas.

Primordial can be traced back to the Latin word *primordium,* or "origin," and applies to something that is only the starting point in a course of development or progression. A primordial landscape is one that bears no sign of human use, and a primordial cell is the first formed and least specialized in a line of cells. The substance out of which the earth was formed and from which all life evolved is commonly called "the primordial ooze" or "the primordial soup"— even by scientists.

Quizzes

A. Fill in each blank with the correct letter:

a.	primer	e.	polyp
b.	polyglot	f.	primordial
c.	primate	g.	polymer
d.	polygraph	h.	primal

1. The only language instruction the child had ever gotten was from a basic _____, but he was already reading at the fifth-grade level.

2.   Rubber is a natural _____ that remains the preferred material for many uses.

3.   The asteroids in our solar system may be remnants of a _____ cloud of dust.

4.   She had never passed a _____ test, since apparently her heart rate always shot up when she was asked a question.

5.   All the _____ species look after their children for much longer than almost any other mammals.

6.   Having gone to school in four countries as a child, she was already a fluent _____.

7.   They were charmed by the _____ innocence of the little village.

8.   The medical tests had revealed a suspicious-looking _____ on his stomach.

B.   Indicate whether the following pairs have the same or different meanings:

1.   polyp / oyster   same ___ / different ___
2.   primate / ape-family member   same ___ / different ___
3.   polymer / molecule with
     repeating units   same ___ / different ___
4.   primer / firstborn   same ___ / different ___
5.   polyglot / speaking many
     languages   same ___ / different ___
6.   primal / highest   same ___ / different ___
7.   polygraph / lie detector   same ___ / different ___
8.   primordial / primitive   same ___ / different ___

HOM/HOMO comes from *homos,* the Greek word for "same," which in English words may also mean "similar." A *homograph* is a word spelled like another word but different in meaning or pronunciation, and a *homosexual* is a person who favors others of the same sex. (This root has nothing to do with the Latin *homo,* meaning "person," as in *Homo sapiens,* the French *homme,* and the Spanish *hombre.*)

homonym \\'hä-mə-ˌnim\\ One of two or more words pronounced and/or spelled alike but different in meaning.

- The *pool* of "a pool of water" and the *pool* of "a game of pool" are homonyms.

Homonym can be troublesome because it may refer to three distinct classes of words. Homonyms may be words with identical pronunciations but different spellings and meanings, such as *to, too,* and *two*. Or they may be words with both identical pronunciations and identical spellings but different meanings, such as *quail* (the bird) and *quail* (to cringe). Finally, they may be words that are spelled alike but are different in pronunciation and meaning, such as the *bow* of a ship and *bow* that shoots arrows. The first and second types are sometimes called *homophones*, and the second and third types are sometimes called *homographs*—which makes naming the second type a bit confusing. Some language scholars prefer to limit *homonym* to the third type.

homogeneous \\ˌhō-mə-'jē-nē-əs\\ (1) Of the same or a similar kind. (2) Of uniform structure or composition throughout.

- Though she was raised in a small town, she found the city more interesting because its population was less homogeneous.

A slab of rock is homogeneous if it consists of the same material throughout, like granite or marble. A neighborhood might be called homogeneous if all the people in it are similar, having pretty much the same background, education, and outlook. *Homogeneity* is fine in a rock, though some people find it a little boring in a neighborhood (while others find it comforting). Note that many people spell this word *homogenous*, and pronounce it that way too.

homologous \\hō-'mä-lə-gəs\\ Developing from the same or a similar part of a remote ancestor.

- Arms and wings are homologous structures that reveal the ancient relationship between birds and four-legged animals.

In his famous discussion of the panda's thumb, Stephen Jay Gould carefully explains how this thumb is not homologous to the human thumb. Although the two digits are used in much the same way (the panda's thumb is essential for stripping bamboo of its tasty leaves, the staple of the panda's diet), the panda's thumb developed from a bone in its wrist and is an addition to the five "fingers" of its paw. The tiny stirrup and anvil bones of our inner ear, however, do seem to be homologous with the bones that allow a garter snake to swallow a frog whole.

homogenize \hō-ˈmä-jə-ˌnīz\ (1) To treat (milk) so that the fat is mixed throughout instead of floating on top. (2) To change (something) so that its parts are the same or similar.

• By now the suburb had gotten so homogenized that he couldn't tell the families on his street apart.

Homogenized milk has been around so long—about a hundred years—that many Americans have never seen milk with the cream on top, and probably think cream separation only happens in expensive yogurt. But *homogenize* was being used before anyone succeeded in getting milk and cream to mix. People who use the word often dislike the idea that everything is becoming the same, whether it's radio shows that are no longer produced locally or schools that rely too much on standardized testing.

DIS comes from Latin, where it means "apart." In English, its meanings have increased to include "opposite" or "not" (as in *distaste, disagreeable*), "deprive of" (*disinfect*), or "exclude or expel from" (*disbar*). The original meaning can still be seen in a word like *dissipate,* which means "to break up and scatter."

---

dissuade \di-ˈswād\ To convince (someone) not to do something.

• The thought of the danger he might be facing on the journey makes her uneasy, and she's trying to dissuade him from going.

Dissuade is the opposite of *persuade*, though it's a less common word. The dissuading may be done by a person or by something else: A bad weather forecast may dissuade a fisherman from going out to sea that day, but a warning on a cigarette pack almost never dissuades a real smoker from having his or her next cigarette.

disorient \dis-ˈȯr-ē-ˌent\ To cause to be confused or lost.

• By now the hikers were completely disoriented, and darkness was falling fast.

The Orient is the East (just as the Occident is the West). The verb *orient* comes from the traditional practice of building Christian churches so that the altar is at the building's easterly end—in other words, "orienting" the church. One reason for this practice is that the Book of Matthew says, "As the lightning comes from the East . . . so also will the Son of Man"—that is, just like the sun in the morning, Jesus in his Second Coming will appear in the East. *Orienteering* is participating in a cross-country race in which each person uses a map and compass to navigate the course. *Orient* comes from the word meaning "to rise" (like the sun), and still today it's easy for a hiker to become disoriented when an overcast sky hides the sun.

discredit \dis-ˈkre-dət\ (1) To cause (someone or something) to seem dishonest or untrue. (2) To damage the reputation of (someone).

- His book had been thoroughly discredited by scholars, and his reputation was badly damaged.

Since one meaning of *credit* is "trust," *discredit* means basically "destroy one's trust." A scientific study may be discredited if it turns out it was secretly written up by someone paid by a drug company. An autobiography may be discredited if someone discovers that the best parts came out of a novel. A lawyer may try to discredit testimony in a trial by revealing that the witness just got out of the slammer. Many political campaigns rely on discrediting one's opponents; desperate politicians have learned that, if they can claim that someone attacking them has been completely discredited, it might work even if it isn't true.

dislodge \dis-ˈläj\ To force out of a place, especially a place of rest, hiding, or defense.

- Senators are attempting to dislodge the bill from the committee, where the chairman has failed to act on it for five months.

A *lodge* is usually a kind of rooming house or hotel, and the verb *lodge* often means staying or sleeping in such a place. Thus, *dislodge* means removing a person or thing from where it's been staying. So, for instance, you might use a toothpick to dislodge a seed from between your teeth, police might use tear gas to dislodge a sniper from his hiding place, and a slate tile dislodged from a roof could be dangerous to someone hanging out on the street below.

Quizzes

A. Choose the closest definition:

1. dislodge   a. drink slowly b. scatter c. make pale
   d. remove
2. homonym   a. word meaning the same as another
   b. word spelled and sounded the same as another
   c. one with same name as another d. one who loves
   another of the same sex
3. discredit   a. cancel a bank card b. show to be
   untrue   c. dissolve d. lower one's grade
4. homogeneous   a. self-loving b. unusually brilliant
   c. having many parts d. consistent throughout
5. dissuade   a. remove b. break up c. advise against
   d. sweep away
6. homologous   a. of different length b. of similar size
   c. of different stages d. of similar origin
7. disorient   a. confuse b. disagree c. take away d. hide
8. homogenize   a. treat as the same b. explain
   thoroughly c. speak the same language d. mix
   thoroughly

**B. Match the definition on the left to the correct word
   on the right:**

1. word spelled like another   a.   disorient
2. pry loose   b.   homogenize
3. having a consistent texture   c.   dissuade
4. perplex   d.   homonym
5. evolutionarily related   e.   discredit
6. damage a reputation   f.   homologous
7. make the same throughout   g.   dislodge
8. convince otherwise   h.   homogeneous

Latin Borrowings

ad hoc \\'ad-'häk\\ Formed or used for a particular purpose or for
immediate needs.

• The faculty formed an ad hoc committee to deal with the question
  of First Amendment rights on campus.

Ad hoc literally means "for this" in Latin, and in English this almost always means "for this specific purpose." Issues that come up in the course of a project often require immediate, ad hoc solutions. An ad hoc investigating committee is authorized to look into a matter of limited scope. An ad hoc ruling by an athletic council is intended to settle a particular case, and is not meant to serve as a model for later rulings. If an organization deals with too many things on an ad hoc basis, it may mean someone hasn't been doing enough planning.

ad hominem \\'ad-'hä-mə-nem\\ Marked by an attack on an opponent's character rather than by an answer to the arguments made or the issues raised.

• Presidential campaigns have often relied on ad hominem attacks rather than serious discussion of important issues.

Ad hominem in Latin means "to the man"—that is, "against the other person." The term comes from the field of rhetoric (the art of speaking and writing). If you have a weak argument, one easy way to defend yourself has always been to attack your opponent verbally in a personal way. Since such attacks require neither truth nor logic to be effective, their popularity has never waned.

alter ego \\'ȯl-tər-'ē-gō\\ (1) A trusted friend or personal representative. (2) The opposite side of a personality.

• The White House chief of staff is a political alter ego, who knows, or should know, who and what the President considers most important.

In Latin, *alter ego* literally means "second I." An alter ego can be thought of as a person's clone or second self. A professional alter ego might be a trusted aide who knows exactly what the boss wants done. A personal alter ego might be a close friend who is almost like a twin. *Alter ego* can also refer to the second, hidden side of one's own self. In Robert Louis Stevenson's classic *The Strange Case of Doctor Jekyll and Mr. Hyde,* Dr. Jekyll is a good-hearted, honorable man; but after taking a potion, his alter ego, the loathsome and diabolical Mr. Hyde, takes over his personality.

de facto \\dē-'fak-tō\\ Being such in practice or effect, although not formally recognized; actual.

• Although there was never a general declaration of war, the two countries were at war in a de facto sense for almost a decade.

Literally meaning "from the fact," *de facto* in English can be applied to anything that has the substance of something without its formal name. A de facto government is one that operates with all of the power of a regular government but without official recognition. De facto segregation isn't the result of laws, but can be just as real and deep-rooted as legally enforced segregation. The de facto leader of a group is just the one who all the rest seem to follow. (Compare *de jure*, p. 398.)

quid pro quo \ˌkwid-ˌprō-ˈkwō\ Something given or received for something else.

• He did something very nice for me years ago, so getting him that job was really a quid pro quo.

In Latin, *quid pro quo* means literally "something for something." Originally, the phrase was used to mean the substitution of an inferior medicine for a good one. Today it often doesn't suggest anything negative; for most people, it just means "a favor for a favor." But in politics the phrase is often used when, for example, a wealthy corporation gives a lot of money to a candidate and expects to get a big favor in return. In such cases, some of us may prefer to describe the money as a *bribe* and the quid pro quo as a *payoff*.

ex post facto \ˌeks-ˌpōst-ˈfak-tō\ Done, made, or formulated after the fact.

• When Carl tells us his "reasons" for why he behaved badly, they're nothing but ex post facto excuses for impulsive behavior.

Ex post facto is Latin for "from a thing done afterward." Approval for a project that's given ex post facto—after the project already has been begun or completed—may just have been given in order to save face. An ex post facto law is one that declares someone's action to be criminal only after it was committed—a procedure forbidden by our Constitution.

modus operandi \ˈmō-dəs-ˌä-pə-ˈran-ˌdī\ A usual way of doing something.

• A criminal who commits repeated crimes can often be identified by his modus operandi.

Modus operandi is Latin for "method of operating." The term is often associated with police work, and it's a favorite of mystery writers. In speech and dialogue, it's often abbreviated to "m.o." (as in "We're beginning to get a handle on the killer's m.o., but we can't go public with it yet"). But it's not only used in criminal contexts. So a frequent gambler who likes to play the horses may have a particular modus operandi for picking winners. And the familiar modus operandi of a cutthroat retailer may be to undersell competitors, drive them out of business, and then raise prices afterwards.

modus vivendi \\'mō-dəs-vi-'ven-dē\\ (1) A practical compromise or arrangement that is acceptable to all concerned. (2) A way of life.

• During the budget crisis, the Democratic governor and the Republican legislature established a good working modus vivendi.

Modus vivendi literally means "manner of living" in Latin, and it sometimes has that meaning in English as well. Usually, though, a modus vivendi is a working arrangement that disputing parties can live with, at least until a more permanent solution can be found. Typically, a modus vivendi is an arrangement that ignores differences and difficulties. So, for example, two people going through a bitter divorce may be able to arrive at a modus vivendi that allows them to at least maintain an appearance of civility and dignity.

Quiz

Choose the closest definition:

1. alter ego   a. church structure b. bad conscience
   c. intimate friend d. self-love
2. modus vivendi   a. pie with ice cream
   b. compromise c. stalemate d. immoral conduct
3. ad hoc   a. for this purpose b. permanent
   c. long-range d. for many reasons
4. ex post facto   a. in anticipation b. sooner or later
   c. coming after d. someday
5. ad hominem   a. based on personalities b. based on
   logic c. based on issues d. based on sexual preference
6. modus operandi   a. procedure b. way of moving
   c. crime d. arrest

7. de facto a. in transit b. in effect c. in debt
   d. in theory
8. quid pro quo a. proven truth b. philosophical
   question c. mystery d. something given in return

Review Quizzes

A. Complete the analogy:
1. anxious : calm :: ambivalent : _____
   a. neutral b. certain c. funloving d. jittery
2. prologue : beginning :: epilogue : _____
   a. start b. end c. book d. drama
3. past : previous :: ex post facto : _____
   a. beforehand b. afterward c. during d. actually
4. local : here :: ambient : _____
   a. there b. somewhere c. nowhere d. everywhere
5. rodent : woodchuck :: primate : _____
   a. zoology b. mammal c. antelope d. baboon
6. support : assist :: dissuade : _____
   a. distrust b. convince c. soothe d. discourage
7. personal : impersonal :: ad hominem : _____
   a. to the time b. to the issue c. to the end d. to the
   maximum
8. floral : flowers :: thermal : _____
   a. weight b. pressure c. terms d. heat

B. Fill in each blank with the correct letter:

a.	ad hoc	i.	dissuade
b.	ambivalent	j.	modus vivendi
c.	modus operandi	k.	primer
d.	epithet	l.	alter ego
e.	thermonuclear	m.	polyglot
f.	quid pro quo	n.	hypochondriac
g.	polymer	o.	ambit
h.	homogeneous		

1. A real _____, she could speak four languages and read
   three others.

2. The independent-minded teenager and her overprotective parents struggled to arrive at a _____ that both sides could accept.

3. The usual _____ for the songwriters was for one to write the lyrics first and then for the other to compose the music.

4. She is such a close friend that she seems like my _____.

5. The Congressman's vote was seen as a _____ for the insurance industry's campaign contributions.

6. She's the only person who could possibly _____ him from proceeding with this foolish plan.

7. Much thought has gone into the designing of _____ power plants that run on nuclear fusion.

8. The development of the first synthetic _____ for use as fabric revolutionized the garment industry.

9. "Gray-eyed" is the standard _____ used to describe the goddess Athena.

10. She had written a little _____ on volunteering, which she was now expanding into a full-length book.

11. Jessica was _____ about going to the party: it sounded exciting, but she wouldn't know any of the other guests.

12. In her middle age she became a thorough _____, always convinced she was suffering from some new disease.

13. You should blend all ingredients thoroughly to produce a _____ mixture.

14. An _____ committee was named to come up with ideas for redecorating the waiting room.

15. He reminded the audience that particle physics didn't really fall within the _____ of his expertise.

C. Indicate whether the following pairs have the same or different meanings:

1. de facto / actually   same ___ / different ___
2. hypothermia / heatstroke   same ___ / different ___
3. primordial / existing from
   the beginning   same ___ / different ___
4. ambient / atmospheric   same ___ / different ___
5. polyphonic / religious   same ___ / different ___
6. primal / first   same ___ / different ___

7.	ambiguous / unclear	same __ / different __
8.	modus operandi / way of life	same __ / different __
9.	homologous / blended	same __ / different __
10.	discredit / mislead	same __ / different __
11.	thermal / soil-related	same __ / different __
12.	epiphyte / parasite	same __ / different __
13.	quid pro quo / synonym	same __ / different __
14.	epitaph / grave inscription	same __ / different __
15.	dislodge / deflate	same __ / different __

UNIT

4

VOR comes from the Latin verb *vorare,* "to eat," and the ending *-ivorous* shows up in words that refer to eaters of certain kinds of food. *Frugivorous* (for "fruit-eating"), *granivorous* (for "grain-eating"), and *graminivorous* (for "grass-eating") aren't too rare, but you won't run across *phytosuccivorous* ("plant-sap-eating") every day.

carnivorous \kär-ˈni-və-rəs\ Meat-eating or flesh-eating.

- He'd gotten tired of his vegetarian guinea pigs and decided he preferred carnivorous pets such as ferrets.

The order of mammals that Linnaeus named the Carnivora includes such families as the dogs, the bears, the raccoons, the weasels, the hyenas, the cats, and the seals. Most *carnivores* eat only meat in the wild, but some have varied diets; some bears, for instance, normally eat far more vegetation than meat. Carnivores have powerful jaws and complex teeth, and most are highly intelligent. Humans, like their ape cousins, are basically *omnivores* (see p. 344).

herbivorous \hər-ˈbi-və-rəs\ Plant-eating.

- In spite of their frightening appearance, marine iguanas are peaceable herbivorous animals that feed mostly on seaweed.

Many herbivorous animals, such as rabbits, deer, sheep, and cows, are noted for their gentle and passive ways. But such behavior is not universal among *herbivores*. Rhinoceroses and elephants, for instance, are capable of inflicting serious damage if threatened, and among dinosaurs, the herbivorous Diplodocus had a thick tail that could be used as a lethal weapon against attacking carnivores. Herbivorous humans are usually called *vegetarians*.

insectivorous \ˌin-ˌsek-ˈtiv-rəs\ Feeding on insects.

* Their rather odd 12-year-old son kept insectivorous plants in his bedroom and fed them live flies.

A wide variety of animals could be called *insectivores*—most of the birds, for example, as well as the spiders. Of the amphibians, frogs and many lizards are largely insectivorous. Even some fish get much of their food from insects. The order of mammals called Insectivora contains the shrews, moles, and hedgehogs, though bats and anteaters are also insectivores. Many insects are themselves insectivores; the dragonfly, for instance, is a swift insectivorous terror that lives up to its name. But it's the insectivorous plants that tend to fascinate us; of the over 600 species, the best known are the Venus flytrap (which snaps shut on its prey), the pitcher plants (which drown insects in a tiny pool of water), and the sundews (which capture insects with their sticky surfaces).

voracious \və-ˈrā-shəs\ Having a huge appetite.

* One of the hardest parts of dieting is watching skinny people with voracious appetites consume large amounts of food without gaining weight.

Voracious can be applied to people, animals, and even things, and doesn't always refer to consuming food. Thus, teenagers are voracious eaters; you may become a voracious reader on vacation; and Americans have long been voracious consumers. The most voracious bats may eat three-quarters of their weight in insects in a single night. Some countries have a voracious appetite for oil. Voracious corporations keep "swallowing" other companies through mergers.

CARN comes from a Latin word meaning "flesh" or "meat." *Carnation* originally meant "the color of flesh," which was once the only color of the flower we call the carnation. In Christian countries, Lent is the period when the faithful traditionally give up something they love, often meat. The days leading up to Lent are known as the *carnival* season, from the Italian *carnelevare*, later shortened to *carnevale*, which meant "removal of meat"—though during carnival, of course, people indulge in just about everything, and the removal of meat only comes later.

---

carnage \\'kär-nij\\ Great destruction of life (as in a battle); slaughter.

• Countries around the world appealed to all sides of the conflict to stop the carnage of the war in Bosnia.

This word was taken over straight from French (a Latin-based language), and has mostly referred to large-scale killing in wartime. But *carnage* needn't refer only to slaughter on the battlefield. With tens of thousands of people dying each year in automobile accidents, it's appropriate to speak of carnage on the nation's highways. And those concerned about the effects of the violence we see constantly on TV and movie screens may refer to that as carnage as well.

carnal \\'kär-nəl\\ Having to do with bodily pleasures.

• The news stories about students on Spring Break tend to focus on the carnal pleasures associated with the annual ritual.

In Christianity in past centuries, *carnal* was often used as the opposite of *spiritual,* describing what are sometimes called "the pleasures of the flesh." Thus, gluttony—the consumption of excessive food and drink—was a deadly carnal sin, whereas the holiest monks and hermits might eat hardly anything and never touch wine. Today *carnal* has a somewhat old-fashioned sound; when we use it, we generally mean simply "sexual."

incarnate \\in-'kär-nət\\ Given bodily or actual form; especially, having human body.

• For the rest of his life, he would regard his childhood nanny as goodness incarnate.

Incarnate often has a religious ring to it, since for centuries it has been used in the Christian church, which regards Jesus as the *incarnation* of God—that is, as God made human. Surprisingly, neither word appears in Bible translations; instead, the Latin word *incarnatus* appears in the Christian creeds (basic statements of belief) and the Catholic Mass. Regardless, *incarnate* soon began to be used with various nouns: "the devil incarnate," "evil incarnate," etc. Notice that *incarnate* is one of the rare adjectives that usually, but not always, follows its noun. *Incarnate* is also a verb, though with a slightly different pronunciation: "This report simply incarnates the prejudices of its authors," "For her followers, she incarnates the virtue of selflessness," etc.

reincarnation \ˌrē-ˌin-ˌkär-'nā-shən\ (1) Rebirth in new bodies or forms of life. (2) Someone who has been born again with a new body after death.

• Even as a child he struck everyone as a reincarnation of his grandfather, not in his features but in his manner and personality.

It's easy to make fun of people who claim to be the reincarnation of Cleopatra or Napoleon, but they don't come from a culture that takes reincarnation seriously. In Hindu belief, a person must pass through a series of reincarnations—some of which may be as insects or fish—before fully realizing that the bodily pleasures are shallow and that only spiritual life is truly valuable; only then do the reincarnations cease. For Hindus, an "old soul" is a person who seems unusually wise from early in life, and whose wisdom must have come from passing through many reincarnations.

Quizzes

A. Indicate whether the following pairs have the same or different meanings:

1. carnage / slaughter   same __ / different __
2. insectivorous / buglike   same __ / different __
3. reincarnation / rebirth   same __ / different __
4. voracious / extremely hungry   same __ / different __
5. carnal / spiritual   same __ / different __
6. herbivorous / vegetarian   same __ / different __
7. incarnate / holy   same __ / different __
8. carnivorous / meat-eating   same __ / different __

B. Fill in each blank with the correct letter:

a. reincarnation   e. voracious
b. insectivorous   f. herbivorous
c. carnage   g. carnal
d. carnivorous   h. incarnate

1. Sheep, cattle, and antelope are _____; unlike dogs and cats, they show no interest in meat.
2. The school tried to shield students from _____ temptations.
3. The smallest mammal is the bumblebee bat, an _____ creature about the size of a dime.

4. Today he speaks of his former stepfather as evil _____, and his mother doesn't argue with him.
5. From the variety of books on his shelves, we could tell he was a _____ reader.
6. Even the ambulance drivers were horrified by the _____ of the accident.
7. As a child she loved to watch them throw meat to the _____ ones, especially the lions and tigers.
8. The current Dalai Lama is said to be the 13th _____ of the first one, who lived in the 15th century.

CRED comes from *credere,* the Latin verb meaning "to believe" or "to entrust." We have a good *credit* rating when institutions trust in our ability to repay a loan, and we carry *credentials* so that others will believe that we are who we say we are.

---

credence \ˈkrē-dəns\ Mental acceptance of something as true or real; belief.

• He scoffed and said no one still gives any credence to the story of the Loch Ness monster.

Credence is close in meaning to *belief,* but there are differences. Unlike *belief, credence* is seldom used in connection with faith in a religion or philosophy. Instead *credence* is often used in reference to reports, rumors, and opinions. And, unlike *belief,* it tends to be used with the words *give, lack, lend,* and *gain.* So a new piece of evidence may lend credence to the alibi of a criminal suspect. Claims that a political candidate can become the next President gain credence only after the candidate wins a few primaries. And although stories about Elvis sightings persist, they lack credence for most people.

credible \ˈkre-də-bəl\ (1) Able to be believed; reasonable to trust or believe. (2) Good enough to be effective.

• Because of her past criminal record, the defense lawyers knew she wouldn't be a credible witness.

Credible evidence is evidence that's likely to be believed. A credible plan is one that might actually work, and a credible excuse is one your parents might actually believe. And just as *credible* means "believable," the noun *credibility* means "believability." (But we no longer use *incredible* to mean the literal opposite of *credible*, just as we no longer use *unbelievable* as the literal opposite of *believable*.) Since *cred* is short for *credibility*, "street cred" is the kind of credibility among tough young people that you can only get by proving yourself on the mean streets of the inner city.

credulity \kri-ˈdü-lə-tē\ Readiness and willingness to believe on the basis of little evidence.

* Thrillers and action movies only succeed if they don't strain our credulity too much.

A particularly far-fetched story may be said to strain credulity, stretch credulity, put demands on our credulity, or make claims on our credulity. Credulity is a quality of innocent children (of all ages) and isn't always a bad thing; it must have been pure credulity that enabled Chicago White Sox and Philadelphia Phillies fans to wait so long for a World Series victory ("This is the year they're going to take it!"), which probably made life bearable for them. The related adjective is *credulous*. F. Scott Fitzgerald once defined advertising as "making dubious promises to a credulous public."

credo \ˈkrē-ˌdō\ (1) A statement of the basic beliefs of a religious faith. (2) A set of guiding principles or beliefs.

* She claims she made her money on Wall Street just by following the old credo "Buy low, sell high."

Credo comes straight from the Latin word meaning "I believe," and is the first word of many religious credos, or *creeds*, such as the Apostles' Creed and the Nicene Creed. But the word can be applied to any guiding principle or set of principles. Of course, you may choose a different credo when you're 52 than when you're 19. But here is the credo of the writer H. L. Mencken, written after he had lived quite a few years: "I believe that it is better to tell the truth than to lie. I believe that it is better to be free than to be a slave. And I believe that it is better to know than to be ignorant."

FID comes from *fides,* the Latin word for "faith" or "trust." *Fidelity* is another word for "faithfulness." *Confidence* is having faith in someone or something. An *infidel* is someone who lacks a particular kind of religious faith. And the once-popular dog's name *Fido* is Latin for "I trust."

affidavit \ˌa-fə-ˈdā-vət\ A sworn statement made in writing.

• The whole family had signed affidavits stating that they believed the will to be valid.

In Latin, *affidavit* means "he (she) has sworn an oath," and an affidavit is always a sworn written document. If it contains a lie, the person making it may be prosecuted. Affidavits are often used in court when it isn't possible for someone to appear in person. Police officers must usually file an affidavit with a judge to get a search warrant. Affidavits (unlike similar signed statements called *depositions*) are usually made without an opposing lawyer being present and able to ask questions.

diffident \ˈdi-fə-dənt\ Lacking confidence; timid, cautious.

• He always found it a struggle to get his most diffident students to speak in front of the class.

Diffident means lacking faith in oneself—in other words, the opposite of *confident*. Distrust in your abilities or opinions usually makes you hesitate to speak or act. Patients who feel diffident around their doctors, for example, don't dare ask them many questions. A helpful friend tries to instill confidence in place of *diffidence*.

fiduciary \fi-ˈdü-shē-ˌer-ē\ (1) Having to do with a confidence or trust. (2) Held in trust for another.

• Pension-fund managers have a fiduciary responsibility to invest the pension's funds for the sole benefit of those who will receive the pensions.

A fiduciary relationship is one in which one person places faith in another. Stockbrokers and real-estate agents have fiduciary duties to their clients, which means they must act in their clients' best financial interests. Members of a company's board of directors have a fiduciary responsibility to protect the financial interests of the company's shareholders. There are legal requirements for those with fiduciary responsibility, and they can be sued for breach of fiduciary duty if they fail.

perfidy \ˈpər-fə-dē\ Faithlessness, disloyalty, or treachery.

• While working for the CIA he was lured into becoming a double agent, and it seems he paid a high price for his perfidy.

The *perfidious* Benedict Arnold plotted with the British to surrender West Point to them during the American Revolution—an act that made his name a synonym for *traitor*. In recent years, the perfidy of the double agents Aldrich Ames (of the CIA) and Robert Hanssen (of the FBI) has become notorious.

Quizzes

A. Fill in each blank with the correct letter:

a.	perfidy	e.	credo
b.	credible	f.	affidavit
c.	diffident	g.	fiduciary
d.	credulity	h.	credence

1. She gave little _____ to his story about his deranged girlfriend and the kitchen knife.
2. Their account of the burglary didn't strike investigators as _____, and the insurance company refused to pay.
3. For her own best friend to take up with her former husband was _____ that could never be forgiven.
4. He's so _____ that you'd never believe he gives talks in front of international organizations.
5. The family trust had been so badly mismanaged that it appeared there had been a violation of _____ responsibility.
6. The company's odd but charming _____ was "Don't be evil."
7. The _____ stated that no oral agreement had ever been made.
8. Her _____ is enormous; no story in the supermarket tabloids is too far-fetched for her.

B. Match the definition on the left to the correct word on the right:

1.	bad faith	a.	perfidy
2.	timid	b.	credible
3.	acceptance	c.	diffident
4.	trust-based	d.	credulity
5.	sworn document	e.	credo
6.	believable	f.	affidavit

7.	principles	g.	fiduciary
8.	trustfulness	h.	credence

CURR/CURS comes from *currere,* the Latin verb meaning "to run." Although words based on this root don't tend to suggest speed, the sense of movement remains. *Current,* for instance, refers to running water in a stream or river, or electrons running through a wire, and an *excursion* is a trip from one place to another.

concurrent \kən-ˈkər-ənt\ Happening or operating at the same time.

* The killer was sentenced to serve three concurrent life terms in prison.

Things that are concurrent usually not only happen at the same time but also are similar to each other. So, for example, multitasking computers are capable of performing concurrent tasks. When we take more than one medication at a time, we run the risks involved with concurrent drug use. And at any multiplex theater several movies are running *concurrently.*

cursory \ˈkər-sə-rē\ Hastily and often carelessly done.

* Having spent the weekend going to parties, she had only given the chapter a cursory reading before class on Monday.

Unlike the other words in this section, *cursory* always implies speed. But it also stresses a lack of attention to detail. Cursory observations are generally shallow or superficial because of their speed. And when citizens complain about a cursory police investigation of a crime, they're distressed by its lack of thoroughness, not its speed.

discursive \dis-ˈkər-siv\ Passing from one topic to another.

* Some days he allowed himself to write long discursive essays in his diary instead of his usual simple reporting of the day's events.

The Latin verb *discurrere* meant "to run about," and from this word we get our word *discursive,* which often means rambling about over a wide range of topics. A discursive writing style generally isn't encouraged by writing teachers. But some of the great 19th-century writers, such as Charles Lamb and Thomas de Quincey, show that the discursive essay, especially when gracefully written and somewhat personal in tone, can be a pleasure to read. And the man often called the inventor of the essay, the great Michel de Montaigne, might touch on dozens of different topics in the course of a long discursive essay.

precursor \\'prē-ˌkər-sər\\ One that goes before and indicates the coming of another.

* Scientists are trying to identify special geological activity that may be a precursor to an earthquake, which will help them predict the quake's size, time, and location.

With its prefix *pre-*, meaning "before," a precursor is literally a "forerunner," and in fact *forerunner* first appeared as the translation of the Latin *praecursor*. But the two words function a little differently today. A forerunner may simply come before another thing, but a precursor generally paves the way for something. So, for example, the Office of Strategic Services in World War II was the immediate precursor of today's Central Intelligence Agency, while the blues music of the 1930s and 1940s was only one of the precursors of the rock and roll of today.

PED comes from the Latin word for "foot." A *pedal* is pushed by the foot; a *pedicure* is a treatment of the feet, toes, and toenails; and a *pedestal* is what a statue stands on—in a sense, its foot.

---

quadruped \\'kwä-drə-ˌped\\ An animal having four feet.

* She always tells her friends that their farm has five kinds of quadrupeds: sheep, goats, cows, horses, and pigs.

The quadrupeds include almost all the mammals. (Among the exceptions are whales, bats, and humans.) The Greek equivalent of this Latin word is *tetrapod*. However, the two are not identical, since the tetrapod classification includes *bipeds* such as birds, in which two of the limbs are no longer used for walking. Insects all have six legs, of course, and in the sea there are eight-legged *octopods* (including the octopus). But there are no animals of any kind with an odd number of legs.

pedigree \\'pe-də-ˌgrē\\ The line of ancestors of a person or animal.

- She talks a lot about her pedigree, but never mentions that a couple of her uncles spent time in prison.

What does someone's ancestry have to do with feet? Because someone once thought that a family tree, or genealogical chart, resembled a crane's foot (in French, *pied de grue*), even though cranes' feet only have four talons or claws, no more than any other bird, while a family tree may have hundreds of branches. The word *pedigree* is usually used for purebred animals—cats, racehorses, and dogs, as well as livestock such as cows and sheep. Some people continue to believe that "purity" in human family trees is a good thing as well, though most of us find the idea a little creepy.

impediment \\im-'pe-də-mənt\\ Something that interferes with movement or progress.

- Her poorly developed verbal ability was the most serious impediment to her advancement.

Impediment comes from a Latin verb that meant "to interfere with" or "to get in the way of progress," as if by tripping up the feet of someone walking. In English, *impediment* still suggests an obstruction or obstacle along a path; for example, a lack of adequate roads and bridges would be called an impediment to economic development. Impediments usually get in the way of something we want. So we may speak of an impediment to communication, marriage, or progress—but something that slows the progress of aging, disease, or decay is rarely called an impediment.

pedestrian \\pə-'des-trē-ən\\ Commonplace, ordinary, or unimaginative.

- While politicians endlessly discussed the great issues facing Russia, the Russians worried about such pedestrian concerns as finding enough food, shelter, and clothing.

Most of us know *pedestrian* as a noun meaning someone who travels on foot. But the adjective sense of *pedestrian* as defined here is actually its original meaning. To be pedestrian was to be drab or dull, as if plodding along on foot rather than speeding on horseback or by coach. *Pedestrian* is often used to describe a colorless or lifeless writing style, but it can also describe politicians, public tastes, personal qualities, or possessions. In comparison with the elaborate stage shows put on by today's rock artists, for instance, most of the stage presentations of 1960s rock stars seem pedestrian.

Quizzes

A. **Fill in each blank with the correct letter:**

a.	concurrent	e.	cursory
b.	pedigree	f.	impediment
c.	precursor	g.	discursive
d.	pedestrian	h.	quadruped

1. The warm days in March were a _____ to spring floods that were sure to come.
2. His rather snobbish grandmother only seemed to be concerned about his fiancée's _____.
3. After only a _____ look at the new car, he knew he had to have it.
4. The presence of her little sister was a definite _____ to her romantic plans for the evening.
5. She came to enjoy the _____ style of the older, rambling essays.
6. From his fleeting glimpse, all he could tell was that it was a small brown _____ that could move very fast.
7. Convention-goers had to decide which of the _____ meetings to attend.
8. His sister's trips to Borneo made his vacations at the seashore seem _____.

B. **Match the definition on the left to the correct word on the right:**

1.	simultaneous	a.	impediment
2.	obstacle	b.	precursor
3.	four-footed animal	c.	quadruped
4.	forerunner	d.	discursive
5.	hasty	e.	pedestrian
6.	ancestry	f.	pedigree
7.	rambling	g.	cursory
8.	ordinary	h.	concurrent

FLECT comes from *flectere,* the Latin verb meaning "to bend." The root sometimes takes the form *flex-*. Things that are *flexible* can be bent, and when you *flex* a muscle, you're usually bending a limb—which, as a trainer at the gym will tell you, requires the use of *flexor* muscles.

deflect \di-ˈflekt\ To turn aside, especially from a straight or fixed course.

• The stealth technology used on bombers and fighter jets works by deflecting radar energy, making them "invisible."

Use of the physical meaning of *deflect* is common. Thus, a soccer goalie's save might involve deflecting the ball rather than catching it, and workers wear eye shields to deflect tiny particles flying out of machines. But the nonphysical meaning may be even more common. A Hollywood actress might deflect criticism about her personal life by giving lavishly to charity, for example, and we've all tried to change the subject to deflect a question we really didn't want to answer.

reflective \ri-ˈflekt\ (1) Capable of reflecting light, images, or sound waves. (2) Thoughtful.

• He likes action movies and going out drinking with friends, but when you get to know him you realize he's basically reflective and serious.

Reflective people are people who *reflect* on things—that is, look back at things that have been done or said in order to think calmly and quietly about them. Most reflective people would agree with Socrates that (as he told the jury that would soon sentence him to death) "The unexamined life is not worth living." Reflective people tend to be a bit philosophical and intellectual. But almost everyone has reflective moods; gazing into a fireplace or a campfire seems to do it to almost everyone.

genuflect \ˈjen-yù-ˌflekt\ To kneel on one knee and then rise as an act of respect.

• At religious shrines in China, pilgrims may not only genuflect but actually lie down flat on the ground.

Genuflection, which contains the root *genu-*, "knee," has long been a mark of respect and obedience. King Arthur's Knights of the Round Table genuflected not only when he knighted them but whenever they greeted him formally, and this custom remains in countries today that are still ruled by royalty. In some churches, each worshipper is expected to genuflect whenever entering or leaving a pew on the central aisle.

inflection \in-'flek-shən\ (1) A change in the pitch, tone, or loudness of the voice. (2) The change in form of a word showing its case, gender, number, person, tense, mood, voice, or comparison.

- She couldn't understand her grandfather's words, but she knew from his inflection that he was asking a question.

Changing the pitch, tone, or loudness of our words are ways we communicate meaning in speech, though not on the printed page. A rising inflection at the end of a sentence generally indicates a question, and a falling inflection indicates a statement, for example. Another way of *inflecting* words is by adding endings: *-s* to make a noun plural, *-ed* to put a verb in the past tense, *-er* to form the comparative form of an adjective, and so on.

POST comes from a Latin word meaning "after" or "behind." A *postscript* (or PS) is a note that comes after an otherwise completed letter, usually as an afterthought. *Postpartum* refers to the period following childbirth, with any related events and complications. To *postdate* a check is to give it a date after the day it was written.

posterior \pō-'stir-ē-ər\ Situated toward or on the back; rear.

- In a human *posterior* and *dorsal* can both refer to the back, but in a fish *posterior* refers to the tail area.

Posterior comes from the Latin word *posterus*, meaning "coming after." *Posterior* is often used as a technical term in biology and medicine to refer to the back side of things, and is the opposite of *anterior*, which refers to the front side. For example, as more people took up running as a sport, doctors began to see an increase in stress fractures along the posterior as well as the anterior surface of the lower leg bones. In some technical fields, *posterior* may mean "later." When used as a noun, *posterior* simply means "buttocks."

posthumous \\'päs-chə-məs\ (1) Published after the death of the author. (2) Following or happening after one's death.

* Though Van Gogh scarcely sold a single painting during his lifetime, he rose to posthumous fame as one of the world's great artists.

Posthumous fame is fame that comes a little late. In fact, its original meaning in English is "born after the death of the father." Bill Clinton was the posthumous son of a father who died in an automobile accident. The word is now mostly used of artistic works that appear after the death of the artist, or the changing reputation of a dead artist. Such posthumous works as Herman Melville's *Billy Budd*, the diary of Anne Frank, and almost all the poetry of Emily Dickinson have become legendary, and in each case they had a major influence on the writer's reputation.

postmodern \\ˌpōst-'mä-dərn\ Having to do with a movement in architecture, art, or literature that is a reaction against modernism and that reintroduces traditional elements and techniques in odd contexts as well as elements from popular culture.

* The postmodern AT&T building in New York, with the "Chippendale" top that reminds viewers of an antique dresser, aroused a storm of criticism.

With its prefix *post-*, *postmodern* describes a movement that has reacted against modernism. Modernism, dating from around the start of the 20th century, represented a sharp break from 19th-century styles. But in the 1970s architects began to be dissatisfied with the stark simplicity of most modern architecture and began including in their mostly modern designs such traditional elements as columns, arches, and keystones and sometimes startling color contrasts such as might have come from advertising and pop culture. In art and literature, as in architecture, *postmodernism* often seems to be making fun of tradition, especially by denying that there's any real distinction between serious and popular art or writing. Wherever it has shown up, postmodernism has been greeted with a mixture of approval, disapproval, and sometimes amusement.

postmortem \\ˌpōst-'mȯr-təm\ (1) Occurring after death. (2) Following the event.

- In their postmortem discussion of the election, the reporters tried to explain how the polls and predictions could have been so completely wrong.

Post mortem is Latin for "after death." In English, *postmortem* refers to an examination, investigation, or process that takes place after death. A postmortem examination of a body (often simply called a *postmortem*) is often needed to determine the time and cause of death; the stiffening called rigor mortis is one postmortem change that doctors look at to determine when death occurred. Today we've come to use *postmortem* to refer to any examination or discussion that takes place after an event.

Quizzes

A. Choose the closest definition:

1. posthumous   a. before the event b. born prematurely c. occurring after death d. early in development
2. reflective   a. merry b. thoughtful c. glowing d. gloomy
3. posterior   a. on the front b. on the back c. underneath d. on top
4. deflect   a. fold over b. kneel c. turn aside d. protect
5. postmodern   a. ultramodern b. traditional c. contemporary d. mixing styles
6. inflection   a. style in art b. change in pitch c. muscle d. part to the rear
7. genuflect   a. kneel b. flex a muscle c. fold back d. change one's tone of voice
8. postmortem   a. after the event b. before the event c. caused by the event d. causing the event

B. Complete the analogy:

1. postscript : letter :: postmortem : _____ a. examination b. death c. body d. morgue
2. clever : dull :: reflective : _____ a. lazy b. educated c. calm d. empty-headed
3. prenatal : before birth :: posthumous : _____ a. after birth b. before life c. after death d. famous

4. reflect : mirror :: deflect : _____
   a. shield b. laser c. metal d. spear
5. accent : syllable :: inflection : _____
   a. note b. hint c. turn d. word
6. wave : friendship :: genuflect : _____
   a. salute b. knee c. power d. obedience
7. exterior : interior :: posterior : _____
   a. frontal b. behind c. beside d. above
8. hip-hop : music :: postmodern : _____
   a. tradition b. design c. style d. architecture

Words from Mythology

calypso \kə-ˈlip-sō\ A folk song or style of singing of West Indian origin that has a lively rhythm and words that are often made up by the singer.

• If you take a Caribbean vacation in December, you end up listening to a lot of Christmas carols played to a calypso beat.

In Homer's *Odyssey,* the nymph Calypso detains Odysseus for seven years on his way home from the Trojan War, using all her wiles to hold him on her lush island. For many people, the calypso music of the West Indian islands, which was eventually brought to America by singers such as the Andrews Sisters and later Harry Belafonte, has some of the same captivating power as the nymph, though the lyrics that are often improvised to the melodies tend to make fun of local people and happenings. The original name for these songs, however, actually seems to be based on a similar-sounding African word, for which, early in the 20th century, someone began substituting this name from Greek mythology.

odyssey \ˈä-də-sē\ (1) A long, wandering journey full of trials and adventures. (2) A spiritual journey or quest.

• Their six-month camping trip around the country was an odyssey they would always remember.

Odysseus, the hero of Homer's *Odyssey,* spends 20 years traveling home from the Trojan War. He has astonishing adventures and learns a great deal about himself and the world; he even descends to the underworld to talk to the dead. Thus, an odyssey is any long, complicated journey, often a quest for a goal, and may be a spiritual or psychological journey as well as an actual voyage.

palladium \pə-ˈlā-dē-əm\ A precious, silver-white metal related to platinum that is used in electrical contacts and as an alloy with gold to form white gold.

• Most wedding rings today are simple bands of gold, platinum, or palladium.

Pallas Athena was one of the poetical names given to the Greek goddess Athena (although it's no longer clear what Pallas was supposed to mean), and the original palladium was a statue of Athena that was believed to have the power to protect the ancient city of Troy. When an asteroid belt was discovered between Mars and Jupiter, most of the asteroids were named after figures in Greek mythology, and one of the first to be discovered was named Pallas in 1803. In the same year, scientists isolated a new silvery metal element, which they named *palladium* in honor of the recently discovered asteroid.

Penelope \pə-ˈne-lə-pē\ A modest domestic wife.

• Critics of Hillary Rodham Clinton in the 1990s would perhaps have preferred her to be a Penelope, quietly tending the White House and staying out of politics.

In the *Odyssey,* Penelope waits 20 long years for her husband Odysseus to return from Troy. During that time, she must raise their son and fend off the attentions of numerous rough suitors. She preserves herself for a long time by saying she cannot remarry until she has finished weaving a funeral shroud for her aging father-in-law; however, what she weaves each day she secretly unravels each night. A Penelope thus appears to be the perfect, patient, faithful wife (and may be using her clever intelligence to keep herself that way).

procrustean \prō-ˈkrəs-tē-ən\ Ruthlessly disregarding individual differences or special circumstances.

• The school's procrustean approach seemed to assume that all children learned in the same way and at the same rate.

In the Greek tale of the hero Theseus, Procrustes was a bandit who ambushed travelers and, after robbing them, made them lie on an iron bed. To make sure they "fit" this bed, he would cut off the parts that hung off the ends or stretch the body if it was too short; either way, the unlucky traveler always died. When he made the mistake of confronting Theseus, Procrustes was made to "fit" his own bed. Something procrustean takes no account of individual differences but cruelly and mercilessly makes everything the same.

protean \\'prō-tē-ən\ (1) Displaying great versatility or variety. (2) Able to take on many different forms or natures.

• A protean athlete, he left college with offers from the professional leagues to play baseball, football, and basketball.

As the story is told in the *Odyssey*, at the end of the Trojan War the sea god Proteus revealed to King Menelaus of Sparta how to get home from Troy with his unfaithful wife, the beautiful Helen of Troy. Before Proteus would give up the information, though, Menelaus had to capture him—no mean feat, since Proteus had the ability to change into any natural shape he chose. The word *protean* came to describe this ability to change into many different shapes or to play many different roles in quick succession.

sibyl \\'si-bəl\ A female prophet or fortune-teller.

• The villagers told him about an aged woman who lived alone in a hut on a nearby mountain, a sibyl who knew the future and would prophesy under the right conditions.

Ancient writers refer to the existence of various women in such countries as Babylonia, Greece, Italy, and Egypt, through whom the gods regularly spoke. These sibyls were easy to confuse with the oracles, women who were likewise mouthpieces of the gods, at such sites as Apollo's temple at Delphi. The most famous sibyl was the Sibyl of Cumae in Italy, a withered crone who lived in a cave. Her prophecies were collected into twelve books, three of which survived to be consulted by the Romans in times of national emergencies. She is one of the five sibyls memorably depicted by Michelangelo on the ceiling of the Sistine Chapel.

siren \\'sī-rən\ A woman who tempts men with bewitching sweetness.

• Reporters treated her like a sex symbol, but she lacked the graceful presence and air of mystery of a real siren.

The sirens were a group of partly human female creatures that lured sailors onto destructive rocks with their singing. Odysseus and his men encountered the sirens on their long journey home from Troy. The only way to sail by them safely was to make oneself deaf to their enchanting song, so Odysseus packed the men's ears with wax, while he himself, ever curious, kept his ears open but had himself tied to the mast to keep from flinging himself into the water or steering his ship toward sure destruction in his desire to see them. A siren today is a sinister but almost irresistible woman. A *siren song*, however, may be any appeal that lures a person to act against his or her better judgment.

Quiz

Fill in each blank with the correct letter:

a. odyssey   e. sibyl
b. calypso   f. procrustean
c. Penelope   g. siren
d. palladium   h. protean

1. They danced and sang to the rhythm of the _____ music long into the night.
2. While he was away on maneuvers, his wife stayed loyally at home like a true _____.
3. Critics condemn modern education as _____, forcing all students into narrow and limited modes of thinking.
4. On their four-month _____ they visited most of the major cities of Asia.
5. The wedding rings were white gold, a mixture of gold and _____.
6. She won her reputation as the office _____ after her third successful prediction of who would get married next.
7. Actors like Robin Williams seem _____ in their ability to assume different characters.
8. She was a _____ of the screen in the 1920s, luring men to their doom in movie after movie.

Review Quizzes

A. Choose the closest definition:

1. carnage   a. meat b. slaughter c. flesh d. battle
2. precursor   a. shadow b. forerunner c. follower d. oath
3. diffident   a. angry b. different c. aggressive d. shy
4. pedestrian   a. useless b. footlike c. unusual d. boring
5. credence   a. creation b. belief c. doubt d. destruction
6. credible   a. believable b. acceptable
        c. praiseworthy d. remarkable
7. pedigree   a. wealth b. education c. breeding d. purity
8. impediment   a. help b. obstacle c. footpath
        d. obligation
9. voracious   a. vast b. hungry c. fierce d. unsatisfied
10. protean   a. meaty b. powerful c. changeable
        d. professional

**B. Indicate whether the following pairs of words have
the same or different meanings:**

1. procrustean / merciful   same ___ / different ___
2. credulity / distrust   same ___ / different ___
3. concurrent / simultaneous   same ___ / different ___
4. cursory / hurried   same ___ / different ___
5. odyssey / journey   same ___ / different ___
6. deflect / absorb   same ___ / different ___
7. perfidy / disloyalty   same ___ / different ___
8. posterior / front   same ___ / different ___
9. siren / temptress   same ___ / different ___
10. herbivorous / plant-eating same ___ / different ___

C. Complete the analogy:

1. fiduciary : trust-based :: carnivorous : _____
        a. vegetarian b. meat-eating c. greedy d. hungry
2. cursory : brief :: carnal : _____
        a. musical b. festive c. deadly d. sexual
3. genuflect : kneel :: affidavit : _____
        a. financial affairs b. courtroom testimony c. legal
        advice d. sworn statement
4. insectivorous : insects :: herbivorous : _____
        a. plants b. herbs c. grains d. flowers

5. carnage : bloodbath :: Penelope : _____
   a. wife b. mother c. daughter d. siren
6. ambivalent : uncertain :: pedestrian : _____
   a. slow b. colorful c. unexciting d. explosive
7. credence : trust :: discursive : _____
   a. fast b. slow-moving c. wide-ranging
   d. all-knowing
8. procrustean : inflexible :: inflection : _____
   a. way of life b. tone of voice c. financial affairs
   d. part of speech

UNIT

5

MAL comes from a Latin word meaning "bad." A *malady* is a bad condition—a disease or illness—of the body or mind. *Malpractice* is bad medical practice. *Malodorous* things smell bad. And a *malefactor* is someone guilty of bad deeds.

malevolent \mə-ˈle-və-lənt\ Having or showing intense ill will or hatred.

• Captain Ahab sees Moby Dick not simply as a whale but as a powerfully malevolent foe.

Malevolence runs deep. Malevolent enemies have bitter and lasting feelings of ill will. Malevolent racism and bigotry can erupt in acts of violence against innocent people. Malevolence can also show itself in hurtful words, and can sometimes be seen in something as small as an angry look or gesture.

malicious \mə-ˈli-shəs\ Desiring to cause pain, injury, or distress to another.

• The boys didn't take the apples with any malicious intent; they were just hungry and didn't know any better.

Malicious and *malevolent* are close in meaning, since both refer to ill will that desires to see someone else suffer. But while *malevolent* suggests deep and lasting dislike, *malicious* usually means petty and spiteful. Malicious gossipers are often simply envious of a neighbor's good fortune. Vandals may take malicious pleasure in destroying and defacing property but usually don't truly hate the owners. *Malice* is an important legal concept, which has to be proved in order to convict someone of certain crimes such as first-degree murder.

malign \mə-'līn\ To make harsh and often false or misleading statements about.

- Captain Bligh of the *Bounty* may be one of the most unjustly maligned figures in British naval history.

Malign is related to verbs like *defame, slander,* and *libel.* The person or group being maligned is the victim of false or misleading statements, even if the *maligner* isn't necessarily guilty of deliberate lying. Someone or something that's frequently criticized is often said to be "much maligned," which suggests that the criticism isn't entirely fair or deserved. *Malign* is also an adjective, and writers often refer to a person's malign influence. The very similar *malignant*, which used to be a common synonym of *malign*, today tends to describe dangerous medical conditions, especially cancerous tumors.

malnourished \,mal-'nər-isht\ Badly or poorly nourished.

- When they finally found the children in the locked cabin, they were pale and malnourished but unharmed.

Malnourished people can be found in all types of societies. Famine and poverty are only two of the common causes of *malnutrition*. In wealthier societies, malnutrition is often the result of poor eating habits. Any diet that fails to provide the nutrients needed for health and growth can lead to malnutrition, and some malnourished people are actually fat.

CATA comes from the Greek *kata,* one of whose meanings was "down." A *catalogue* is a list of items put down on paper, and a *catapult* is a weapon for hurling missiles down on one's enemies.

cataclysm \'ka-tə-,kli-zəm\ (1) A violent and massive change of the earth's surface. (2) A momentous event that results in great upheaval and often destruction.

- World War I was a great cataclysm in modern history, marking the end of the old European social and political order.

The -*clysm* part of *cataclysm* comes from the Greek word meaning "to wash," so *cataclysm*'s original meaning was "flood, deluge," and especially Noah's Flood itself. A cataclysm causes great and lasting changes. An earthquake or other natural disaster that changes the landscape is one kind of cataclysm, but a violent political revolution may also be a *cataclysmic* event. Many cataclysms could instead be called *catastrophes*.

catacomb \\'ka-tə-ˌkōm\\ An underground cemetery of connecting passageways with recesses for tombs.

- The early Christian catacombs of Rome provide a striking glimpse into the ancient past for modern-day visitors.

About forty Christian catacombs have been found near the roads that once led into Rome. After the decline of the Roman empire these cemeteries were forgotten, not to be rediscovered until 1578. *Catacomb* has come to refer to different kinds of underground chambers and passageways. The catacombs of Paris are abandoned stone quarries that were not used for burials until 1787. The catacombs built by a monastery in Palermo, Sicily, for its deceased members later began accepting bodies from outside the monastery; today you may wander through looking at hundreds of mummified corpses propped against the catacomb walls, dressed in tattered clothes that were once fashionable.

catalyst \\'ka-tə-list\\ (1) A substance that speeds up a chemical reaction or lets it take place under different conditions. (2) Someone or something that brings about or speeds significant change or action.

- The assassination of Archduke Ferdinand in Sarajevo in 1914 turned out to be the catalyst for World War I.

Chemical catalysts are substances that, in very small amounts, can bring about important chemical changes in large quantities of material. The *catalytic* converter in your car's exhaust system, for instance, uses tiny amounts of platinum to swiftly convert the engine's dangerous gases to carbon dioxide and water vapor. And it's easy to see how the meaning of *catalyst* could broaden to include nonchemical situations. We can now say, for example, that the Great Depression served as the catalyst for such important social reforms as Social Security.

catatonic \ˌka-tə-ˈtä-nik\ (1) Relating to or suffering from a form of schizophrenia. (2) Showing an unusual lack of movement, activity, or expression.

• After an hour, extreme boredom had produced a catatonic stupor in those of the audience who were still awake.

Catatonia is primarily a form of the terrible mental disease known as schizophrenia, though it may show up in patients with a variety of other mental conditions. A common symptom is extreme muscular rigidity; catatonic patients may be "frozen" for hours or even days in a single position. Its causes remain mysterious. Serious though the condition is, most nondoctors use *catatonic* humorously to describe people who seem incapable of moving or changing expression.

Quizzes

A. Choose the closest definition:

1. malevolent   a. wishing evil b. wishing well
   c. blowing violently d. badly done
2. cataclysm   a. loud applause b. feline behavior
   c. disaster d. inspiration
3. malign   a. speak well of b. speak to c. speak ill of
   d. speak of repeatedly
4. catacomb   a. underground road b. underground
   cemetery c. underground spring d. underground
   treasure
5. malicious   a. vague b. explosive c. confusing d. mean
6. catatonic   a. refreshing b. slow c. motionless
   d. boring
7. malnourished   a. fed frequently b. fed poorly
   c. fed excessively d. fed occasionally
8. catalyst   a. literary agent b. insurance agent
   c. cleaning agent d. agent of change

B. Indicate whether the following pairs of words have the same or different meanings:

1. catacomb / catastrophe　　same ___ / different ___
2. malnourished / overfed　　same ___ / different ___
3. cataclysm / disaster　　　same ___ / different ___

4.	malign / slander	same ___ / different ___
5.	catatonic / paralyzed	same ___ / different ___
6.	catalyst / cemetery	same ___ / different ___
7.	malicious / nasty	same ___ / different ___
8.	malevolent / pleasant	same ___ / different ___

PROT/PROTO comes from Greek and has the basic meaning "first in time" or "first formed." *Protozoa* are one-celled animals, such as amoebas and paramecia, that are among the most basic members of the biological kingdom. A *proton* is an elementary particle that, along with neutrons, can be found in all atomic nuclei. A *protoplanet* is a whirling mass of gas and dust that astronomers believe may someday become a planet.

---

protagonist \prō-ˈta-gə-nist\ The main character in a literary work.

• Macbeth is the ruthlessly ambitious protagonist of Shakespeare's play, but it is his wife who pulls the strings.

Struggle, or conflict, is central to drama. The protagonist or hero of a play, novel, or film is involved in a struggle of some kind, either against someone or something else or even against his or her own emotions. So the hero is the "first struggler," which is the literal meaning of the Greek word *prōtagōnistēs*. A character who opposes the hero is the *antagonist,* from a Greek verb that means literally "to struggle against."

protocol \ˈprō-tə-ˌkȯl\ (1) A code of diplomatic or military rules of behavior. (2) A set of rules for the formatting of data in an electronic communications system.

• The guests at the governor's dinner were introduced and seated according to the strict protocol governing such occasions.

The basic meaning of *proto-* is a little harder to follow in this word. *Protocol* comes from a Greek word for the first sheet of a papyrus roll. In English, *protocol* originally meant "a first draft or record," and later specifically the first draft of a diplomatic document, such as a treaty. The "diplomatic" connection led eventually to its current meaning of "rules of behavior." Someone wearing Bermuda shorts and sandals to a state dinner at the White House would not be acting "according to protocol," and royal protocol forbids touching the queen of England except to shake her hand. But *protocol* is also now used for other sets of rules, such as those for doing a scientific experiment or for handling computer data.

protoplasm \\'prō-tō-ˌpla-zəm\\ The substance that makes up the living parts of cells.

• A mixture of organic and inorganic substances, such as protein and water, protoplasm is regarded as the physical basis of life.

After the word *protoplasm* was coined in the mid-19th century for the jellylike material that is the main substance of a cell, it began to be used widely, especially by scientists and others who imagined that the first life-forms must have arisen out of a great seething *protoplasmic* soup. Since protoplasm includes all the cell's living material, inside and outside the nucleus, it is a less useful scientific word today than more precise terms such as *cytoplasm*, which refers only to the living material outside the nucleus. But many remain fascinated by the image of that soup bubbling away as the lightning flashes and the volcanoes erupt.

prototype \\'prō-tō-ˌtīp\\ (1) An original model on which something is patterned. (2) A first, full-scale, usually working version of a new type or design.

• There was great excitement when, after years of top-secret development, the prototype of the new Stealth bomber first took to the skies.

A prototype is someone or something that serves as a model or inspiration. A successful fund-raising campaign can serve as a prototype for future campaigns, for example, and the legendary Robin Hood is the *prototypical* honorable outlaw, the inspiration for countless other romantic heroes. But the term is perhaps most widely used in the world of technology; every new "concept car," for example, starts off as a unique prototype.

ANTE is Latin for "before" or "in front of." *Antediluvian,* which describes something very old or outdated, literally means "before the flood"—that is, Noah's Flood. And *antebellum* literally means "before the war," usually the American Civil War.

antechamber \\'an-ti-ˌchām-bər\\ An outer room that leads to another and is often used as a waiting room.

- The antechamber to the lawyer's office was both elegant and comfortable, designed to inspire trust and confidence.

One expects to find an antechamber outside the private chambers of a Supreme Court Justice or leading into the great hall of a medieval castle. In the private end of the castle the lord's or lady's bedchamber would have its own antechamber, which served as a dressing room and sitting room, but could also house bodyguards if the castle came under siege. *Anteroom* is a less formal synonym, one that's often applied to the waiting rooms of professional offices today.

antedate \\'an-ti-ˌdāt\\ (1) To date something (such as a check) with a date earlier than that of actual writing. (2) To precede in time.

- Nantucket Island has hundreds of beautifully preserved houses that antedate the Civil War.

Dinosaurs antedated the first human beings by almost 65 million years, though this stubborn fact never used to stop cartoonists and screenwriters from having the two species inhabit the same story line. Dictionary editors are constantly noticing how the oral use of a word may antedate its first appearance in print by a number of years. Antedating a check or a contract isn't illegal unless it's done for the purpose of fraud (the same is true of its opposite, *postdating*).

antecedent \\ˌan-tə-'sē-dᵊnt\\ (1) A word or phrase that is referred to by a pronoun that follows it. (2) An event or cause coming before something.

- As I remember, she said "My uncle is taking my father, and he's staying overnight," but I'm not sure what the antecedent of "he" was.

A basic principle of clear writing is to keep your antecedents clear. Pronouns are often used in order not to repeat a noun (so instead of saying "Sheila turns 22 tomorrow, and Sheila is having a party," we replace the second "Sheila" with "she"). But sloppy writers sometimes leave their antecedents unclear (for instance, "Sheila helps Kathleen out, but she doesn't appreciate it," where it isn't clear who "she" is). Watch out for this possible problem when using not just *he* and *she* but also *they, them, it, this,* and *that.* And keep in mind that *antecedent* isn't just a grammar term. You may talk about the

antecedents of heart disease (such as bad eating habits), the antecedents of World War II (such as the unwise Treaty of Versailles), and
even your own antecedents (your mother, grandfather, etc.).

anterior \an-ˈtir-ē-ər\ (1) Located before or toward the front or
head. (2) Coming before in time or development.

• When she moved up to join the first-class passengers in the plane's
  anterior section, she was delighted to recognize the governor in
  the next seat.

Anterior generally appears in either medical or scholarly contexts.
Anatomy books refer to the anterior lobe of the brain, the anterior
cerebral artery, the anterior facial vein, etc. Scholar and lawyers
may use *anterior* to mean "earlier in time or order." For example,
supporters of states' rights point out that the individual states enjoyed
certain rights anterior to their joining the union. And prenuptial
agreements are designed to protect the assets that one or both parties
acquired anterior to the marriage.

Quizzes

A. Fill in each blank with the correct letter:

a. antedate   e. prototype
b. protoplasm   f. antecedent
c. anterior   g. protocol
d. protagonist   h. antechamber

1. The _____ of *The Wizard of Oz* is a Kansas farm girl
   named Dorothy.
2. According to official _____, the Ambassador from
   England ranks higher than the Canadian Consul.
3. A butterfly's antennae are located on the most _____
   part of its body.
4. There under the microscope we saw the cell's _____ in
   all its amazing complexity.
5. She was tempted to _____ the letter to make it seem
   that she had not forgotten to write it but only to mail it.
6. The engineers have promised to have the _____ of the
   new sedan finished by March.

7. Please step into the judge's _____; she'll be with you in a few minutes.

8. The British would say "The company are proud of their record," since they treat "the company" as a plural _____.

B. Match the definition on the left to the correct word on the right:

1. to date before
2. cell contents
3. what comes before
4. rules of behavior
5. toward the front
6. model
7. waiting room
8. hero or heroine

  a. protocol
  b. antechamber
  c. protagonist
  d. antecedent
  e. protoplasm
  f. antedate
  g. prototype
  h. anterior

ORTHO comes from *orthos,* the Greek word for "straight," "right," or "true." *Orthotics* is a branch of therapy that straightens out your stance or posture by providing artificial support for weak joints or muscles. And *orthograde* animals, such as human beings, walk with their bodies in a "straight" or vertical position.

orthodontics \,ȯr-thə-ˈdän-tiks\ A branch of dentistry that deals with the treatment and correction of crooked teeth and other irregularities.

• A specialty in orthodontics would require three more years of study after completing her dentistry degree.

Orthodontics has been practiced since ancient times, but the elaborate techniques familiar to us today were introduced only in recent decades. Braces, retainers, and headgear are used to fix such conditions as crowding of the teeth and overbites. According to a 1939 text, "Speech defects, psychiatric disturbances, personality changes, . . . all are correctable through *orthodontic* measures," though many adolescents, having endured the embarrassment of rubber bands breaking and even of entangling their braces while kissing, might disagree.

orthodox \\'òr-thə-ˌdäks\\ (1) Holding established beliefs, especially in religion. (2) Conforming to established rules or traditions; conventional.

- The O'Briens remain orthodox Catholics, faithfully observing the time-honored rituals of their church.

An orthodox religious belief or interpretation is one handed down by a church's founders or leaders. When capitalized, as in *Orthodox Judaism*, *Orthodox* refers to a branch within a larger religious organization that claims to honor the religion's original or traditional beliefs. The steadfast holding of established beliefs that is seen in religious *orthodoxy* is apparent also in other kinds of orthodox behavior. Orthodox medical treatment, for example, follows the established practices of mainstream medicine. *Unorthodox* thinking is known in business language as "thinking outside the box."

orthopedics \\ˌòr-thə-'pē-diks\\ The correction or prevention of deformities of the skeleton.

- For surgery to correct the child's spinal curvature, they were referred to the hospital's orthopedics section.

Just as an orthodontist corrects crookedness in the teeth, an *orthopedist* corrects crookedness in the skeleton. *Orthopedics* is formed in part from the Greek word for "child," and many *orthopedic* patients are in fact children. But adults also often have need of orthopedic therapy, as when suffering from a joint disease like arthritis or when recovering from a broken arm or leg.

orthography \\òr-'thä-grə-fē\\ The spelling of words, especially spelling according to standard usage.

- Even such eloquent writers as George Washington and Thomas Jefferson were deficient in the skill of orthography.

Even as recently as the 19th century, the orthography of the English language was still unsettled. Not until spelling books like Noah Webster's and textbooks like "McGuffey's Readers" came along did uniform spelling become established in the U.S. Before that, there was much *orthographic* variation, even among the more educated. The many people who still have problems with spelling can take heart from Mark Twain, who once remarked, "I don't give a damn for a man that can spell a word only one way."

RECT comes from the Latin word *rectus,* which means "straight" or "right." To *correct* something is to make it right. A *rectangle* is a four-sided figure with straight parallel sides. *Rectus,* short for Latin *rectus musculus,* may refer to any of several straight muscles, such as those of the abdomen.

---

rectitude \'rek-tə-ˌtüd\ Moral integrity.

* The school superintendent was stern and not terribly popular, but no one questioned her moral rectitude.

We associate straightness with honesty, so if we suspect someone is lying we might ask if they're being "straight" with us, and we might call a lawbreaker *crooked* or label him a *crook. Rectitude* may sound a little old-fashioned today, but the virtue it represents never really goes out of style.

rectify \'rek-tə-ˌfī\ To set right; remedy.

* The college is moving to rectify this unfortunate situation before anyone else gets hurt.

We rectify something by straightening it out or making it right. We might rectify an injustice by seeing to it that a wrongly accused person is cleared. An error in a financial record can be rectified by replacing an incorrect number with a correct one. If the error is in our tax return, the Internal Revenue Service will be happy to rectify it for us; we might then have to rectify the impression that we were trying to cheat on our taxes.

rectilinear \ˌrek-tə-ˈli-nē-ər\ (1) Moving in or forming a straight line. (2) Having many straight lines.

* After admiring Frank Lloyd Wright's rectilinear buildings for years, the public was astonished by the giant spiral of the Guggenheim Museum.

Rectilinear patterns or constructions are those in which straight lines are strikingly obvious. In geometry, *rectilinear* usually means "perpendicular"; thus, a rectilinear polygon is a many-sided shape whose angles are all right angles (the footprints of most houses, with their extensions and garages, are good examples). But *rectilinear* is particularly used in physics. Rectilinear motion is motion in which the speed remains constant and the path is a straight line; and rectilinear rays, such as light rays, travel in a straight line.

directive \də-ˈrek-tiv\ Something that guides or directs; especially, a general instruction from a high-level body or official.

• At the very beginning of the administration, the cabinet secretary had sent out a directive to all border-patrol personnel.

As the definition states, a directive *directs*. A directive from a school principal might provide guidance about handling holiday celebrations in class. A directive from the Vatican might specify new wording for the Mass in various languages. Even the European Union issues directives to its member countries, which they often ignore.

Quizzes

A.   Choose the closest definition:

1.   orthodox   a. straight b. pier c. conventional
     d. waterfowl
2.   rectify   a. redo b. make right c. modify
     d. make longer
3.   orthopedics   a. foot surgery b. children's medicine
     c. medical dictionaries d. treatment of skeletal defects
4.   directive   a. leader b. sign c. order d. straightener
5.   orthography   a. correct color b. correct map c. correct
     direction d. correct spelling
6.   rectitude   a. roughness b. integrity c. certainty
     d. sameness
7.   orthodontics   a. dentistry for children b. dentistry for
     gums c. dentistry for crooked teeth d. dentistry for
     everyone
8.   rectilinear   a. employing straight lines b. employing
     curved lines c. employing 45° angles d. employing
     circles

**B.   Indicate whether the following pairs have the same
       or different meanings:**

1.   orthodox / crucial   same ___ / different ___
2.   rectitude / honesty   same ___ / different ___

3.	orthopedics / broken bones	same ___ / different ___
4.	directive / question	same ___ / different ___
5.	orthography / architecture	same ___ / different ___
6.	rectilinear / straight	same ___ / different ___
7.	orthodontics / fixing of crooked teeth	same ___ / different ___
8.	rectify / damage	same ___ / different ___

EU comes from the Greek word for "well"; in English words it can also mean "good" or "true." A veterinarian who performs *euthanasia* is providing a very sick or hopelessly injured animal a "good" or easy death.

---

eugenic \yu̇-'je-nik\ Relating to or fitted for the production of good offspring through controlled breeding.

• Eugenic techniques have been part of sheep breeding for many years.

The word *eugenic*, like the name *Eugene*, includes the Greek root meaning "born" (see GEN, p. 409). Breeders of farm animals have long used eugenic methods to produce horses that run faster, for example, or pigs that provide more meat. Through *eugenics,* Holstein cows have become one of the world's highest producers of milk. But eugenics also has a dark side. The idea of human eugenics was taken up enthusiastically by the Nazis in the 20th century, with terrible consequences.

euphemism \'yü-fə-ˌmi-zəm\ An agreeable or inoffensive word or expression that is substituted for one that may offend or disgust.

• The Victorians, uncomfortable with the physical side of human existence, had euphemisms for most bodily functions.

The use of euphemisms is an ancient part of the English language, and perhaps of all languages, and all of us use them. *Golly* and *gosh* started out as euphemisms for *God,* and *darn* is a familiar euphemism for *damn. Shoot, shucks,* and *sugar* are all *euphemistic* substitutes for a well-known vulgar word. *Pass away* for *die, mis-*

speak for *lie*, *downsize* for *fire*, *senior citizen* for *old person*—the list goes on and on.

euphoria \yu̇-ˈfȯr-ē-ə\ A strong feeling of well-being or happiness.

• Swept up in the euphoria of a Super Bowl victory, the whole city seemed to have poured out into the streets.

Euphoria is the feeling of an intense (and usually temporary) "high." Doctors use the word for the kind of abnormal or inappropriate high spirits that might be caused by a drug or by mental illness, but euphoria is usually natural and appropriate. When we win enough money in the lottery to buy several small Pacific islands, or even just when the home team wins the championship, we have good reason to feel *euphoric*.

eulogy \ˈyu̇-lə-jē\ (1) A formal speech or writing especially in honor of a dead person. (2) High praise.

• The book was a fond eulogy to the 1950s, when Americans had joined social organizations of all kinds.

With its *-logy* ending (see LOG, p. 203), *eulogy* means literally something like "good speech." We are told to speak only good of the dead, but a *eulogist* actually makes a speech in the dead person's honor—or often instead for someone living, who might actually be there in the audience. The most famous eulogies include Lincoln's Gettysburg Address and Pericles' funeral oration for the Athenian warriors; but these are only two of the many great eulogies, which continue to be delivered not only at funerals and memorial services but at retirement parties, anniversary parties, and birthday parties.

DYS comes from Greek, where it means "bad" or "difficult." So *dysphagia* is difficult swallowing, and *dyspnea* is difficult or labored breathing. *Dysphasia* is an inability to use and understand language because of injury to or disease of the brain. *Dys-* is sometimes close in meaning to *dis-* (see DIS, p. 60), but try not to confuse the two.

---

dystopia \dis-ˈtō-pē-ə\ An imaginary place where people lead dehumanized and often fearful lives.

- For a 10-year-old British boy, boarding school could be a grim dystopia, with no comforts, harsh punishments, and constant bullying.

Dystopia was created from Utopia, the name of an ideal country imagined by Sir Thomas More in 1516. For More, the suffix *-topia* meant "place" (see TOP, p. 338), and *u-* (from the Greek root *ou*) meant "no," but also perhaps "good" (see EU, p. 103). In other words, More's Utopia was too good to be true. It's probably no accident that *dystopia* was first used around 1950, soon after George Orwell published his famous novel *Nineteen Eighty-Four* and 16 years after Aldous Huxley published *Brave New World*. These two are still the most famous of the 20th century's many depressingly *dystopian* novels. And what about all those bleak futuristic films: *Blade Runner, Brazil, The Matrix,* and the rest? What does it mean when no one will paint a picture of a happy future?

dyslexia \dis-ˈlek-sē-ə\ A disturbance or interference with the ability to read or to use language.

- She managed to deal with her dyslexia through careful tutoring all throughout elementary school.

Dyslexia is a neurological disorder that usually affects people of average or superior intelligence. *Dyslexic* individuals have an impaired ability to recognize and process words and letters. Dyslexia usually shows itself in the tendency to read and write words and letters in reversed order; sometimes similar reversals occur in the person's speech. Dyslexia has been shown to be treatable through patient instruction in proper reading techniques.

dyspeptic \dis-ˈpep-tik\ (1) Relating to or suffering from indigestion. (2) Having an irritable temperament; ill-humored.

- For decades the dyspeptic columnist served as the newspaper's— and the city's—resident grouch.

Dyspepsia comes from the Greek word for "bad digestion." Interestingly, the Greek verb *pessein* can mean either "to cook" or "to digest"; bad cooking has been responsible for a lot of dyspepsia. Dyspepsia can be caused by many diseases, but dyspeptic individuals are often the victims of their own habits and appetites. Worry, overeating, inadequate chewing, and excessive smoking and drinking can all bring on dyspepsia. Today we generally use *dyspeptic* to mean "irritable"—that is, in the kind of mood that could be produced by bad digestion.

dysplasia \dis-ˈplā-zhə\ Abnormal development of cells or organs, or an abnormal structure resulting from such growth.

- The infant was born with minor hip dysplasia, which was fixed by a routine operation.

Of the dozens of medical terms that begin with the *dys-* prefix, *dysplasia* (with the suffix *-plasia*, meaning "development") is one of the more common, though not many nondoctors know it. Structural dysplasias are usually something you're born with; they often involve the hip or the kidneys. But cell dysplasia is often associated with cancer. And a *dysplastic* mole—a mole that changes shape in an odd way—is always something to be concerned about.

Quizzes

A. Fill in each blank with the correct letter:

a. euphemism   e. dyslexia
b. dysplasia   f. euphoria
c. eulogy   g. dystopia
d. dyspeptic   h. eugenic

1. There is many a _____ for the word *die*, and many more for the word *drunk*.
2. The novel paints a picture of a _____ in which the effects of climate change have wrecked the social order.
3. Her _____ for her longtime friend was the most moving part of the ceremony.
4. Because his _____ was discovered early, he was able to receive the special reading instruction he needed.
5. The end of the war was marked by widespread _____ and celebration.
6. Ebenezer Scrooge, in *A Christmas Carol,* is a thoroughly _____ character.
7. Though the dog is the product of generations of _____ breeding, she is high-strung and has terrible eyesight.
8. The tests had detected some suspicious cell _____, but her doctors told her not to worry since it was at a very early stage.

> **B. Match the word on the left to the correct definition on the right:**
>
> 1. dysplasia   a. nightmarish society
> 2. euphemism   b. crabby
> 3. dyslexia   c. abnormal growth
> 4. eugenic   d. speech of praise
> 5. dystopia   e. polite term
> 6. euphoria   f. reading disorder
> 7. dyspeptic   g. promoting superior
> 8. eulogy   offspring
>   h. great happiness

Latin Borrowings

a fortiori \ˌä-ˌfȯr-tē-ˈȯr-ē\ All the more certainly.

• If drug users are going to be subject to mandatory sentences, then, a fortiori, drug dealers should be subject to them also.

A fortiori in Latin literally means "from the stronger (argument)." The term is used when drawing a conclusion that's even more obvious or convincing than the one just drawn. Thus, if teaching English grammar to native speakers is difficult, then, a fortiori, teaching English grammar to nonnative speakers will be even more challenging.

a posteriori \ˌä-ˌpōs-tir-ē-ˈȯr-ē\ Relating to or derived by reasoning from known or observed facts.

• Most Presidents will come to the a posteriori conclusion that a booming economy is entirely due to their own economic policies.

A posteriori, Latin for "from the latter," is a term from logic, which usually refers to reasoning that works backward from an effect to its causes. This kind of reasoning can sometimes lead to false conclusions. The fact that sunrise follows the crowing of a rooster, for example, doesn't necessarily mean that the rooster's crowing caused the sun to rise.

a priori \ˌä-prē-ˈȯr-ē\ Relating to or derived by reasoning from self-evident propositions.

- Her colleagues rejected the a priori argument because it rested on assumptions they felt weren't necessarily true.

A priori, Latin for "from the former," is traditionally contrasted with *a posteriori* (see above). The term usually describes lines of reasoning or arguments that proceed from the general to the particular, or from causes to effects. Whereas a posteriori knowledge is knowledge based solely on experience or personal observation, a priori knowledge is knowledge that comes from the power of reasoning based on self-evident truths. So, for example, "Every mother has had a child" is an a priori statement, since it shows simple logical reasoning and isn't a statement of fact about a specific case (such as "This woman is the mother of five children") that the speaker knew about from experience.

bona fide \\'bō-nə-ˌfīd\\ (1) Made in good faith, without deceit. (2) Authentic or genuine.

- According to the broker, they've made a bona fide offer to buy the property.

Bona fide means "in good faith" in Latin. When applied to business deals and the like, it stresses the absence of fraud or deception. A bona fide sale of securities is an entirely aboveboard transaction. Outside of business and law, *bona fide* implies mere sincerity and earnestness. A bona fide promise is one that the person has every intention of keeping. A bona fide proposal of marriage is one made by a suitor who isn't kidding around. *Bona fide* also has the noun form *bona fides*; when someone asks about someone else's *bona fides*, it usually means evidence of their qualifications or achievements.

carpe diem \\'kär-pā-'dē-ˌem\\ Enjoy the pleasures or opportunities of the moment without concern about the future.

- When he learned the phrase "Carpe diem" in high-school Latin class, he knew he'd found the motto he would live by for the rest of his life.

Carpe diem, a phrase that comes from the Roman poet Horace, means literally "Pluck the day," though it's usually translated as "Seize the day." A free translation might be "Enjoy yourself while you have the chance." For some people, *Carpe diem* serves as the closest thing to a philosophy of life as they'll ever have.

caveat emptor \\'ka-vē-ˌät-'emp-tər\\ Let the buyer beware.

- The best rule to keep in mind when buying anything from a pushcart is: "Caveat emptor."

"Without a warranty, the buyer must take the risk" is the basic meaning of the phrase *caveat emptor*. In the days when buying and selling was carried on in the local marketplace, the rule was a practical one. Buyer and seller knew each other and were on equal footing. The nature of modern commerce and technology placed the buyer at a disadvantage, however, so a stack of regulations have been written by federal, state, and local agencies to protect the consumer against dangerous or defective products, fraudulent practices, and the like. But the principle that a buyer needs a warranty if he is to avoid risk remains an important legal concept. Note that a *caveat* is a small warning or explanation intended to avoid misinterpretation.

corpus delicti \ˈkȯr-pəs-di-ˈlik-ˌtī\ (1) The substantial and basic fact or facts necessary to prove that a crime has been committed. (2) The material substance, such as the murdered body, on which a crime has been committed.

- The police believed they had solved the crime, but couldn't prove their case without the corpus delicti.

Corpus delicti literally means "body of the crime" in Latin. In its original sense, the body in question refers not to a corpse but to the body of essential facts that, taken together, prove that a crime has been committed. In popular usage, *corpus delicti* also refers to the actual physical object upon which a crime has been committed. In a case of arson, it would be a ruined building; in a murder case, the victim's corpse.

curriculum vitae \kə-ˈri-kyu̇-ləm-ˈvē-ˌtī\ A short summary of one's career and qualifications, typically prepared by an applicant for a position; résumé.

- The job advertisement asked for an up-to-date curriculum vitae and three recommendations.

The Latin phrase *curriculum vitae,* often abbreviated CV, literally means "the course of one's life." The term is usually used for applications for jobs in the sciences and medicine and for teaching positions in colleges and universities. A shorter term is simply *vita*, meaning "life." In other fields, *résumé* is more commonly used in the U.S.; in England, however, *curriculum vitae* is the usual term for any job application.

Quiz

Fill in each blank with the correct letter:

a. a priori
b. curriculum vitae
c. caveat emptor
d. a posteriori
e. carpe diem
f. a fortiori
g. corpus delicti
h. bona fide

1. To ensure that all reservations are _____, the cruise line requires a nonrefundable deposit.
2. If Britain can't afford a space program, then _____ neither can a much poorer country like India.
3. The philosopher published his own _____ proof of the existence of God.
4. Their motto is "_____," and the two of them have more fun than anyone else I know.
5. She sent out a _____ full of impressive educational and professional credentials.
6. All of the elements were available to establish the _____ of the defendant's crime.
7. This art critic takes the _____ position that if Pablo Picasso painted it, it's a masterpiece of modern art.
8. When you go out to buy a used car, the best advice, warranty or no warranty, is still "_____."

Review Quizzes

A. Complete the analogy:

1. antagonist : villain :: protagonist : _____
   a. maiden b. wizard c. knight d. hero
2. radical : rebellious :: orthodox : _____
   a. routine b. conventional c. sane d. typical
3. fake : fraudulent :: bona fide : _____
   a. copied b. certain c. authentic d. desirable
4. slang : vulgar :: euphemism : _____
   a. habitual b. polite c. dirty d. dumb

5. identify : name :: rectify : _____
   a. make over b. make new c. make right d. make up
6. better : inferior :: anterior : _____
   a. before b. beside c. above d. behind
7. warranty : guarantee :: caveat emptor : _____
   a. explanation b. warning c. endorsement d. contract
8. jovial : merry :: dyspeptic : _____
   a. grumpy b. sleepy c. dopey d. happy
9. lively : sluggish :: catatonic : _____
   a. active b. petrified c. feline d. tired
10. benevolent : wicked :: malevolent : _____
    a. evil b. silly c. noisy d. kindly

B. Fill in each blank with the correct letter:

a. antechamber   i. curriculum vitae
b. a posteriori   j. catacomb
c. euphoria   k. dysplasia
d. malign   l. eugenic
e. a fortiori   m. malnourished
f. orthography   n. protoplasm
g. prototype   o. orthodontics
h. directive

1. Before car makers produce a new model, they always build and test a _____.
2. Her short stories are her main qualification for the job, but the college needs her _____ as well.
3. They were shown into an elegant _____ where they awaited their audience with the king.
4. After graduation from dental school, Kyle took a postgraduate course in _____.
5. That yappy little dog makes the _____ assumption that he's what keeps me from breaking into the house.
6. The jellylike substance in cells is called _____.
7. These abused and _____ children can't be expected to pay attention in class.
8. In poor countries, hip _____ is rarely fixed in the early years.
9. They felt such _____ that they almost wept with joy.
10. Since they earned high honors for achieving a 3.7 average, _____ we should do so for getting a 3.8.

11. He argues that _____ is more important than ever, since the success of your Web searches depends on your spelling.

12. It is common for boxers to _____ each other in crude terms before a big match.

13. Their department had received a _____ that morning regarding flexibility in the work schedule.

14. When they went to Rome, they made sure to visit at least one underground _____.

15. _____ experimentation has produced a new breed of sheep with thick, fast-growing wool.

C. **Indicate whether the following pairs have the same or different meanings:**

1. corpus delicti / basic evidence   same __ / different __
2. rectify / straighten   same __ / different __
3. malicious / mean   same __ / different __
4. protocol / rules of behavior   same __ / different __
5. a priori / determined later   same __ / different __
6. dyslexia / speech patterns   same __ / different __
7. cataclysm / religious teachings   same __ / different __
8. antedate / occur before   same __ / different __
9. orthopedics / shoe repair   same __ / different __
10. rectilinear / curvy   same __ / different __
11. orthodox / Christian   same __ / different __
12. carpe diem / look ahead   same __ / different __
13. prototype / model   same __ / different __
14. catalyst / distributor   same __ / different __
15. rectitude / stubbornness   same __ / different __

UNIT

6

EQU comes from the Latin word *aequus*, meaning "equal." To *equalize* means to make things equal. Things that are *equivalent* have the same value, use, or meaning. All three sides of an *equilateral* triangle are of the same length. And an *equation* (for instance, 21 + 47 = 68) is a statement that two mathematical expressions are equal.

---

equable \\'e-kwə-bəl\\ (1) Tending to remain calm. (2) Free from harsh changes or extreme variation.

• Her friends thought it odd that such an equable woman had married a man so moody and unpredictable.

Equable usually describes either climate or personality. The word seems to be used less today than in decades past, maybe because the personality type is less admired than it used to be. A steady, calm, equable personality may not produce much excitement but usually makes for a good worker and a good parent, and maybe even a longer life. In the words of the poet Robert Service: "Avoid extremes: be moderate / In saving and in spending. / An equable and easy gait / Will win an easy ending."

adequacy \\'a-di-kwə-sē\\ Being equal to some need or requirement.

• Environmentalists doubt the adequacy of these regulations to protect the wilderness areas.

When we question the adequacy of health-care coverage, or parking facilities, or school funding, we're asking if they are *equal* to our need. The adjective *adequate* means "enough" or "acceptable"—though in sentences like "His performance was adequate," it really means "no better than acceptable."

equilibrium \ˌē-kwə-ˈli-brē-əm\ (1) A state in which opposing forces are balanced so that one is not stronger or greater than the other. (2) A state of emotional balance or calmness.

• The news had come as a shock, and it took him several minutes to recover his equilibrium.

Equilibrium contains a root from the Latin *libra*, meaning "weight" or "balance." As a constellation, zodiac symbol, and astrological sign, Libra is usually pictured as a set of balance scales, often held by the blindfolded goddess of justice, which symbolizes fairness, equality, and justice. *Equilibrium* has special meanings in biology, chemistry, physics, and economics, but in all of them it refers to the balance of competing influences.

equinox \ˈē-kwə-ˌnäks\ A day when day and night are the same length.

• She and her friends got together for an equinox party twice a year to celebrate the arrival of the fall and the spring.

If you know that *nox* means "night" in Latin, it's not hard to remember the meaning of *equinox*. There are two equinoxes in the year: the spring equinox, around March 21, and the fall equinox, around September 23. The equinoxes are contrasted with the *solstices*, when the sun is farthest north and south of the equator. The summer solstice occurs around June 22 (the longest day of the year), the winter solstice around December 22 (the shortest day).

QUIS is derived from the Latin verb meaning "to seek or obtain." The roots *quer, quir,* and *ques* are derived from the same Latin verb and give us words such as *inquiry* and *question*.

---

inquisition \ˌin-kwə-ˈzi-shən\ A questioning or examining that is often harsh or severe.

• The President's first choice for the job turned him down, fearing the Senate hearings would turn into an inquisition into her past.

While an *inquiry* can be almost any search for truth, the related word *inquisition* suggests a long, thorough investigation that involves extensive and harsh questioning. Though the two words originally had about the same meaning, today *inquisition* tends to remind us of the Spanish Inquisition, an ongoing trial conducted by church-appointed *inquisitors* that began in the Middle Ages and sought out nonbelievers, Jews, and Muslims, thousands of whom were sentenced to torture and to burning at the stake.

perquisite \\'pər-kwə-zət\ (1) A privilege or profit that is provided in addition to one's base salary. (2) Something claimed as an exclusive possession or right.

- A new car, a big house, and yearly trips to Europe were among the perquisites that made the presidency of Wyndam College such an attractive position.

Though the Latin source of *perquisite* originally meant "something insistently asked for," the "ask" meaning has mostly vanished from the English word. A perquisite, often called simply a *perk,* is instead something of value that the holder of a particular job or position is entitled to, usually without even asking. The President of the United States, for instance, enjoys as perquisites the use of Camp David and Air Force One. Perhaps because perquisites are usually available to only a small number of people, the word sometimes refers to non-job-related privileges that are claimed as exclusive rights.

acquisitive \ə-'kwi-zə-tiv\ Eager to acquire; greedy.

- With each year the couple became more madly acquisitive, buying jewelry, a huge yacht, and two country estates.

Unlike most tribal peoples and the populations of some older countries, we Americans live in an acquisitive society, a society devoted to getting and spending. And America often makes successfully acquisitive people into heroes; even Ebenezer Scrooge, that model of miserly greed and *acquisitiveness*, was once defended by a White House chief of staff. An acquisitive nation may seek to *acquire* other territories by force. But mental *acquisition* of specialized knowledge or skills—or new vocabulary!—doesn't deprive others of the same information.

requisition \ˌre-kwə-'zi-shən\ A demand or request (such as for supplies) made with proper authority.

- The teachers had grown impatient with having to submit a requisition for even routine classroom supplies.

Requisition was originally a noun but is now probably more common as a verb. So we either can speak of sending our office's purchasing department a requisition for computers, or of *requisitioning* more computers from the department. The word has an official sound to it. However, one of Hollywood's bittersweet love stories begins when Omar Sharif, playing a World War II freedom fighter, says to Ingrid Bergman, who is the owner of a stately old yellow Rolls Royce, "I've come to requisition your car."

Quizzes

A. Indicate whether the following pairs of terms have the same or different meanings:

1. equilibrium / weight   same ___ / different ___
2. inquisition /curiosity   same ___ / different ___
3. equable / steady   same ___ / different ___
4. perquisite / salary   same ___ / different ___
5. equinox /May Day   same ___ / different ___
6. acquisitive / greedy   same ___ / different ___
7. requisition / requirement   same ___ / different ___
8. adequacy / surplus   same ___ / different ___

B. Fill in each blank with the correct letter:

a. equinox   e. adequacy
b. requisition   f. acquisitive
c. equilibrium   g. equable
d. perquisite   h. inquisition

1. They're a quiet, pleasant couple, with very _____ temperaments.
2. You couldn't even get a pencil unless you filled out a _____.
3. In a healthy economy, supply and demand are in a state of approximate _____.
4. Daylight saving time begins in March, shortly before the _____ and the arrival of spring.
5. There was more than enough water, but he worried about the _____ of their food supplies.
6. The whole family was _____ by nature, and there were bitter legal battles over the will.

7. His status as newcomer did carry the special _____ of being able to ask a lot of questions.
8. Louisa feared an _____ into her background and previous involvements.

PLE/PLEN comes from a Latin word meaning "to fill." It can be seen in the words *plenty*, meaning basically "filled," and *complete*, meaning "thoroughly filled."

plenary \\'plē-nə-rē\\ (1) Including all who have a right to attend. (2) Complete in all ways.

• For the convention's plenary session, five thousand members gathered to hear a star speaker.

Plenary often shows up in writing referring to the "plenary power" held by a government, and is particularly used for powers mentioned in a constitution. For example, under the U.S. Constitution, the Congress has plenary power to wage war, which means that no one else—not the courts, not the states, not the president—has any power whatsoever to second-guess Congress about warmaking. But in recent years, that hasn't stopped some presidents from starting conflicts that looked a lot like wars to most people. At a conference, the plenary sessions (unlike the various smaller "presentations," "workshops," "forums," and "seminars" that otherwise fill the day) try to bring everyone together in the same room.

complement \\'käm-plə-mənt\\ (1) Something that fills up or makes perfect; the amount needed to make something complete. (2) A counterpart.

• On the committee, the two young people provided an energetic complement to the older members.

A complement fills out or balances something. We think of salt as the complement of pepper (maybe mostly because of their colors), and the right necktie is a perfect complement to a good suit. *Complement* can also mean "the full quantity, number, or amount"; thus, a ship's complement of officers and crew is the whole force necessary for full operation. *Complement* is actually most common as a verb; we may say, for example, that a bright blue scarf *complements* a cream-colored outfit beautifully. Don't confuse *complement* with *compliment*, which means an expression of respect or affection.

deplete \di-ˈplēt\ To reduce in amount by using up.

• Years of farming on the same small plot of land had left the soil depleted of minerals.

The *de-* prefix often means "do the opposite of," so *deplete* means the opposite of "fill." Thus, for example, a kitchen's food supplies can be rapidly depleted by hungry teenagers. But *deplete* often suggests something more serious. Desertions can deplete an army; layoffs can deplete an office staff; and too much time in bed can rapidly deplete your muscular strength.

replete \ri-ˈplēt\ Fully or abundantly filled or supplied.

• The professor's autobiography was replete with scandalous anecdotes about campus life in the 1950s.

Replete implies that something is filled almost to capacity. Autumn landscapes in New England are replete with colorful foliage. Supermarket tabloids are always replete with details of stars' lives, whether real or imaginary. And a professor may complain that most of the papers she received were replete with errors in grammar and punctuation.

METR/METER comes to us from Greek by way of Latin; in both languages it refers to "measure." A *thermometer* measures heat; a *perimeter* is the measure around something; and things that are *isometric* are equal in measure.

---

metric \ˈme-trik\ (1) Relating to or based on the metric system. (2) Relating to or arranged in meter.

• Americans have resisted using the metric system for years, but are now slowly getting accustomed to a few of the metric units.

The metric system was invented in France in the years following the French Revolution, and a version of it is now used in most of the world to measure distance, weight, and volume. Basic metric units include the *kilogram* (the basic unit of weight), the *liter* (the basic unit of volume), and of course the *meter* (the basic unit of length— see below). *Metric*—or more often *metrical*—can also refer to the basic underlying rhythm of songs and poetry. So while the scientists' measurements are usually metric, the poets' are usually metrical.

meter \ˈmē-tər\ (1) The basic metric unit of length, equal to about 39.37 inches. (2) A systematic rhythm in poetry or music.

- The basic meter of the piece was 3/4, but its rhythms were so complicated that the 3/4 was sometimes hard to hear.

Meter is a metric measurement slightly longer than a yard; thus, a 100-meter dash might take you a second longer than a 100-yard dash. But the word has a different sense in music, where people aren't separated by whether they use the metric system. For a musician, the meter is the regular background rhythm, expressed by the "time signature" written at the beginning of a piece or section: 2/2, 2/4, 3/8, 4/4, 6/8, etc. Within a meter, you can create rhythms that range from the simple to the complex. So, for example, "America the Beautiful" is in 4/4 meter (or "4/4 time"), but so are most of the rhythmically complex songs written by Paul Simon, Burt Bacharach, or Stevie Wonder. In ordinary conversation, though, most people use "rhythm" to include meter and everything that's built on top of it. In poetry, meter has much the same meaning; however, poetic meters aren't named with numbers but instead with traditional Greek and Latin terms such as *iambic* and *dactylic*.

odometer \ō-ˈdä-mə-tər\ An instrument used to measure distance traveled.

- Jennifer watched the odometer to see how far she would have to drive to her new job.

Odometer includes the root from the Greek word *hodos*, meaning "road" or "trip." An odometer shares space on your dashboard with a speedometer, a tachometer, and maybe a "tripmeter." The odometer is what crooked car salesmen tamper with when they want to reduce the mileage a car registers as having traveled. One of life's little pleasures is watching the odometer as all the numbers change at the same time.

tachometer \ta-ˈkä-mə-tər\ A device used to measure speed of rotation.

- Even though one purpose of a tachometer is to help drivers keep their engine speeds down, some of us occasionally try to see how high we can make the needle go.

A tachometer is literally a "speed-measurer," since the Greek root *tach-* means "speed." This is clear in the names of the *tachyon,* a particle of matter that travels faster than the speed of light (if it actually exists, it's so fast that it's impossible to see with any instrument), and *tachycardia,* a medical condition in which the heart races uncontrollably. Since the speed that an auto tachometer measures is speed of rotation of the crankshaft, the numbers it reports are revolutions per minute, or rpm's.

Quizzes

A. Match the word on the left to the correct definition on the right:

1.	meter	a.	drain
2.	tachometer	b.	brimming
3.	metric	c.	counterpart
4.	replete	d.	beat pattern
5.	odometer	e.	distance measurer
6.	deplete	f.	rotation meter
7.	plenary	g.	general
8.	complement	h.	relating to a measuring system

B. Choose the closest definition:

1. deplete   a. straighten out b. draw down c. fold d. abandon
2. replete   a. refold b. repeat c. abundantly provided d. fully clothed
3. odometer   a. intelligence measurer b. heart-rate measurer c. height measurer d. mile measurer
4. tachometer   a. rpm measurer b. sharpness measurer c. fatigue measurer d. size measurer
5. complement   a. praise b. number required c. abundance d. usual dress
6. metric   a. relating to poetic rhythm b. relating to ocean depth c. relating to books d. relating to particles of matter
7. plenary   a. for hours b. for life c. for officials d. for everyone
8. meter   a. weight b. rhythm c. speed d. force

AUD, from the Latin verb *audire,* is the root that has to do with hearing. What is *audible* can be heard. An *audience* is a group of listeners, sometimes seated in an *auditorium.* And *audio* today can mean almost anything that has to do with sound.

auditor \ˈȯ-də-tər\ A person who formally examines and verifies financial accounts.

• It seems impossible that so many banks could have gotten into so much trouble if their auditors had been doing their jobs.

The *auditing* of a company's financial records by independent examiners on a regular basis is necessary to prevent "cooking the books," and thus to keep the company honest. We don't normally think of auditors as listening, since looking at and adding up numbers is their basic line of work, but auditors do have to listen to people's explanations, and perhaps that's the historical link. Hearing is more obviously part of another meaning of *audit*, the kind that college students do when they sit in on a class without taking exams or receiving an official grade.

auditory \ˈȯ-də-ˌtȯr-ē\ (1) Perceived or experienced through hearing. (2) Of or relating to the sense or organs of hearing.

• With the "surround-sound" systems in most theaters, going to a movie is now an auditory experience as much as a visual one.

Auditory is close in meaning to *acoustic* and *acoustical*, but *auditory* usually refers more to hearing than to sound. For instance, many dogs have great auditory (not acoustic) powers, and the *auditory nerve* lets us hear by connecting the inner ear to the brain. *Acoustic* and *acoustical* instead refer especially to instruments and the conditions under which sound can be heard; so architects concern themselves with the acoustic properties of an auditorium, and instrument makers with those of a clarinet or piano.

audition \ȯ-ˈdi-shən\ A trial performance to evaluate a performer's skills.

• Auditions for Broadway shows attract so many hopeful unknown performers that everyone in the business calls them "cattle calls."

Most stars are discovered at auditions, where a number of candidates read the same part and the director chooses. Lana Turner famously skipped the audition process and was instead discovered by an agent sipping a soda in a Sunset Boulevard café at age 16. *Audition* can also be a verb; so, for example, after Miss Turner gained her stardom, actors had to audition to be her leading man. But when musicians audition for a job in an orchestra, it's usually behind a screen so that the judges won't even know their sex and therefore can't do anything but listen.

inaudible \i-ˈnȯ-də-bəl\ Not heard or capable of being heard.

- The coach spoke to her in a low voice that was inaudible to the rest of the gymnastics team.

With its negative prefix *in-*, *inaudible* means the opposite of *audible*. What's clearly audible to you may be inaudible to your elderly grandfather. Modern spy technology can turn inaudible conversations into audible ones with the use of high-powered directional microphones, so if you think you're being spied on, make sure there's a lot of other noise around you. And if you don't want everyone around you to know you're bored, keep your sighs inaudible.

SON is the Latin root meaning "sound." *Sonata*, meaning a piece for one or two instruments, was originally an Italian verb meaning "sounded" (when singers were involved, the Italians used a different verb). And *sonorous* means full, loud, or rich in sound.

---

sonic \ˈsä-nik\ (1) Having to do with sound. (2) Having to do with the speed of sound in air (about 750 miles per hour).

- A sonic depth finder can easily determine the depth of a lake by bouncing a sound signal off the bottom.

A sonic boom is an explosive sound created by a shock wave formed at the nose of an aircraft. In 1947 a plane piloted by Chuck Yeager burst the "sound barrier" and created the first sonic boom. In the decades afterward sonic booms became a familiar sound to Americans. (Because of steps that were eventually taken, sonic booms are rarely heard anymore.) Today *sonic* is often used by ambitious rock musicians to describe their experimental sounds.

dissonant \ˈdi-sə-nənt\ (1) Clashing or discordant, especially in music. (2) Incompatible or disagreeing.

- Critics of the health-care plan pointed to its two seemingly dissonant goals: cost containment, which would try to control spending, and universal coverage, which could increase spending.

Since *dissonant* includes the negative prefix *dis-,* what is dissonant sounds or feels unresolved, unharmonic, and clashing. Early in the 20th century, composers such as Arnold Schoenberg and his students developed the use of *dissonance* in music as a style in itself. But to many listeners, the sounds in such music are still unbearable, and most continue to prefer music based on traditional tonality. *Dissonant* is now often used without referring to sound at all. *Cognitive dissonance*, for example, is what happens when you believe two different things that can't actually both be true.

resonance \\'re-zə-nəns\\ (1) A continuing or echoing of sound. (2) A richness and variety in the depth and quality of sound.

- The resonance of James Earl Jones's vocal tones in such roles as Darth Vader made his voice one of the most recognizable of its time.

Many of the finest musical instruments possess a high degree of resonance which, by producing additional vibrations and echoes of the original sound, enriches and amplifies it. Violins made by the Italian masters Stradivari and Guarneri possess a quality of resonance that later violinmakers have never precisely duplicated. And you may have noticed how a particular note will start something in a room buzzing, as one of the touching surfaces begins to *resonate* with the note. Because of that, *resonance* and *resonate*—along with the adjective *resonant*—aren't always used to describe sound. For example, you may say that a novel resonates strongly with you because the author seems to be describing your own experiences and feelings.

ultrasonic \\ˌəl-trə-'sä-nik\\ Having a frequency higher than what can be heard by the human ear.

- My grandfather's dog is always pricking up its ears at some ultrasonic signal, while he himself is so deaf he can't even hear a bird singing.

Ultrasound, or *ultrasonography,* works on the principle that sound is reflected at different speeds by tissues or substances of different densities. Ultrasound technology has been used medically since the 1940s. *Sonograms,* the pictures produced by ultrasound, can reveal heart defects, tumors, and gallstones; since low-power ultrasonic waves don't present any risks to a body, they're most often used to display fetuses during pregnancy in order to make sure they're healthy. *Ultrasonics* has many other uses, including underwater *sonar* sensing. High-power ultrasonics are so intense that they're actually used for drilling and welding.

Quizzes

A. **Indicate whether the following pairs of words have the same or different meanings:**

1.	dissonant / jarring	same ___ / different ___
2.	inaudible / invisible	same ___ / different ___
3.	resonance / richness	same ___ / different ___
4.	audition / tryout	same ___ / different ___
5.	ultrasonic / radical	same ___ / different ___
6.	auditor / performer	same ___ / different ___
7.	sonic / loud	same ___ / different ___
8.	auditory / hearing-related	same ___ / different ___

B. **Match the word on the left to the correct definition on the right:**

1.	inaudible	a.	involving sound
2.	auditory	b.	impossible to hear
3.	ultrasonic	c.	beyond the hearing range
4.	resonance	d.	a critical hearing
5.	auditor	e.	relating to hearing
6.	sonic	f.	unharmonious
7.	dissonant	g.	financial examiner
8.	audition	h.	continuing or echoing sound

ERR, from the Latin verb *errare,* means "to wander" or "to stray." The root is seen in the word *error,* meaning a wandering or straying from what is correct or true. *Erratum* (plural, *errata*) is Latin for "mistake"; so an errata page is a book page that lists mistakes found too late to correct before the book's publication.

errant \\'er-ənt\ (1) Wandering or moving about aimlessly. (2) Straying outside proper bounds, or away from an accepted pattern or standard.

* Modern-day cowboys have been known to use helicopters to spot errant calves.

Errant means both "wandering" and "mistaken." A *knight-errant* was a wandering knight who went about slaying dragons or rescuing damsels in distress (at least when he was on good behavior). *Arrant* is a old-fashioned spelling of *errant*; an *arrant knave* (the phrase comes from Shakespeare) is an extremely untrustworthy individual. An errant sock might be one that's gotten lost; an errant politician might be one who's been caught cheating; and an errant cloud might be one that floats by all alone in a deep-blue sky on a summer day.

aberrant \ə-'ber-ənt\ Straying or differing from the right, normal, or natural type.

* Sullivan's increasingly aberrant behavior was leading his friends to question his mental stability.

Something aberrant has wandered away from the usual path or form. The word is generally used in a negative way; aberrant behavior, for example, may be a symptom of other problems. But the discovery of an aberrant variety of a species can be exciting news to a biologist, and identifying an aberrant gene has led the way to new treatments for diseases.

erratic \i-'ra-tik\ (1) Having no fixed course. (2) Lacking in consistency.

* In the 1993 World Series, the Phillies weren't helped by the erratic performance of their ace relief pitcher, "Wild Thing."

Erratic can refer to literal "wandering." A missile that loses its guidance system may follow an erratic path, and a river with lots of twists and bends is said to have an erratic course. *Erratic* can also mean "inconsistent" or "irregular." So a stock market that often changes direction is said to be acting *erratically;* an erratic heartbeat can be cause for concern; and if your car idles erratically it may mean that something's wrong with the spark-plug wiring.

erroneous \i-ˈrō-nē-əs\ Mistaken, incorrect.

- For years her parents had had an erroneous idea of her intelligence, because she didn't begin to talk until the age of six.

Erroneous basically means "containing errors," and, since most of us are constantly suffering from mistaken notions, the word is often used in front of words such as "assumption" and "idea." It's also used to describe the kind of mistaken information that can lead to erroneous theories, erroneous conclusions, and erroneous decisions.

CED comes from the Latin verb *cedere*, meaning "to proceed" or "to yield." *Proceed* itself employs the root, as does *recede*, and their related nouns *procession* and *recession* employ another form of the Latin verb.

---

cede \ˈsēd\ To give up, especially by treaty; yield.

- Their 88-year-old father reluctantly ceded control over his finances to two of the children this year.

Cede is often a formal term used in discussing territory and rights, but is also used less formally. So, for example, Spain ceded Puerto Rico to the U.S. in 1898, following the Spanish-American War, and the U.S. ceded control of the Panama Canal to Panama in 1999. Critics warn that we are ceding leadership in alternative-energy technology to China. Citizens of one European country or another are always worrying that their own country is ceding too much power to the European Union. A tennis player doesn't have any choice when she cedes her no. 1 ranking to a rival.

concede \kən-ˈsēd\ To admit grudgingly; yield.

- To his friends, Senator Beasley concedes that his reelection campaign was badly run and that he made several damaging errors.

After the votes have been counted, one candidate traditionally concedes the election to his or her opponent by giving a *concession* speech. If you're lucky, your boss will concede that she was wrong the last time she criticized you. But in the middle of an argument, we're not all so good at conceding that the other guy might have a good point.

accede \akˈ-sēd\ (1) To give in to a request or demand. (2) To give approval or consent.

- This time Congress refused to accede to the demands of the president, and began cutting the funding for the war.

To accede usually means to yield, often under pressure and with some reluctance, to the needs or requests of others. Voters usually accede to a tax increase only when they're convinced it's the only real solution to a shortfall in government funding. A patient may accede to surgery only after the doctor assures him it's better than the alternatives. If you accede to your spouse's plea to watch the new reality show at 9:00, you may get to choose something better at 10:00.

precedent \\'pre-sə-dənt\\ Something done or said that may be an example or rule to guide later acts of a similar kind.

- When Judy bought Christmas presents for all her relatives one year, she claimed that it set no precedent, but it did.

A precedent is something that *precedes*, or comes before. The Supreme Court relies on precedents—that is, earlier laws or decisions that provide some example or rule to guide them in the case they're actually deciding. When hostages are being held for ransom, a government may worry about setting a bad precedent if it gives in. And a company might "break with precedent" by naming a foreigner as its president for the first time.

Quizzes

A. Complete the analogy:

1. descending : ascending :: errant : _____
   a. moving b. wandering c. fixed d. straying
2. grab : seize :: cede : _____
   a. hang on b. hand over c. hang up d. head out
3. fruitful : barren :: erroneous : _____
   a. productive b. pleasant c. targeted d. correct
4. disagree : argue :: concede : _____
   a. drive b. hover c. yield d. refuse
5. stable : constant :: erratic : _____
   a. fast b. invisible c. mistaken d. unpredictable
6. swerve : veer :: accede : _____
   a. agree b. descent c. reject d. demand

7. typical : normal :: aberrant : _____
    a. burdened b. roving c. odd d. missing
8. etiquette : manners :: precedent : _____
    a. courtesy b. tradition c. rudeness d. behavior

B. Fill in each blank with the correct letter:

a. aberrant   e. erratic
b. errant   f. erroneous
c. precedent   g. cede
d. concede   h. accede

1. Her low opinion of him turned out to be based on several _____ assumptions.
2. The judges could find no _____ to guide them in deciding how to deal with the case.
3. Like many malaria sufferers, she experienced _____ changes in her temperature.
4. Occasionally an _____ cow would be found on the back lawn, happily grazing on the fresh clover.
5. She's very stubborn, and in an argument she'll never _____ a single point.
6. After several incidents of disturbingly _____ behavior, his parents began taking him to a psychiatrist.
7. After lengthy negotiations, the union will probably _____ to several of the company's terms.
8. The treaty requires that both sides _____ several small tracts of land.

Words from Mythology and History

Augean stable \ȯ-ˈjē-ən-ˈstā-bəl\ A condition or place marked by great accumulation of filth or corruption.

• Leaders of many of the newly formed nations of Eastern Europe found that the old governments of their countries had become Augean stables that they must now clean out.

Augeus, the mythical king of Elis, kept great stables that held 3,000 oxen and had not been cleaned for thirty years when Hercules was assigned the job as one of his famous "twelve labors." This task was enormous even for someone so mighty, so Hercules shifted the course of two rivers to make them pour through the stables. *Augean* by itself has come to mean "extremely difficult or distasteful," and to "clean the Augean stable" usually means either to clear away corruption or to perform a large and unpleasant task that has long called for attention. So today we refer to "Augean tasks," "Augean labor," or even "Augean clutter." And the British firm Augean PLC is—what else?—a waste-management company.

Croesus \\'krē-səs\\ A very rich person.

- Warren Buffett's extraordinary record of acquiring and investing made him an American Croesus.

Croesus, which tends to appear in the phrase "rich as Croesus," was the name of a king of Lydia, an ancient kingdom in what is now western Turkey, who died around 546 B.C. Lydia was probably the first country in history to use coins, and under the wealthy and powerful Croesus the first coins of pure silver and gold were produced, which may have added to the legends surrounding his wealth. But it was Croesus who the Greek lawgiver Solon was thinking about when he said "Count no man happy until his death"—and indeed Croesus was finally overthrown and may even have been burned alive.

dragon's teeth \\'dra-gənz-'tēth\\ Seeds of conflict.

- Many experts believed that, in invading a Middle Eastern country that hadn't attacked us, we were sowing dragon's teeth.

The Phoenician prince Cadmus once killed a dragon, and was instructed by the goddess Athena to plant its teeth in the ground. From the many teeth, there immediately sprang up an army of fierce armed men. The goddess then directed him to throw a precious stone into their midst, and they proceeded to slaughter each other until only the five greatest warriors were left; these became Cadmus's generals, with whom he constructed the great city-state of Thebes. When we "sow dragon's teeth," we're creating the conditions for future trouble.

Hades \\'hā-dēz\\ The underground home of the dead in Greek mythology.

- In a dramatic scene, he crawls up out of the ground coated in black petroleum as though emerging from Hades.

In Greek mythology, Hades is both the land of the dead and the god who rules there. Hades the god (who the Greeks also called Pluto) is the brother of Zeus and Poseidon, who rule the skies and the seas. The realm called Hades, where he rules with his wife Persephone, is the region under the earth, full of mineral wealth and fertility and home to dead souls. *Hades* today is sometimes used as a polite term for *Hell* ("It's hotter than Hades in here!").

lethargic \lə-'thär-jik\ (1) Lazily sluggish. (2) Indifferent or apathetic.

• Once again the long Sunday dinner had left most of the family feeling stuffed and lethargic.

The philosopher Plato wrote that before a dead person could leave the underworld to begin a new life, he or she had to drink from the river Lethe, whose name means "forgetfulness" in Greek, and forget all aspects of one's former life and the time spent in Hades (usually pretty awful, according to Plato). But *lethargic* and its noun *lethargy* never actually refer to forgetting; instead, they describe the weak, ghostly state of the dead spirits—so weak that they may require a drink of blood before they can even speak.

Midas touch \'mī-dəs-'təch\ The talent for making money in every venture.

• Investors are always looking for an investment adviser with the Midas touch, but after a couple of good years each adviser's brilliance usually seems to vanish.

Midas was a legendary king of Phrygia (in modern-day Turkey). In return for a good deed, he was granted one wish by the god Dionysus, and asked for the power to turn everything he touched into gold. When he discovered to his horror that his touch had turned his food and drink—and even his daughter—to gold, he begged Dionysus to take back the gift, and Dionysus agreed to do so. When "Midas touch" is used today, the moral of this tale of greed is usually ignored.

Pyrrhic victory \'pir-ik-'vik-tə-rē\ A victory won at excessive cost.

• That win turned out to be a Pyrrhic victory, since our best players sustained injuries that would sideline them for weeks.

In 279 B.C. Pyrrhus, the king of Epirus, a country in northwest Greece, defeated the Romans at the Battle of Ausculum, but lost all of his best officers and many men. He is said to have exclaimed after the battle, "One more such victory and we are lost." Pyrrhic victories are more common than we tend to think. Whenever we win an argument but in so doing manage to offend the friend we were arguing with, or whenever a country invades another country but rouses widespread opposition in surrounding countries in the process, it's probably a Pyrrhic victory that has been achieved.

stygian \'sti-jē-ən\ Extremely dark, dank, gloomy, and forbidding.

• When the power went out in the building, the halls and stairwells were plunged in stygian darkness.

The Greek underworld of Hades was cold and dark, rather than blazing like the Christian image of Hell. The river Styx, whose name meant "hateful" in Greek, was the chief river of the underground, and the souls of the dead were ferried across its poisonous waters into Hades by the boatman Charon. The Styx was so terrible that even the gods swore by its name in their most solemn oaths. The name Stygia, borrowed from *stygian*, is used for a country in fantasy games today; but a stygian atmosphere, a stygian tunnel, stygian darkness, and so on, still describe the dreary cheerlessness of the Greek underworld.

Quiz

Choose the word that does not belong:
1. lethargic   a. lazy b. sluggish c. energetic
   d. indifferent
2. Croesus   a. rich b. powerful c. impoverished
   d. successful
3. Midas touch   a. talented b. unsuccessful c. rich
   d. prosperous
4. Pyrrhic victory   a. unqualified b. costly
   c. dangerous d. destructive
5. Augean stable   a. purity b. corruption c. filth
   d. Herculean
6. Hades   a. underworld b. heaven c. dead d. eternity

7. dragon's teeth   a. dangerous b. troublesome
   c. sensible d. conflict
8. stygian   a. glamorous b. gloomy c. grim d. dank

Review Quizzes

A. **Match each word on the left to its *antonym* on the right:**

1.	cede	a.	true
2.	erroneous	b.	generous
3.	dissonant	c.	energetic
4.	lethargic	d.	fill
5.	replete	e.	imbalance
6.	acquisitive	f.	typical
7.	deplete	g.	acquire
8.	equilibrium	h.	hearable
9.	inaudible	i.	empty
10.	aberrant	j.	harmonious

B. **Complete the analogies:**

1. allow : forbid :: cede : _____ a. take b. agree
   c. soothe d. permit
2. lively : energetic :: erratic : _____ a. calm
   b. changeable c. steady d. weary
3. complain : whine :: accede : _____ a. go over b. give
   in c. give out d. go along
4. noisy : raucous :: dissonant : _____ a. musical
   b. symphonic c. harsh d. loud
5. amount : quantity :: complement _____ a. remainder
   b. extra c. extension d. minority
6. spendthrift : thrifty :: acquisitive : _____ a. wealthy
   b. uncertain c. curious d. unselfish

C. **Fill in each blank with the correct letter:**

a.	auditor	f.	erratic
b.	tachometer	g.	Midas touch
c.	dragon's teeth	h.	accede
d.	complement	i.	Pyrrhic victory
e.	Croesus	j.	metric

1. My grandfather has never had any money, but his brother is rich as _____.

2. Every scientist in the world uses a version of the _____ system, but the American public has always resisted it.

3. An _____ had been going over the company's financial records all week.

4. The triumphant corporate takeover proved to be a _____, since the resulting debt crippled the corporation for years.

5. The children made only _____ progress because they kept stopping to pick flowers.

6. Some of the faculty have decided to quietly _____ to the students' request for less homework.

7. She's been sowing _____ with her mean gossip, and by now no one in the department is speaking to anyone else.

8. When the traffic gets too noisy, I have to glance at the _____ to see if the engine is racing.

9. Fresh, hot bread is the perfect _____ to any dinner.

10. Her wealthy father had always had the _____, and his money-making genius was still a mystery to her.

UNIT

7

VIS comes from a Latin verb meaning "see." *Vision* is what enables us to see, *visual* images are *visible* to our eyes, and a *visitor* is someone who comes to see something. The same verb actually gives us another root, *vid-,* as in Julius Caesar's famous statement about his military exploits, "Veni, vidi, vici" ("I came, I saw, I conquered"), and such common English words as *video.*

vista \\'vi-stə\ (1) A distant view. (2) An extensive mental view, as over a stretch of time.

• The economic vista for the next two years looks excellent, according to a poll of business economists.

Vista is generally used today for broad sweeping views of the kind you might see from a mountaintop. But the word originally meant an avenue-like view, narrowed by a line of trees on either side. And *vista* has also long been used (like *view* and *outlook*) to mean a mental scan of the future—as if you were riding down a long grand avenue and what you could see a mile or so ahead of you was where you'd be in the very near future.

vis-à-vis \\ˌvē-zä-'vē\ In relation to or compared with.

• Many financial reporters worry about the loss of U.S. economic strength vis-à-vis our principal trading partners.

Vis-à-vis comes from Latin by way of French, where it means literally "face-to-face." In English it was first used to mean a little horse-drawn carriage in which two people sat opposite each other. From there it acquired various other meanings, such as "dancing partner." Today it no longer refers to actual physical faces and bodies, but its modern meaning comes from the fact that things that are face-to-face can easily be compared or contrasted. So, for example, a greyhound is very tall vis-à-vis a Scottie, and the Red Sox have often fared badly vis-à-vis the Yankees.

visionary \\'vi-zhə-ˌner-ē\ (1) A person with foresight and imagination. (2) A dreamer whose ideas are often impractical.

- His followers regarded him as an inspired visionary; his opponents saw him as either a con man or a lunatic.

A visionary is someone with a strong *vision* of the future. Since such visions aren't always accurate, a visionary's ideas may either work brilliantly or fail miserably. Even so, *visionary* is usually a positive word. Martin Luther King, Jr., for instance, was a visionary in his hopes and ideas for a just society. The word is also an adjective; thus, for example, we may speak of a *visionary* project, a visionary leader, a visionary painter, or a visionary company.

envisage \in-'vi-zij\ To have a mental picture of; visualize.

- A mere three weeks after they had started dating, the two were already arguing, and none of us could envisage the relationship lasting for long.

One of the imagination's most valuable uses is its ability to see something in the "mind's eye"—that is, to *visualize, envision,* or envisage something. Envisaging a possibility may be one of the chief abilities that separate human beings from the other animals. What we envisage may be physical (such as a completed piece of furniture) or nonphysical (such as finishing college). Envisaging life with a puppy might lead us down to the pound to buy one, and envisaging the sinking of an island nation may focus our minds on climate change.

SPECT comes from the Latin verb *specere*, meaning "to look at," and produces several familiar English words. *Spectacles* can be glasses that you look through; but a spectacle can also be a remarkable sight—in Roman times, perhaps a *spectacular* chariot race or a *spectacularly* bloody battle between gladiators and wild beasts, mounted for the pleasure of its *spectators*.

aspect \\'a-ˌspekt\\ (1) A part of something. (2) A certain way in which something appears or may be regarded.

- Many experts believe the mental aspect of distance racing is more important than the physical aspect.

Since *aspectus* in Latin means "looked at," an aspect of something is basically the direction from which it's looked at. So we may say that travel is your favorite aspect of your job, or that eating well is one aspect of a healthy life. If you look at a stage set from the front, it looks completely different than from behind, where all the mechanisms are visible, and both aspects are important. The word can be very useful when you're analyzing something, and it's used a great deal in the writings of scholars.

prospect \\'prä-ˌspekt\\ (1) The possibility that something will happen in the future. (2) An opportunity for something to happen.

- There was little prospect of a breakthrough in the negotiations before the elections.

Since the Latin prefix *pro-* often means "forward" (see PRO, p. 631), *prospect* refers to looking forward. The prospect of a recession may lead investors to pull their money out of the stock market. Graduates of a good law school usually have excellent prospects for finding employment. *Prospective* students roam campuses with their parents in the year before they plan to enter college.

perspective \\pər-'spek-tiv\\ (1) Point of view; the angle, direction, or standpoint from which a person looks at something. (2) The art or technique of painting or drawing a scene so that objects in it seem to have depth and distance.

- From the perspective of the lowly soldier, the war looked very different.

To the modern mind, it's hard to believe that perspective had to be "discovered," but before the 1400s paintings simply lacked accurate perspective. Instead, important people and objects were simply shown larger than less important ones; and although distant objects were sometimes shown smaller than near ones, this wasn't done in a regular and accurate way. Just as odd, many paintings didn't represent the other meaning of *perspective* either—that is, a scene might not be shown as if it were being seen from one single place. Today, *perspective* is used much like *standpoint*. Just as *standpoint* once used to mean simply the physical place where you stand but today also means the way you "see" things as a result of who you are and what you do, the same could be said about *perspective*.

prospectus \prə-ˈspek-təs\ A printed statement that describes something (such as a new business or a stock offering) and is sent out to people who may be interested in buying or investing.

- The prospectus for the mutual fund says nothing about how its profit forecasts were calculated.

Like *prospect*, *prospectus* looks forward. Thus, a prospectus originally outlined something that didn't yet exist, describing what it would become. This might even be a book; the great dictionary of Noah Webster, like that of Samuel Johnson, was first announced in the form of a prospectus, so that well-to-do people might actually subscribe to it—that is, pay for it in advance so that Webster would have money to live on while writing it. Soon, *prospectus* was being used to mean a description of a private school or college, intended to attract new students. Today the word very often means a description of a stock offering or mutual fund, whether new or not.

Quizzes

A. Fill in each blank with the correct letter:

a. perspective
b. vis-à-vis
c. prospectus
d. prospect

e. envisage
f. aspect
g. visionary
h. vista

1. When she considered Cleveland _____ other cities where she might have to live, she always chose Cleveland.
2. The _____ of spending an evening with such an unhappy couple was just depressing.
3. His ambitious plans for the city marked him as a true _____.
4. The most troubling _____ of the whole incident was the public reaction.
5. The _____ for the new development was full of glowing descriptions that made both of us suspicious.

6. Turning a corner, they found themselves gazing out on the broad _____ of the river valley.

7. Some judges only look at crimes like these from the _____ of the police.

8. Her therapist keeps asking her if she could _____ getting back together with her husband.

B. **Match the definition on the left to the correct word on the right:**

1.	compared to	a.	perspective
2.	advance description	b.	envisage
3.	prophet	c.	vis-à-vis
4.	imagine	d.	aspect
5.	standpoint	e.	prospectus
6.	outlook	f.	visionary
7.	element	g.	prospect
8.	view	h.	vista

VOC comes from the Latin words meaning "voice" and "speak." So a *vocal* ensemble is a singing group. A *vocation* was originally a "calling" from God to do religious work as a priest, monk, or nun, though today most people use the word just to mean a career. And a *vocabulary* is a set of words for speaking.

equivocate \i-ˈkwi-və-ˌkāt\ (1) To use ambiguous language, especially in order to deceive. (2) To avoid giving a direct answer.

• As the company directors continued to equivocate, the union prepared to return to the picket lines.

With its root *equi-*, meaning "equal," *equivocate* suggests speaking on both sides of an issue at the same time. An *equivocal* answer is one that manages not to take a stand; an *unequivocal* answer, by contrast, is strong and clear. Politicians are famous for equivocating, but *equivocation* is also typical of used-car salesmen, nervous witnesses in a courtroom, and guys whose girlfriends ask them how committed they are to a relationship.

irrevocable \i-ˈre-və-kə-bəl\ Impossible to call back or retract.

• She had told him she wasn't going to see him again, but he couldn't believe her decision was irrevocable.

Irrevocable has a formal sound to it and is often used in legal contexts. Irrevocable trusts are trust funds that cannot be dissolved by the people who created them (the other kind is a *revocable* trust). An irrevocable credit is an absolute obligation from a bank to provide credit to a customer. Irrevocable gifts, under U.S. tax law, are gifts that are given by one living person to another and can't be reclaimed by the giver. But the word isn't always legal; we've all had to make irrevocable decisions, decisions that commit us absolutely to something.

advocate \\'ad-və-ˌkāt\\ To speak in favor of.

• Our lawyer is advocating a suit against the state, but most of us would rather try some other approaches first.

The verb *advocate* may be followed by *for* ("advocated for better roads," "advocated for merging the two school districts") or by a noun or gerund ("advocating an increase in the military budget," "advocated closing the budget gap"). But *advocate* isn't only a verb: An *advocate* is someone who advocates for you, or argues on your side. Originally, this was often a lawyer in court, and in Britain *advocate* is still a term for "lawyer."

vociferous \\vō-'si-fə-rəs\\ Making noisy or emphatic outcries.

• Whenever the referee at these soccer games makes a questionable call, you hear vociferous protests from half the parents.

A vociferous group shouts loudly and insistently, and they're usually not too happy about something. So, for example, we often hear about vociferous critics, vociferous demands, vociferous opponents, or a vociferous minority. When a small group makes itself vociferous enough, everyone else may even start thinking it's actually a majority.

PHON is a Greek root meaning "sound," "voice," or "speech." It's probably most familiar in the form of the English suffix *-phone*, in words that begin with a Greek or Latin root as well. Thus, the *tele-* in *telephone* means "far," the *micro-* in *microphone* means "small," the *xylo-* in *xylophone* means "wood," and so on.

phonics \'fä-niks\ A method of teaching beginners to read and pronounce words by learning the characteristic sounds of letters, letter groups, and especially syllables.

• My son's school switched to phonics instruction several years ago, and reading achievement in the early grades has been improving.

In the field of beginning reading, there are two basic schools of thought in the U.S. today. One emphasizes "whole language" teaching, which relies on teaching a lot of reading; the other emphasizes phonics, teaching how letters and syllables correspond to sounds. Phonics instruction may be especially difficult in English, since English has the most difficult spelling of any Western language. Consider the various ways we create the *f* sound in *cough, photo,* and *giraffe,* or the *sh* sound in *special, issue, vicious,* and *portion,* or the *k* sound in *tack, quite,* and *shellac,* and how we pronounce the *o* in *do, core, lock,* and *bone,* or the *ea* in *lead, ocean, idea,* and *early.* Teaching phonics obviously isn't an easy job, but it's probably an important one.

phonetic \fə-'ne-tik\ Relating to or representing the sounds of the spoken language.

• In almost every Spanish word the pronunciation is clear from the spelling, so the phonetic part of learning Spanish isn't usually a big challenge.

The English alphabet is phonetic—that is, the letters represent sounds. The Chinese alphabet, however, isn't phonetic, since its symbols represent ideas rather than sounds. But even in English, a letter doesn't always represent the same sound; the "a" in *cat, father,* and *mate,* for example, represents three different sounds. Because of this, books about words often use specially created phonetic alphabets in which each symbol stands for a single sound in order to represent pronunciations. So in this book, *cat, father,* and *mate* would be *phonetically* represented as 'kat, 'fä-<u>th</u>ər, and 'māt.

polyphonic \ˌpä-lē-'fä-nik\ Referring to a style of music in which two or more melodies are sung or played against each other in harmony.

• Whenever he needed something calming, he would put on some quiet polyphonic music from the Renaissance and just let the voices waft over him.

Since *poly-* means "many" (see POLY, p. 54), polyphonic music has "many voices." In *polyphony,* each part has its own melody, and they weave together in a web that may become very dense; a famous piece by Thomas Tallis, composed around 1570, has 40 separate voice parts. Polyphony reached its height during the 16th century with Italian madrigals and the sacred music of such composers as Tallis, Palestrina, and Byrd. Usually when we speak of polyphony we're talking about music of Bach's time and earlier; but the principles remain the same today, and songwriters such as the Beatles have sometimes used polyphony as well.

cacophony \kə-ˈkä-fə-nē\ Harsh or unpleasant sound.

- In New York she was often dragged off by her boyfriend to downtown jazz concerts, where she struggled to make sense of what sounded like nothing but cacophony.

Cacophony employs the Greek prefix *caco-,* meaning "bad," but not everything we call *cacophonous* is necessarily bad. Grunge, thrash, hardcore, and goth music are unlistenable to some people and very popular to others. Open-air food markets may be marked by a cacophony of voices but also by wonderful sights and sounds. On the other hand, few people can really enjoy, for more than a few minutes, the cacophony of jackhammers, car horns, and truck engines that assaults the city pedestrian on a hot day in August.

Quizzes

A. Complete the analogy:

1. initial : beginning :: irrevocable : _____
   a. usual b. noisy c. final d. reversible
2. arithmetic : numbers :: phonics : _____
   a. letters b. notes c. meanings d. music
3. prefer : dislike :: advocate : _____
   a. oppose b. support c. assist d. boost
4. multistoried : floor :: polyphonic : _____
   a. poetry b. melody c. story d. harmony
5. reject : accept :: equivocate : _____
   a. decide b. specify c. detect d. delay
6. melodic : notes :: phonetic : _____
   a. sounds b. signs c. ideas d. pages

7. monotonous : boring :: vociferous : _____
   a. vegetarian b. angry c. favorable d. noisy
8. stillness : quiet :: cacophony : _____
   a. melodious b. dissonant c. creative d. birdlike

B. Indicate whether the following pairs have the same or different meanings:

1. advocate / describe   same ___ / different ___
2. phonetic / phonelike   same ___ / different ___
3. equivocate / refuse   same ___ / different ___
4. polyphonic / many-voiced   same ___ / different ___
5. irrevocable / unfortunate   same ___ / different ___
6. cacophony / din   same ___ / different ___
7. vociferous / calm   same ___ / different ___
8. phonics / audio   same ___ / different ___

CUR, from the Latin verb *curare,* means basically "care for." Our verb *cure* comes from this root, as do *manicure* ("care of the hands") and *pedicure* ("care of the feet").

---

curative \\'kyùr-ə-tiv\\ Having to do with curing diseases.

* As soon as the antibiotic entered his system, he imagined he could begin to feel its curative effects.

Medical researchers are finding curative substances in places that surprise them. Folklore has led to some "new" *cures* of old diseases, and natural substances never before tried have often proved effective. Quinine, which comes from a tree in the Andes, was the original drug for malaria; aspirin's main ingredient came from willow bark; and Taxol, a drug used in treating several cancers, was originally extracted from the bark of a yew tree. The curative properties of these natural drugs are today duplicated in the laboratory.

curator \\'kyùr-ˌā-tər\\ Someone in charge of something where things are on exhibit, such as a collection, a museum, or a zoo.

* In recent decades, zoo curators have tried to make the animals' surroundings more and more like their natural homes.

In a good-sized art museum, each curator is generally responsible for a single department or collection: European painting, Asian sculpture, Native American art, and so on. *Curatorial* duties include acquiring new artworks, caring for and repairing objects already owned, discovering frauds and counterfeits, lending artworks to other museums, and mounting exhibitions of everything from Greek sculpture to 20th-century clothing.

procure \prō-'kyùr\ To get possession of; obtain.

• Investigators were looking into the question of how the governor had procured such a huge loan at such a favorable rate.

While *procure* has the general meaning of "obtain," it usually implies that some effort is required. It may also suggest getting something through a formal set of procedures. In many business offices, a particular person is responsible for procuring supplies, and government agencies have formal *procurement* policies. When teenagers use an older friend to procure the wrong kind of supplies for their parties, they often risk getting into trouble.

sinecure \'si-nə-ˌkyùr\ A job or position requiring little work but usually providing some income.

• The job of Dean of Students at any college is no sinecure; the hours can be long and the work draining.

Sinecure contains the Latin word *sine,* "without," and thus means "without care." In some countries, the government in power may be free to award sinecure positions to their valued supporters; in other countries, this would be regarded as corruption. The positions occupied by British royalty are called sinecures by some people, who claim they enjoy their enormous wealth in return for nothing at all. But their many supporters point to the amount of public-service, charitable, and ceremonial work they perform, not to mention the effort they put into promoting Britain to the world.

PERI, in both Latin and Greek, means "around." A *period* is often a span of time that keeps coming around regularly, day after day or year after year. With a *periscope,* you can see around corners. *Peristalsis* is the process that moves food around the intestines; without it, digestion would grind to a halt.

---

perimeter \pə-'ri-mə-tər\ The boundary or distance around a body or figure.

- In a medieval siege, an army would surround the perimeter of a city's high walls, denying the population any food from outside as it assaulted the walls with catapults and battering rams.

The perimeter of a prison is ringed with high walls and watchtowers, and the entire perimeter of Australia is bounded by water. In geometry, you may be asked to calculate the perimeter of various geometrical shapes. In basketball, the perimeter is the area beyond the free-throw circle; a "perimeter player" tends to stay outside that circle. Try not to confuse this word with *parameter,* which usually means a rule or limit that controls what something is or how it can be done.

periodontal \\,per-ē-ō-'dän-təl\\ Concerning or affecting the tissues around the teeth.

- Years of bad living had filled his teeth with cavities, but it was periodontal disease that finished them off.

In dentistry, cavities are important but they aren't the whole story; what happens to your gums is every bit as vital to your dental health. When you don't floss regularly to keep plaque from forming on your teeth and gums, the gums will slowly deteriorate. Dentists called *periodontists* specialize in the treatment of periodontal problems, and when the gums have broken down to the point where they can't hold the teeth in place a periodontist may need to provide dental implants, a costly and unpleasant process. But even a periodontist can't keep your gums healthy; that job is up to you.

peripatetic \\,per-ə-pə-'te-tik\\ (1) Having to do with walking. (2) Moving or traveling from place to place.

- She spent her early adult years as a peripatetic musician, traveling from one engagement to another.

The philosopher Aristotle had his school at the Lyceum gymnasium in Athens. The Lyceum may have resembled the Parthenon in being surrounded by a row of columns, or colonnade, which the Greeks would have called a *peripatoi.* Aristotle was also said to have paced slowly while teaching, and the Greek word for "pacing" was *peripatos.* And finally, *peripatos* meant simply "discussion." Whatever the source of the word, Aristotle and his followers became known as the *Peripatetics,* and the "pacing" sense led to *peripatetic*'s English meaning of traveling or moving about. Johnny Appleseed is a good example of a peripatetic soul, and peripatetic executives and salespeople today stare into their laptop computers while endlessly flying from city to city.

peripheral \pə-'ri-fə-rəl\ (1) Having to do with the outer edges, especially of the field of vision. (2) Secondary or supplemental.

• Like most good fourth-grade teachers, he had excellent peripheral vision, and the kids were convinced that he had eyes in the back of his head.

Your peripheral vision is the outer area of your field of vision, where you can still detect movement and shapes. It can be very valuable when, for instance, you're driving into Chicago at rush hour, especially when switching lanes. When people call an issue in a discussion peripheral, they mean that it's not of primary importance, and they're probably suggesting that everyone get back to the main topic. *Peripheral* is now also a noun: computer peripherals are the added components—printers, webcams, microphones, etc.—that increase a computer's capacities.

Quizzes

A. Fill in each blank with the correct letter:

a. curative
b. sinecure
c. procure
d. curator

e. peripheral
f. perimeter
g. peripatetic
h. periodontal

1. The _____ benefits of antibiotics have saved many lives.
2. _____ vision is part of what most eye doctors test in their patients.
3. What he had hoped to be an undemanding _____ turned out to be the hardest but most rewarding job of his career.
4. Because of deer, she needed to put up a fence along the _____ of the garden.
5. We asked our purchasing manager to _____ new chairs for the office.
6. In his youth he had been amazingly _____, hitchhiking thousands of miles on three continents.

7. The museum's _____ of African art narrates a guided tour of the exhibit.

8. Regular flossing can prevent most _____ disease.

B. Choose the closest definition:

1. sinecure   a. hopeful sign b. unsuccessful search c. careless act d. easy job

2. curator   a. doctor b. lawyer c. caretaker d. spectator

3. periodontal   a. visual b. inside a tooth c. around a tooth d. wandering

4. peripatetic   a. wandering b. unemployed c. surrounding d. old-fashioned

5. procure   a. say b. obtain c. look after d. heal

6. curative   a. purifying b. healing c. saving d. repairing

7. perimeter   a. factor b. characteristic c. supplement d. boundary

8. peripheral   a. supplementary b. around a tooth c. wandering d. dangerous

---

SENS comes from the Latin noun *sensus,* meaning "feeling" or "sense." *Sense* itself obviously comes straight from the Latin. A *sensation* is something you sense. And if you're *sensitive*, you feel or sense things sharply, maybe even too sharply.

---

sensor \\'sen-ˌsȯr\\ A device that detects a physical quantity (such as a movement or a beam of light) and responds by transmitting a signal.

• The outdoor lights are triggered by a motion sensor that detects changes in infrared energy given off by moving human bodies.

Sensors are used today almost everywhere. Radar guns bounce microwaves off moving cars. A burglar alarm may use a photosensor to detect when a beam of light has been broken, or may use ultrasonic sound waves that bounce off moving objects. Still other sensors may detect pressure (barometers) or chemicals (Breathalyzers and smoke detectors). Stud finders, used by carpenters to locate wooden studs under a wall, may employ magnets or radar. Wired gloves, which relay information about the position of the fingers, are used in virtual-reality environments. A cheap car alarm may be nothing but a shock sensor, in which a strong vibration will cause two metal surfaces to come together.

desensitize \dē-ˈsen-sə-ˌtīz\ To cause (someone or something) to react less to or be less affected by something.

* Even squeamish nursing students report becoming desensitized to the sight of blood after a few months of training.

Physical desensitizing is something that biologists have long been aware of. Basic training in the armed forces tries to desensitize new recruits to pain. We can desensitize ourselves to the summer heat by turning off the air conditioning, or become desensitized to the cold by walking barefoot in the snow. But *desensitize* is more often used when talking about negative emotions. Parents worry that their children will be desensitized to violence by playing video games. Soldiers may become desensitized to death on the battlefield. Desensitizing may be natural and desirable under some circumstances, but maybe not so good in others.

extrasensory \ˌek-strə-ˈsens-rē\ Not acting or occurring through any of the known senses.

* A kind of extrasensory capacity seems to tell some soldiers when danger is near.

Since *extra* means "outside, beyond" (see EXTRA, p. 163), *extrasensory* means basically "beyond the senses." Extrasensory perception, or ESP, usually includes communication between minds involving no obvious contact (*telepathy*), gaining information about something without using the normal senses (*clairvoyance*), or predicting the future (*precognition*). According to polls, about 40% of Americans believe in ESP, and many of them have had personal experiences that seem to prove its existence. When someone jumps into your mind months or years after you had last thought of him or her, and the next day you learn that the person has just died, it can be hard to convince yourself it was just coincidence. Still, scientific attempts to prove the existence of ESP have never been terribly successful.

sensuous \ˈsen-shù-wəs\ (1) Highly pleasing to the senses. (2) Relating to the senses.

* Part of what audiences loved about her was the delight she took in the sensuous pleasures of well-prepared food.

Sensuous and *sensual* are close in meaning but not identical, and *sensuous* was actually coined by the poet John Milton so that he wouldn't have to use *sensual*. *Sensuous* usually implies pleasing of the senses by art or similar means; great music, for example, can be a source of sensuous delight. *Sensual,* on the other hand, usually describes gratification of the senses or physical appetites as an end in itself; thus we often think (perhaps unfairly) of wealthy Romans leading lives devoted to sensual pleasure. You can see why the Puritan Milton might have wanted another word.

SOPH come from the Greek words meaning "wise" and "wisdom." In English the root sometimes appears in words where the wisdom is of the "wise guy" variety, but in words such as *philosophy* we see it used more respectfully.

---

sophistry \\'sä-fə-strē\\ Cleverly deceptive reasoning or argument.

* For lawyers and politicians, the practice of sophistry from time to time is almost unavoidable.

The Sophists were a group of Greek teachers of rhetoric and philosophy, famous during the 5th century B.C., who moved from town to town offering their teaching for a fee. The Sophists originally represented a respectable school of philosophy, but some critics claimed that they tried to persuade by means of clever but misleading arguments. The philosopher Plato wrote negatively about them, and the comic dramatist Aristophanes made fun of them, showing them making ridiculously fine distinctions about word meanings. We get our modern meanings of *sophist, sophistry*, and the adjective *sophistical* mostly from the opinions of these two men.

sophisticated \\sə-'fis-tə-ˌkā-təd\\ (1) Having a thorough knowledge of the ways of society. (2) Highly complex or developed.

* In *Woman of the Year,* Katharine Hepburn plays a sophisticated journalist who can handle everything except Spencer Tracy.

A sophisticated argument is thorough and well-worked-out. A satellite is a sophisticated piece of technology, complex and designed to accomplish difficult tasks. A sophisticated person, such as Humphrey Bogart in *Casablanca,* knows how to get around in the world.

But *sophistication* isn't always admired. As you might guess, the word is closely related to *sophistry* (see above), and its original meanings weren't very positive, and still today many of us aren't sure we really like *sophisticates.*

sophomoric \ˌsä-fə-ˈmȯr-ik\ Overly impressed with one's own knowledge, but in fact undereducated and immature.

- We can't even listen to those sophomoric songs of his, with their attempts at profound wisdom that just demonstrate how little he knows about life.

Sophomoric seems to include the roots *soph-,* "wise," and *moros,* "fool" (seen in words such as *moron*), so the contrast between wisdom and ignorance is built right into the word. Cambridge University introduced the term *sophomore* for its second-year students in the 17th century (though it's no longer used in Britain), maybe to suggest that a sophomore has delusions of wisdom since he's no longer an ignorant freshman. In America today, *sophomore* is ambiguous since it can refer to either high school or college. But *sophomoric* should properly describe something—wit, behavior, arguments, etc.—that is at least trying to be *sophisticated.*

theosophy \thē-ˈä-sə-fē\ A set of teachings about God and the world based on mystical insight, especially teachings founded on a blend of Buddhist and Hindu beliefs.

- He had experimented with a number of faiths, starting with Buddhism and ending with a mixture of Eastern and Western thought that could best be called theosophy.

The word *theosophy,* combining roots meaning "God" and "wisdom," appeared back in the 17th century, but the well-known religious movement by that name, under the leadership of the Russian Helena Blavatsky, appeared only around 1875. Blavatsky's theosophy combined elements of Plato's philosophy with Christian, Buddhist, and Hindu thought (including reincarnation), in a way that she claimed had been divinely revealed to her. The *Theosophical* Society, founded in 1875 to promote her beliefs, still exists, as does the *Anthroposophical* Society, founded by her follower Rudolf Steiner.

Quizzes

A. Indicate whether the following pairs of words have the same or different meanings:

1. sophisticated / worldly-wise   same ___ / different ___
2. sensuous / sensitive   same ___ / different ___
3. theosophy / mythology   same ___ / different ___
4. extrasensory / extreme   same ___ / different ___
5. sophistry / wisdom   same ___ / different ___
6. desensitize / deaden   same ___ / different ___
7. sophomoric / wise   same ___ / different ___
8. sensor / scale   same ___ / different ___

B. Match the word on the left to the correct definition on the right:

1. theosophy   a. immaturely overconfident
2. extrasensory   b. detector
3. sensuous   c. doctrine of God and the world
4. sophomoric   d. pleasing to the senses
5. sophistry   e. false reasoning
6. desensitize   f. not using the senses
7. sophisticated   g. make numb
8. sensor   h. highly complex

Words from Mythology and History

Achilles' heel \ə-ˈki-lēz-ˈhēl\ A vulnerable point.

- By now his rival for the Senate seat had discovered his Achilles' heel, the court records of the terrible divorce he had gone through ten years earlier.

When the hero Achilles was an infant, his sea-nymph mother dipped him into the river Styx to make him immortal. But since she held him by one heel, this spot did not touch the water and so remained mortal and vulnerable, and it was here that Achilles was eventually mortally wounded. Today, the tendon that stretches up the calf from the heel is called the *Achilles tendon*. But the term *Achilles' heel* isn't used in medicine; instead, it's only used with the general meaning "weak point"—for instance, to refer to a section of a country's borders that aren't militarily protected, or to a *Jeopardy* contestant's ignorance in the Sports category.

arcadia \är-ˈkā-dē-ə\ A region or setting of rural pleasure and peacefulness.

• The Pocono Mountains of Pennsylvania are a vacationer's arcadia.

Arcadia, a beautiful rural area in Greece, became the favorite setting for poems about ideal innocence unaffected by the passions of the larger world, beginning with the works of the Roman poet Virgil. There, shepherds play their pipes and sigh with longing for flirtatious nymphs; shepherdesses sing to their flocks; and goat-footed nature gods play in the fields and woods. Today, city dwellers who hope to retire to a country house often indulge in *arcadian* fantasies about what rural life will be like.

Cassandra \kə-ˈsan-drə\ A person who predicts misfortune or disaster.

• They used to call him a Cassandra because he often expected the worst, but his predictions tended to come true.

Cassandra, the daughter of King Priam of Troy, was one of those beautiful young maidens with whom Apollo fell in love. He gave her the gift of prophecy in return for the promise of her sexual favors, but at the last minute she refused him. Though he could not take back his gift, he angrily pronounced that no one would ever believe her predictions; so when she prophesied the fall of her city to the Greeks and the death of its heroes, she was laughed at by the Trojans. A modern-day Cassandra goes around predicting gloom and doom—and may turn out to be right some of the time.

cyclopean \ˌsī-klə-ˈpē-ən\ Huge or massive.

• They're imagining a new medical center on a cyclopean scale—a vast ten-block campus with thirty high-rise buildings.

The Cyclopes of Greek mythology were huge, crude giants, each with a single eye in the middle of his forehead. Odysseus and his men had a terrible encounter with a Cyclops, and escaped utter disaster only by stabbing a burning stick into the monster's eye. The great stone walls at such ancient sites as Troy and Mycenae are called cyclopean because the stones are so massive and the construction (which uses no cement) is so expert that it was assumed that only a superhuman race such as the Cyclopes could have achieved such a feat.

draconian \drə-'kō-nē-ən\ Extremely severe or cruel.

• The severe punishments carried out in Saudi Arabia, including flogging for drunkenness, hand amputation for robbery, and beheading for drug trafficking, strike most of the world as draconian.

Draconian comes from the name of Draco, a leader of Athens in the 7th century B.C. who in 621 B.C. produced its first legal code. The punishments he prescribed were extraordinarily harsh; almost anyone who couldn't pay his debts became a slave, and even minor crimes were punishable by death. So severe were these penalties that it was said that the code was written in blood. In the next century, the wise leader Solon would revise all of Draco's code, retaining the death penalty only for the crime of murder.

myrmidon \'mər-mə-ˌdän\ A loyal follower, especially one who executes orders unquestioningly.

• To an American, these soldiers were like myrmidons, all too eager to do the Beloved Leader's bidding.

In the Trojan War, the troops of the great hero Achilles were called Myrmidons. As bloodthirsty as wolves, they were the fiercest fighters in all Greece. They were said to have come from the island of Aegina, where, after the island's entire population had been killed by a plague, it was said to have been repopulated by Zeus, by turning all the ants in a great anthill into men. Because of their insect origin, the Myrmidons were blindly loyal to Achilles, so loyal that they would die without resisting if ordered to. The Trojans would not be the last fighting force to believe that a terrifying opposing army was made up of men who were not quite human.

nemesis \'ne-mə-səs\ A powerful, frightening opponent or rival who is usually victorious.

• During the 1970s and '80s, Japanese carmakers became the nemesis of the U.S. auto industry.

The Greek goddess Nemesis doled out rewards for noble acts and vengeance for evil ones, but it's only her vengeance that anyone remembers. According to the Greeks, Nemesis did not always punish an offender right away, but might wait as much as five generations to avenge a crime. Regardless, her cause was always just and her eventual victory was sure. But today a nemesis doesn't always dispense justice; a powerful drug lord may be the nemesis of a Mexican police chief, for instance, just as Ernst Stavro Blofeld was James Bond's nemesis in three of Ian Fleming's novels.

Trojan horse \\'trō-jǝn-'hȯrs\\ Someone or something that works from within to weaken or defeat.

- Researchers are working on a kind of Trojan horse that will be welcomed into the diseased cells and then destroy them from within.

After besieging the walls of Troy for ten years, the Greeks built a huge, hollow wooden horse, secretly filled it with armed warriors, and presented it to the Trojans as a gift for the goddess Athena, and the Trojans took the horse inside the city's walls. That night, the armed Greeks swarmed out and captured and burned the city. A Trojan horse is thus anything that looks innocent but, once accepted, has power to harm or destroy—for example, a computer program that seems helpful but ends up corrupting or demolishing the computer's software.

Quiz

Fill in each blank with the correct letter:

a. myrmidon   e. Achilles' heel
b. draconian   f. nemesis
c. cyclopean   g. Cassandra
d. Trojan horse   h. arcadia

1. He's nothing but a _____ of the CEO, one of those creepy aides who's always following him down the hall wearing aviator sunglasses.
2. A "balloon mortgage," in which the low rates for the first couple of years suddenly explode into something completely unaffordable, should be feared as a _____.
3. They marveled at the massive ancient _____ walls, which truly seemed to have been built by giants.

4. On weekends they would flee to their little _____ in rural New Hampshire, leaving behind the trials of the working week.
5. In eighth grade his _____ was a disagreeable girl named Rita who liked playing horrible little tricks.
6. His gloomy economic forecasts earned him a reputation as a _____.
7. Historians point to the _____ treaty terms of World War I as a major cause of World War II.
8. Believing the flattery of others and enjoying the trappings of power have often been the _____ of successful politicians.

Review Quizzes

A. Choose the correct synonym and the correct antonym:

1. peripheral   a. central b. logical c. sincere d. secondary
2. curative   a. humane b. unhealthful c. sensible d. healing
3. irrevocable   a. final b. undoable c. unbelievable d. vocal
4. perimeter   a. essence b. edge c. center d. spurt
5. nemesis   a. ally b. no one c. enemy d. bacteria
6. sophomoric   a. silly b. wise c. cacophonous d. collegiate
7. Achilles' heel   a. paradise b. heroism c. strong point d. vulnerability
8. peripatetic   a. stay-at-home b. exact c. wandering d. imprecise
9. vociferous   a. speechless b. steely c. sweet-sounding d. loud
10. visionary   a. idealist b. cinematographer c. conservative d. writer
11. sophisticated   a. rejected b. advanced c. worldly-wise d. innocent
12. equivocate   a. equalize b. dither c. decide d. enjoy

B.   Choose the closest definition:

1. phonetic   a. called b. twitched c. sounded
   d. remembered
2. sophistry   a. deception b. musical composition
   c. sound reasoning d. pleasure
3. procure   a. appoint b. obtain c. decide d. lose
4. vista   a. summit b. outlook c. mountain d. avenue
5. cacophony   a. fraud b. argument c. racket d. panic
6. vis-à-vis   a. compared to b. allowed to c. rented to
   d. talked to
7. perspective   a. judgment b. self-examination
   c. standpoint d. landscape
8. peripheral   a. auxiliary b. central c. relating to the
   sun d. philosophical
9. draconian   a. clever b. massive c. disastrous d. severe
10. polyphonic   a. multi-melodic b. uniformly
    harmonic c. relatively boring d. musically varied
11. cyclopean   a. whirling b. gigantic c. rapid
    d. circular
12. envisage   a. surround b. imagine c. investigate
    d. envy
13. periodontal   a. relating to feet b. around the sun
    c. around the teeth d. around a corner
14. curator   a. caretaker b. watcher c. doctor d. purchaser
15. Cassandra   a. optimist b. economist c. pessimist
    d. oculist

C.   Fill in each blank with the correct letter:

a.	equivocate	f.	Trojan horse
b.	sensuous	g.	arcadia
c.	cacophony	h.	theosophy
d.	extrasensory	i.	sinecure
e.	nemesis	j.	desensitize

1. The job turned out to be a _____, and no one cared if
   he played golf twice a week.
2. The huge Senate bill was a _____, filled with items
   that almost none of the senators were aware of.
3. We opened the door onto a haze of cigarette smoke and
   a _____ of music and laughter.

4. In an old book on _____ she found a philosophy very similar to the one she and her boyfriend were exploring.

5. She was sure her old _____ was plotting to get her fired.

6. After a month of barefoot running, he had managed to thoroughly _____ the soles of his feet.

7. The letter described their new Virginia farm as a kind of _____ of unspoiled nature.

8. Whenever they asked for a definite date, he would _____ and try to change the subject.

9. She lay in the bath with her eyes closed in a kind of _____ daydream.

10. Husband and wife seemed to communicate by _____ means, each always guessing what the other needed before anything was said.

UNIT

8

PORT comes from the Latin verb *portare*, meaning "to carry." Thus, something *portable* can be carried around. A *porter* carries your luggage, whether through a train station or high into the Himalayas. When we *transport* something, we have it carried from one place to another. And goods for *export* are carried away to another country.

---

portage \\'pȯr-tij\\ The carrying of boats or goods overland from one body of water to another; also, a regular route for such carrying.

• The only portage on the whole canoe route would be the one around the great waterfall on our second day.

Portage was borrowed from French back in the 15th century to mean "carrying, transporting" or "freight," and it has kept its simple "carrying" sense to the present day. But its first known use in its "carrying of boats" sense came in 1698, and the obstacle that the canoes couldn't be steered over was none other than Niagara Falls. Though canoes are much lighter today than they used to be, a long portage that includes a lot of camping gear can still test a camper's strength.

portfolio \\pȯrt-'fō-lē-ō\\ (1) A flat case for carrying documents or artworks. (2) The investments owned by a person or organization.

- In those days, a graphic artist who had recently moved to New York would just schlep his portfolio around to every magazine office in the city.

Portfolio is partly based on the Latin *folium*, meaning "leaf, sheet." A portfolio usually represents a portable showcase of your talents. Today actual portfolios are used less than they used to be by artists, since most commercial artists have a Web site dedicated to showing off their art. But *portfolio* in its other common meaning is extremely common. Not so long ago, a broker would keep each of his or her clients' investments in a separate notebook or portfolio. Today the investment portfolio, like an artist's portfolio, usually takes the form of a Web page, even though everyone still uses the same old word.

comport \kəm-ˈpȯrt\ (1) To be in agreement with. (2) To behave.

- This new evidence comports with everything we know about what happened that night.

With its prefix *com-*, "with," the Latin word *comportare* meant "to bring together." So it's easy to see how in English we could say that a college's policy comports with state law, or that a visit to your parents doesn't comport with your other weekend plans, or that your aunt and uncle won't listen to anything on TV that doesn't comport with their prejudices. The "behave" sense of the word comes through French, and its essential meaning is how a person "carries" him- or herself. So you may say, for instance, that your 17-year-old comported himself well (for once!) at the wedding reception, or that an ambassador always comports herself with dignity—that is, her *comportment* is always dignified—or that your class comported itself in a way that was a credit to the school.

deportment \di-ˈpȯrt-mənt\ Manner of conducting oneself socially.

- At social events she would constantly sneak glances at Alexandra, in quiet admiration of her elegant and graceful deportment.

We've all seen pictures of girls walking around balancing books on their heads in an effort to achieve the poise of a princess or a film star. Classes in deportment were once a standard part of a young lady's upbringing, offered in all the girls' colleges; and you can still take private deportment classes, where you'll learn about posture and body language, how to move, sit, stand, shake hands, dress, drink and eat, and much more. But deportment isn't all about refined female grace. In fact, *deport* is often used as a synonym for *comport*, but usually in a positive way; thus, people are often said to deport themselves well, confidently, with dignity, like gentlemen or ladies, and so on.

PEND comes from the Latin verb *pendere,* meaning "to hang" or "to weigh." (In the Roman era, weighing something large often required hanging it from a hook on one side of the balance scales.) We find the root in English words like *appendix,* referring to that useless and sometimes troublesome tube that hangs from the intestine, or that section at the back of some books that might contain some useful additional information.

---

pendant \\'pen-dənt\\ Something that hangs down, especially as an ornament.

* Around her neck she was wearing the antique French pendant he had given her, with its three rubies set in silver filigree.

Most pendants are purely decorative. But a pendant may also hold a picture or a lock of hair of a lover or a child. And, perhaps because they hang protectively in front of the body and near the heart, pendants have often had symbolic and magical purposes. Thus, a pendant may be a charm or amulet, or its gems or metals may be felt to have health-giving properties. In architecture, a pendant is an ornament that hangs down from a structure, but unlike a necklace pendant it's usually solid and inflexible.

append \\ə-'pend\\ To add as something extra.

* She appended to the memo a list of the specific items that the school was most in need of.

Append is a somewhat formal word. Lawyers, for example, often speak of appending items to other documents, and lawmakers frequently append small bills to big ones, hoping that everyone will be paying attention only to the main part of the big bill and won't notice. When we append a small separate section to the end of a report or a book, we call it an *appendix*. But in the early years of e-mail, the words we decided on were *attach* and *attachment*, probably because appendixes are thought of as unimportant, whereas the attachment is often the whole reason for sending an e-mail.

appendage \ə-'pen-dij\ (1) Something joined on to a larger or more important body or thing. (2) A secondary body part, such as an arm or a leg.

* She often complained that she felt like a mere appendage of her husband when they socialized with his business partners.

Appendix isn't the only noun that comes from *append*. Unlike *appendix*, *appendage* doesn't suggest the end of something, but simply something attached. The word is often used in biology to refer to parts of an animal's body: an insect's antennae, mouthparts, or wings, for example. The appendages of some animals will grow back after they've been removed; a salamander, for example, can regrow a finger, and the tiny sea squirt can regrow all its appendages—and even its brain.

suspend \sə-'spend\ (1) To stop something, or to force someone to give up some right or position, for a limited time. (2) To hang something so that it is free on all sides.

* The country has been suspended from the major trade organizations, and the effects on its economy are beginning to be felt.

When something is suspended, it is "left hanging"; it is neither in full operation nor permanently ended. *Suspense* is a state of uncertainty and maybe anxiety. When we watch a play or movie, we enjoy experiencing a "suspension of disbelief"; that is, we allow ourselves to believe we're watching reality, even though we aren't truly fooled. *Suspension* can also mean physical hanging; thus, in a suspension bridge, the roadway actually hangs from huge cables. When some substance is "in suspension," its particles are "hanging" in another substance, mixed into it but not actually dissolved, like fine sand in water, or sea spray in the air at the seashore.

Quizzes

A. Choose the closest definition:

1. pendant   a. porch   b. salary   c. flag   d. ornament
2. portfolio   a. mushroom   b. folder   c. painting
     d. carriage
3. suspend   a. study carefully   b. watch closely   c. slip
     gradually   d. stop temporarily
4. deportment   a. manner   b. section   c. departure
     d. promotion
5. append   a. close up   b. predict   c. attach   d. reconsider
6. portage   a. small dock   b. river obstacle   c. light boat
     d. short carry
7. comport   a. bend   b. behave   c. join   d. transport
8. appendage   a. hanger   b. body organ   c. limb
     d. companion

B. Fill in each blank with the correct letter:

a. portage	e. appendage
b. portfolio	f. pendant
c. deportment	g. append
d. comport	h. suspend

1. He found himself peering at her silver _____, trying to make out the odd symbols that formed the design.
2. Their _____ consisted mostly of high-tech stocks.
3. On the organizational chart, the group appears way down in the lower left corner, looking like a minor _____ of the company.
4. The biggest challenge would be the half-mile _____ around the river's worst rapids.
5. This is the entire report, to which we'll _____ the complete financial data when we submit it.
6. She never fails to impress people with her elegant _____ in the most difficult social situations.
7. Whenever his mother got wind of more bad behavior, she would _____ his allowance for a month.
8. These figures don't _____ with the ones you showed us yesterday.

PAN comes from a Greek word meaning "all"; as an English prefix, it can also mean "completely," "whole," or "general." A *panoramic* view is a complete view in every direction. A *pantheon* is a temple dedicated to all the gods of a religion. A *pandemic* outbreak of a disease may not affect the entire human population, but enough to produce a catastrophe.

panacea \ˌpa-nə-ˈsē-ə\ A remedy for all ills or difficulties; cure-all.

• Educational reform is sometimes viewed as the panacea for all of society's problems.

Panacea comes from a Greek word meaning "all-healing," and Panacea was the goddess of healing. In the Middle Ages and the Renaissance, alchemists who sought to concoct the "elixir of life" (which would give eternal life) and the "philosopher's stone" (which would turn ordinary metals into gold) also labored to find the panacea. But no such medicine was ever found, just as no solution to all of a society's difficulties has ever been found. Thus, *panacea* is almost always used to criticize the very idea of a total solution ("There's no panacea for the current problems plaguing Wall Street").

pandemonium \ˌpan-də-ˈmō-nē-əm\ A wild uproar or commotion.

• Pandemonium erupted in the stadium as the ball shot past the goalie into the net.

In John Milton's *Paradise Lost,* the fallen Satan has his heralds proclaim "A solemn Councel forthwith to be held / At Pandaemonium, the high Capital / Of Satan and his Peers." Milton got the name for his capital of hell, where Satan gathered together all his demons, by linking *pan* with the Latin word *daemonium,* "evil spirit." For later writers, *pandemonium* became a synonym for hell itself, since hell was then often seen as a place of constant noise and confusion, but also for any wicked and lawless place. Nowadays it's used to refer to the uproar itself rather than the place where it occurs.

pantheism \ˈpan-thē-ˌi-zəm\ A system of belief that regards God as identical with the forces and laws of the universe.

- Most of her students seemed to accept a vague kind of pantheism, without any real belief that God had ever appeared in human form.

Pantheistic ideas—and most importantly the belief that God is equal to the universe, its physical matter, and the forces that govern it—are found in the ancient books of Hinduism, in the works of many Greek philosophers, and in later works of philosophy and religion over the centuries. Much modern New Age spirituality is pantheistic. But most Christian thinkers reject pantheism because it makes God too impersonal, doesn't allow for any difference between the creation and the creator, and doesn't seem to allow for humans to make meaningful moral choices.

panoply \'pa-nə-plē\ (1) A magnificent or impressive array. (2) A display of all appropriate accessory items.

- The full panoply of a royal coronation was a thrilling sight for the throngs of sidewalk onlookers and the millions of television viewers.

The fully armed Greek soldier was an impressive sight, even if Greek armor never became as heavy as that of medieval knights on horseback (who couldn't possibly have marched in such outfits). *Panoplia* was the Greek word for the full suit of armor, and the English *panoply* originally likewise referred to the full suit of armor worn by a soldier or knight. Today *panoply* may refer to full ceremonial dress or lavish ceremonial decoration of any kind. And it can also refer to striking spectacle of almost any kind: the breathtaking panoply of autumn foliage, or the stirring panoply of a military parade, for example.

EXTRA is Latin for "outside" or "beyond." So anything *extraterrestrial* or *extragalactic* takes place beyond the earth or the galaxy. Something *extravagant,* such as an *extravaganza,* goes way beyond the normal. And *extra* is naturally a word itself, a shortening of *extraordinary,* "beyond the ordinary."

---

extradite \'ek-strə-ˌdīt\ To deliver an accused criminal from one place to another where the trial will be held.

- Picked up by the Colorado police for burglary, he's being extradited to Mississippi to face trial for murder.

Extradition from one state to another is generally a straightforward process. But extradition may become more complicated when two countries are involved, even though most countries have signed treaties stating that they will send criminals to the country where they are wanted. Many countries often won't send their own citizens to another country for trial; countries that don't permit the death penalty may not agree to send a suspect back to face such a penalty; and most countries won't extradite someone accused of political crimes. When extradition seems unlikely, a country may actually kidnap someone from another country, but this is illegal and rare.

extrapolate \ik-ˈstra-pə-ˌlāt\ To extend or project facts or data into an area not known in order to make assumptions or to predict facts or trends.

- Economists predict future buying trends partly by extrapolating from current economic data.

Scientists worry about the greenhouse effect because they have extrapolated the rate of carbon-dioxide buildup and predicted that its effect on the atmosphere will become increasingly severe. On the basis of their *extrapolations,* they have urged governments and businesses to limit factory and automobile emissions. Notice that it's acceptable to speak of extrapolating existing data (to produce new data), extrapolating *from* existing data (to produce new data), or extrapolating new data (from existing data)—in other words, it isn't easy to use this word wrong.

extrovert \ˈek-strə-ˌvərt\ A person mainly concerned with things outside him- or herself; a sociable and outgoing person.

- These parties are always full of loud extroverts, and I always find myself hiding in a corner with my drink.

Extrovert (sometimes spelled *extravert*) means basically "turned outward"—that is, toward things outside oneself. The word was coined by the eminent psychologist C. G. Jung in the early 20th century. The opposite personality type, in Jung's view, was the *introvert.* Extroverts seem to be favored by societies such as ours, even though introverts seem to be on average more mentally gifted. Psychologists have said that the only personality traits that can be identified in newborn infants are shyness and lack of shyness, which are fairly close to—but not really the same as—*introversion* and *extroversion.*

extraneous \ek-'strā-nē-əs\ (1) Existing or coming from the outside. (2) Not forming an essential part; irrelevant.

- Be sure your essays are well focused, with any discussion of extraneous topics kept to a minimum.

Extraneous and *strange* both come from the same Latin word, *extraneus*, which basically meant "external" or "coming from outside." But unlike *strange*, *extraneous* is a slightly formal word, often used by scientists and social scientists. Researchers always try to eliminate extraneous factors (or "extraneous variables") from their studies. A researcher conducting a psychological test, for example, would try to make sure that the people were tested under the same conditions, and were properly divided according to gender, age, health, and so on.

Quizzes

A. Fill in each blank with the correct letter:

a. extrapolate
b. panoply
c. extraneous
d. panacea

e. extradite
f. pantheism
g. extrovert
h. pandemonium

1. From these figures, economists can _____ data that shows a steady increase in employment.
2. Being a natural _____, he took to his new career as a salesman easily.
3. The new voice-mail system comes with the usual full _____ of options.
4. _____ broke out at the news of the victory.
5. The treaty with Brazil doesn't require us to _____ a criminal who's a native-born American.
6. He's locked himself in his studio to ensure that there won't be any _____ distractions.
7. She had always believed in vitamins as a _____, but they weren't always able to fight off infections.
8. He attended the Presbyterian church, even though for many years his real beliefs had been a mixture of Buddhism and _____.

B. Indicate whether the following pairs of terms have the same or different meanings:

1. panacea / antibiotic   same ___ / different ___
2. pandemonium / chaos   same ___ / different ___
3. pantheism / priesthood   same ___ / different ___
4. panoply / display   same ___ / different ___
5. extrapolate / project   same ___ / different ___
6. extraneous / necessary   same ___ / different ___
7. extradite / hand over   same ___ / different ___
8. extrovert / schizophrenic   same ___ / different ___

PHOT comes from the Greek word for "light." *Photography* uses light to create an image on film or paper, and a *photocopy* is an image made by using light and tiny electrically charged ink particles.

---

photoelectric \ˌfō-tō-i-ˈlek-trik\ Involving an electrical effect produced by the action of light or other radiation.

• They wanted to avoid the kind of smoke detector that uses radioactive materials, so they've installed the photoelectric kind instead.

The *photoelectric effect* occurs when light (or similar radiation such as X-rays) falls on a material such as a metal plate and causes it to emit electrons. The discovery of the photoelectric effect led to important new theories about matter (and to a Nobel Prize for Albert Einstein). *Photoelectric cells,* or *photocells*, are used in burglar-alarm light detectors and garage-door openers (both employ a beam of light that is broken when something moves across it), and also to play soundtracks on movie film (where a light beam shines through the soundtrack encoded on the film and is "read" by the photocells).

photovoltaic \ˌfō-tō-väl-ˈtā-ik\ Involving the direct generation of electricity when sunlight or other radiant energy falls on the boundary between dissimilar substances (such as two different semiconductors).

• Photovoltaic technology is being applied to thin film that can produce as much energy as solar cells while using far less semi-conducting material.

The *-voltaic* part of *photovoltaic* comes from the name of Alessandro Volta, inventor of the electric battery. Thus, unlike photoelectric cells, which use electricity for certain small tasks, photovoltaic (or PV) cells actually produce electricity. Solar cells, the standard type of photovoltaic cells (often called simply *photocells*), operate without chemicals and with no moving parts to create energy directly from sunlight. Much research is now being done on creating an alternative technology—solar film, which could be stuck onto almost any surface, or possibly even sprayed on.

photon \\ˈfō-ˌtän\ A tiny particle or bundle of radiant energy.

- The idea that light consists of photons is difficult until you begin to think of a ray of light as being caused by a stream of tiny particles.

It was Albert Einstein who first theorized that the energy in a light beam exists in small bits or particles, and scientists today know that light sometimes behaves like a wave (somewhat like sound or water) and sometimes like a stream of particles. The energies of photons range from high-energy gamma rays and X-rays down to low-energy infrared and radio waves, though all travel at the same speed. The amazing power of lasers is the result of a concentration of photons that have been made to travel together in order to hit their target at the same time.

photosynthesis \\ˌfō-tō-ˈsin-thə-sis\ The process by which green plants use light to produce organic matter from carbon dioxide and water.

- Sagebrush survives in harsh climates because it's capable of carrying on photosynthesis at very low temperatures.

The Greek roots of *photosynthesis* combine to produce the basic meaning "to put together with the help of light." Photosynthesis is what first produced oxygen in the atmosphere billions of years ago, and it's still what keeps it there. Sunlight splits the water molecules (made of hydrogen and oxygen) held in a plant's leaves and releases the oxygen in them into the air. The leftover hydrogen combines with carbon dioxide to produce carbohydrates, which the plant uses as food—as do any animals or humans who might eat the plant.

LUC comes from the Latin noun *lux,* "light," and the verb *lucere,* "to shine or glitter." In ancient Rome, *Lucifer,* meaning "Light-bearer," was the name given to the morning star, but the name was eventually transferred by Christians to Satan. This tradition, which dates back to the period before Christ, said that Lucifer had once been among the angels but had wanted to be the great light in the sky, and for his pride had been cast out of heaven and thus became the opponent of everything good.

lucid \\'lü-səd\\ (1) Very clear and easy to understand. (2) Able to think clearly.

• On his last visit he had noticed that his elderly mother hadn't seemed completely lucid.

Mental *lucidity* is easy to take for granted when we're young, though alcohol, drugs, and psychological instability can confuse the mind at any age. We all hope to live to 100 with our mental abilities intact, which is entirely possible; avoiding the condition called dementia (which includes the well-known Alzheimer's disease) often involves a combination of decent genes, physical and mental activity, and a good diet. Writing *lucidly,* on the other hand, can take a lot of work at any age; you've probably had the experience of trying to read a set of instructions and wondering if the writer even grew up speaking English.

elucidate \\i-'lü-sə-ˌdāt\\ To clarify by explaining; explain.

• A good doctor should always be willing to elucidate any medical jargon he or she uses.

The basic meaning of *elucidate* is "to shed light on." So when you elucidate, you make transparent or clear something that had been murky or confusing. *Elucidation* of a complex new health-care policy may be a challenge. Elucidation of the terms of use for a credit card may be the last thing its provider wants to do. The physicist Carl Sagan had a gift for elucidating astronomical science to a large audience, his *lucid* explanations making clear how stars are born and die and how the universe may have begun.

lucubration \\ˌlü-kyů-'brā-shən\\ (1) Hard and difficult study. (2) The product of such study.

- Our professor admitted that he wasn't looking forward to reading through any more of our lucubrations on novels that no one enjoyed.

Lucubration came to mean "hard study" because it originally meant study done by lamplight, and in a world without electric lights, such study was likely to be the kind of hard work that would only a dedicated student like Abe Lincoln would make a habit of. The word has a literary feel to it, and it's often used with a touch of sarcasm.

translucent \tranz-ˈlü-sənt\ Partly transparent; allowing light to pass through without permitting objects beyond to be seen clearly.

- Architects today often use industrial glass bricks in their home designs, because translucent walls admit daylight while guarding privacy.

With its prefix *trans-*, meaning "through," *translucent* describes material that light shines through without making anything on the other side clearly visible, unlike a *transparent* material. Frosted glass, often used in bathroom windows, is translucent, as is stained glass. Red wine in a crystal goblet, when held before a candle in a dark corner of a quiet restaurant, usually proves to be translucent as well.

Quizzes

A. Fill in each blank with the correct letter:

a. photovoltaic   e. photoelectric
b. lucid   f. lucubration
c. photon   g. photosynthesis
d. translucent   h. elucidate

1. A soft light filtered through the _____ white curtains separating the two rooms.
2. _____ cells on the roof capture the sun's energy, and with the small windmill nearby they produce more energy than the house needs.
3. Few of us can truly imagine that light can be reduced to a tiny packet of energy called a _____.
4. In graduate school, his lively social life was replaced with three years of intense _____.

5. A large tree with a 40-inch trunk may produce two-thirds of a pound of oxygen every day through _____.

6. His 88-year-old aunt is in a nursing home, and he never knows which days she'll be _____.

7. The alarm system depends on _____ technology that detects when someone breaks a beam of light in a doorway.

8. Whenever anyone asks the professor to _____, he just makes everything more complicated instead of less.

B. Match the definition on the left to the correct word on the right:

1.	involving the interaction of light with matter	a.	lucubration
		b.	photoelectric
2.	production of carbohydrates	c.	translucent
3.	clarify	d.	elucidate
4.	passing light but only blurred images	e.	photovoltaic
		f.	photosynthesis
5.	elemental particle	g.	photon
6.	brightly clear	h.	lucid
7.	hard study		
8.	using light to generate electricity		

MOR/MORT comes from Latin words meaning "to die" and "death." A *mortuary* is a place where dead bodies are kept until burial, and a *postmortem* examination is one conducted on a recently dead body. The Latin phrase "Memento mori" means "Remember that you must die"; so a *memento mori* is the name we give to a reminder of death; the skulls you can find carved on gravestones in old cemeteries are examples.

---

mortality \mȯr-'ta-lə-tē\ (1) The quality or state of being alive and therefore certain to die. (2) The number of deaths that occur in a particular time or place.

• Mortality rates were highest among those who those who lived closest to the plant.

Young people tend to assume they will never die; but a person's sense of his or her mortality generally increases year by year, and often increases greatly after a serious accident or illness. Still, many people refuse to change behaviors that would improve their chances of living into old age. Mortality rates are calculated by government agencies, insurance companies, and medical researchers. Infant mortality rates provide a good indicator of a country's overall health; in recent years, the rates in countries like Iceland, Singapore, and Japan have been much better than in the U.S.

moribund \\'mȯr-ə-bənd\\ (1) In the process of dying or approaching death. (2) Inactive or becoming outmoded.

• Church attendance in Britain has fallen in recent years, but no one would say the Anglican church is moribund.

Moribund is still sometimes used in its original literal sense of "approaching death," but it's much more often used to describe things. When the economy goes bad, we hear about moribund mills and factories and towns; the economy itself may even be called moribund. Critics may speak of the moribund state of poetry, or lament the moribund record or newspaper industry.

amortize \\'a-mər-ˌtīz\\ To pay off (something such as a mortgage) by making small payments over a period of time.

• For tax purposes, they chose to amortize most of the business's start-up costs over a three-year period.

Amortize is most common as a legal term, and many of us first come across it when we take out a mortgage or start a business. Financial officers and tax lawyers can choose how to legally amortize various types of business expenses, some of which may seem much better than others. In mortgage *amortization*, much of what you pay month by month is actually interest on the mortgage debt, especially at the beginning. So what does amortizing have to do with death? Basically, to amortize a debt means to "kill" it slowly over time.

mortify \\'mȯr-tə-ˌfī\\ (1) To subdue or deaden (the body) especially by self-discipline or self-inflicted pain. (2) To embarrass greatly.

• Our 14-year-old is mortified whenever he sees us dancing, especially if any of his school friends are around.

Mortify once actually meant "put to death," but no longer. Its "deaden" sense is most familiar to us in the phrase "mortifying the flesh," which refers to a custom once followed by devout Christians, who would starve themselves, deprive themselves of every comfort, and even whip themselves in order to subdue their bodily desires and punish themselves for their sins. But the most common use of *mortify* today is the "humiliate" sense; its connection with death is still apparent when we speak of "dying of embarrassment."

TROPH comes from the Greek *trophe*, meaning "nourishment." This particular *troph-* root doesn't show up in many everyday English words (the *troph-* in words like *trophy, apostrophe,* and *catastrophe* has a different meaning), but instead tends to appear in scientific terms.

---

atrophy \\ˈa-trə-fē\ (1) Gradual loss of muscle or flesh, usually because of disease or lack of use. (2) A decline or degeneration.

• After a month in a hospital bed, my father required a round of physical therapy to deal with his muscular atrophy.

From its literal Greek roots, *atrophy* would mean basically "lack of nourishment." Although the English word doesn't usually imply any lack of food, it always refers to a wasting away. Those who have been bedridden for a period of time will notice that their muscles have *atrophied*. And muscular atrophy is a frequent result of such diseases as cancer and AIDS. We also use *atrophy* in a much more general sense. After being out of work a few years, you may find your work skills have atrophied; someone who's been living an isolated life may discover the same thing about his or her social skills; and a democracy can atrophy when its citizens cease to pay attention to how they're being governed.

hypertrophy \hī-ˈpər-trə-fē\ (1) Excessive development of an organ or part. (2) Exaggerated growth or complexity.

• Opponents claimed that the Defense Department, after years of being given too much money by the Congress, was now suffering from hypertrophy.

When the prefix *hyper-*, "above, beyond" (see HYPER, p. 457), is joined to *-trophy*, we get the opposite of *atrophy*. An organ or part becomes *hypertrophic* when it grows so extremely that its function is affected. Muscle hypertrophy is common in men who do strength training, and is often harmless; but extreme muscle hypertrophy generally involves taking steroids, which can do great damage to the body. Hypertrophy of the heart sounds as if it might be healthy, but instead it's usually a bad sign. As the example sentence shows, *hypertrophy*, like *atrophy*, can be used in nonmedical ways as well.

dystrophy \\'di-strə-fē\\ Any of several disorders involving the nerves and muscles, especially muscular dystrophy.

• The most common of the muscular dystrophies affects only males, who rarely live to the age of 40.

Since the prefix *dys-* means "bad" or "difficult" (see DYS, p. 104), *dystrophy* is always a negative term. Originally it meant "a condition caused by improper nutrition," but today the term is instead used for a variety of other conditions, particularly conditions that noticeably affect the muscles. Of the many types of muscular dystrophy, the best known is Duchenne's, a terrible disease that strikes about one in 3,300 males and produces severe wasting of the muscles. However, the muscular dystrophies generally affect many other organs and systems as well. And the other dystrophies, which tend to involve the eyes or hands, don't much resemble the muscular dystrophies.

eutrophication \\yü-ˌtrō-fə-'kā-shən\\ The process by which a body of water becomes enriched in dissolved nutrients.

• Local naturalists are getting worried about the increasing eutrophication they've been noticing in the lake.

Eutrophication, which comes from the Greek *eutrophos*, "well-nourished" (see EU, p. 103), has become a major environmental problem. Nitrates and phosphates, especially from lawn fertilizers, run off the land into rivers and lakes, promoting the growth of algae and other plant life, which take oxygen from the water, causing the death of fish and mollusks. Cow manure, agricultural fertilizer, detergents, and human waste are often to blame as well. In the 1960s and '70s, the eutrophication of Lake Erie advanced so extremely that it became known as the "dead lake." And many areas of the oceans worldwide—some more than 20,000 square miles in extent—have become "dead zones," where almost no life of any kind exists.

Quizzes

A. Choose the closest definition:

1. mortality   a. deadliness b. danger c. disease
   d. death rate
2. hypertrophy   a. excessive growth b. low birth rate
   c. increased speed d. inadequate nutrition
3. amortize   a. bring back b. pay down c. make love
   d. die off
4. atrophy   a. expansion b. swelling c. exercise
   d. wasting
5. mortify   a. weaken b. bury c. embarrass d. kill
6. dystrophy   a. bone development b. muscular
   wasting c. nerve growth d. muscle therapy
7. moribund   a. deathlike b. unhealthy c. lethal d. dying
8. eutrophication   a. inadequate moisture b. excessive
   growth c. loss of sunlight d. healthy nourishment

B. Fill in each blank with the correct letter:

a. eutrophication   e. moribund
b. atrophy   f. mortify
c. hypertrophy   g. mortality
d. dystrophy   h. amortize

1. By the 1960s, most of the textile industry had moved
   south, and the mill town seemed _____.
2. In muscular _____, the wasting begins in the legs and
   advances to the arms.
3. Most people don't spend much time thinking about
   their _____ until they're in their thirties or forties.
4. They should be able to _____ their mortgage
   completely by the time they retire.
5. Muscular _____ as extreme as that is only possible
   with steroids.
6. Some religious sects still engage in acts designed
   to _____ the flesh.
7. By then the pond had almost entirely filled in with
   plant life, a result of the _____ caused by the factory's
   discharges.
8. In the four weeks before he has the cast taken off, his
   muscles will _____ quite a lot.

Words from Mythology and History

aeolian harp \ē-'ō-lē-ən-'härp\ A box-shaped instrument with strings that produce musical sounds when the wind blows on them.

• Poets have long been fascinated by the aeolian harp, the only instrument that produces music without a human performer.

According to the ancient Greeks, Aeolus was the king or guardian of the winds. He lived in a cave with his many, many sons and daughters, and sent forth whatever wind Zeus asked for. When Odysseus stopped there on his way home from Troy, he received a bag of winds to fill his sails. But while he was asleep, his men, thinking it contained treasure, opened the bag and released the raging winds, which blew their ships all the way back to their starting point. An aeolian harp produces enchanting harmonies when the wind passes over it. According to Homer, it was the god Hermes who invented the harp, by having the wind blow over the dried sinews attached to the shell of a dead tortoise.

cynosure \'sī-nə-ˌshủr\ (1) A guide. (2) A center of attention.

• Near the club's dance floor, a young rock star was hanging out, the cynosure of a small crowd of admirers.

In Greek *kynosoura* means "dog's tail," and in Latin *Cynosura* came to mean the constellation Ursa Minor (Little Bear)—what we usually call the Little Dipper. The first star on the dog's or bear's "tail," or the dipper's "handle," is Polaris, the North Star, long used as a guide for seamen or travelers lost on a clear night, since, unlike the other stars, it always remains in the same position in the northern sky, while the other constellations (and even the rest of its own constellation) slowly revolve around it. Since *Cynosura* also came to mean the star itself, the English *cynosure* now may mean both "guide" and "center of attention."

laconic \lə-'kä-nik\ Using extremely few words.

• Action-film scripts usually seem to call for laconic leading men who avoid conversation but get the job done.

Ancient Sparta was located in the region of Greece known as Laconia, and the Greek word *lakonikos* could mean both "Laconian" and "Spartan." The disciplined and militaristic Spartans, the finest warriors of their time, were known for putting up with extreme conditions without complaint. So English writers who knew their ancient history came to use *laconic* to describe the habit of saying few words. Today we can refer not only to a laconic person but also to laconic wit, a laconic answer, or a laconic phrase—such as "Men of few words require few laws," uttered by a Spartan king.

mnemonic \ni-ˈmä-nik\ Having to do with the memory; assisting the memory.

- Sales-training courses recommend various mnemonic devices as a way of remembering peoples' names.

The Greek word for memory is *mnemosyne*, and Mnemosyne was the goddess of memory and the mother of the Muses. So something that helps the memory is a mnemonic aid, or simply a *mnemonic*. Such traditional mnemonic devices as "Every Good Boy Does Fine" (for the notes on the lines of a musical staff with a treble clef) or the "Thirty days hath September" rhyme help to recall simple rules or complicated series that might otherwise slip away. (For extra credit, guess what "King Henry Died Drinking Chocolate Milk" or "King Philip Could Only Find Green Socks" stands for.) Notice that the first *m* isn't pronounced, unlike in other *-mne-* words such as *amnesia* and *amnesty*.

platonic \plə-ˈtä-nik\ (1) Relating to the philosopher Plato or his teachings. (2) Involving a close relationship from which romance and sex are absent.

- The male and female leads in sitcoms often keep their relationship platonic for the first few seasons, but romance almost always wins out in the end.

The philosopher Plato presented his theories in a series of dramatic conversations between Socrates and other people, now called the "Platonic dialogues." Among many other important concepts, he taught that everything here on earth is a pale imitation—like a shadow—of its ideal form, and this ideal form is now often called the "platonic form." But *platonic* is probably usually seen in the phrase "platonic love." Because Socrates (through Plato) teaches that the philosophical person should turn his passion for a lover into appreciation of beauty and love of a higher power and of the universe, close but nonsexual friendship between two people who might be thought to be romantically attracted is today known as platonic love or friendship.

sapphic \\'sa-fik\\ (1) Lesbian. (2) Relating to a poetic verse pattern associated with Sappho.

- The Roman poets Catullus and Horace composed wonderful love poems in sapphic verse.

The poet Sappho wrote poems of self-reflection but also of passion, some of it directed to the women attending the school she conducted on the Greek island of Lesbos around 600 B.C. Even though most of the poems survive only as fragments, they have been greatly admired for many centuries. They were written in an original rhythmical pattern, which has become known as sapphic verse. Later admirers, such as the Roman poets Catullus and Horace, honored her by adopting the sapphic meter for their own poetry. Because of Sappho, the island of Lesbos also gave its name to lesbianism, which writers often used to call sapphic love.

Socratic \\sō-'kra-tik\\ Having to do with the philosopher Socrates or with his teaching method, in which he systematically questioned the student in conversation in order to draw forth truths.

- She challenges her students by using the Socratic method, requiring them to think and respond constantly in every class.

Socrates lived and taught in Athens in the 5th century B.C., but left no writings behind, so all we know of him comes through the works of his disciple Plato, almost all of which claim to be accounts of Socrates' conversations with others. Today Socrates is best remembered for his method of teaching by asking increasingly difficult questions, the so-called *Socratic method*. This generally involves the use of *Socratic induction,* a way of gradually arriving at generalizations through a process of questions and answers, and *Socratic irony,* in which the teacher pretends ignorance while questioning his students skillfully to make them aware of their errors in understanding.

solecism \\'sō-lə-ˌsi-zəm\\ (1) A grammatical mistake in speaking or writing. (2) A blunder in etiquette or proper behavior.

- The poor boy committed his first solecism immediately on entering by tracking mud over the Persian rug in the dining room.

In ancient Asia Minor (now Turkey), there was a city called Soloi where the inhabitants spoke Greek that was full of grammatical errors. So errors in grammar, and later also small errors in formal social behavior, came to be known (at least by intellectuals) as solecisms. The British magazine *The Economist* publishes a list of solecisms to be avoided in its prose, including the use of "try and" when you mean "try to," "hone in on" when you mean "home in on," and so forth. Social solecisms, such as mentioning how inferior the wine is to someone who turns out to be the hostess's sister, are more commonly called by a French name, *faux pas*.

Quiz

Fill in each blank with the correct letter:

a. solecism   e. cynosure
b. sapphic   f. aeolian harp
c. platonic   g. mnemonic
d. Socratic   h. laconic

1. She always learns her students' names quickly by using her own _____ devices.
2. Every so often, a breeze would spring up and the _____ in the window would emit its beautiful harmonies.
3. New Yorkers tend to think of their city as the _____ of the nation.
4. The _____ method is inappropriate for normal courtroom interrogation.
5. After encountering the fifth _____ in the report, we began to lose faith in the writer.
6. Her father-in-law was _____ in her presence but extremely talkative around his son.
7. As an experiment, he had written a poem in _____ verse, but he suspected that the rhythm was more suited to Greek.
8. The dinner was good, but saying that it approached the _____ ideal of a meal was probably too much.

Review Quizzes

A. Fill in each blank with the correct letter.

a. elucidate   f. laconic
b. appendage   g. moribund
c. solecism   h. deportment
d. pantheism   i. mortality
e. comport   j. atrophy

1. After spending four years at home, she's afraid her professional skills have begun to _____.
2. Her impressive résumé doesn't _____ well with her ignorance of some basic facts about the business.
3. He can't go to a cocktail party without committing at least one _____ and offending a couple of people.
4. Like most farmers, he's fairly _____, but when he says something it's usually worth listening to.
5. For kids their age they have excellent manners, and everyone admires their _____ around adults.
6. It was a large beetle with an odd _____ coming off the top of its head.
7. The book's introduction helps _____ how the reader can make the best use of it.
8. _____ has been a common element in religious belief in the West over many centuries.
9. The newspaper has suffered declines in both advertisements and readership over the last few years and is clearly _____.
10. The _____ rates from these kinds of cancer have been going down as new treatments have been adopted.

B. Indicate whether the following pairs of words have the same or different meanings:

1. mnemonic / ideal   same ___ / different ___
2. hypertrophy / overgrowth   same ___ / different ___
3. extrapolate / project   same ___ / different ___
4. mortify / stiffen   same ___ / different ___
5. appendage / attachment   same ___ / different ___
6. cynosure / guide   same ___ / different ___
7. extrovert / champion   same ___ / different ___
8. append / attach   same ___ / different ___

9.	amortize / pay down	same ___ / different ___
10.	lucid / glittering	same ___ / different ___
11.	atrophy / enlarge	same ___ / different ___
12.	translucent / cross-lighted	same ___ / different ___
13.	solecism / goof	same ___ / different ___
14.	pandemonium / uproar	same ___ / different ___
15.	extraneous / superb	same ___ / different ___
16.	lucubration / nightmare	same ___ / different ___
17.	photosynthesis / reproduction	same ___ / different ___
18.	panacea / remedy	same ___ / different ___
19.	elucidate / charm	same ___ / different ___
20.	deportment / behavior	same ___ / different ___

C. Match the definition on the left to the correct word on the right:

1.	question-and-answer	a.	panoply
2.	elementary particle of light	b.	pendant
3.	stop temporarily	c.	sapphic
4.	hanging ornament	d.	comport
5.	impressive display	e.	translucent
6.	nonsexual	f.	platonic
7.	behave	g.	photon
8.	dying	h.	Socratic
9.	lesbian	i.	suspend
10.	light-diffusing	j.	moribund

UNIT

9

HER comes from the Latin verb *haerere,* meaning "to stick." Another form of the verb produces the root *hes-*, seen in such words as *adhesive,* which means basically "sticky" or "sticking," and *hesitate,* which means more or less "stuck in one place."

adherent \ad-ˈhir-ənt\ (1) Someone who follows a leader, a party, or a profession. (2) One who believes in a particular philosophy or religion.

• The general's adherents heavily outnumbered his opponents and managed to shout them down repeatedly.

Just as tape *adheres* to paper, a person may adhere to a cause, a faith, or a belief. Thus, you may be an adherent of Hinduism, an adherent of environmentalism, or an adherent of the Republican Party. A plan for cutting taxes always attracts adherents easily, regardless of what the cuts may result in.

cohere \kō-ˈhir\ To hold together firmly as parts of the same mass.

• His novels never really cohere; the chapters always seem like separate short stories.

When you finish writing a paper, you may feel that it coheres well, since it's sharply focused and all the ideas seem to support each other. When all the soldiers in an army platoon feel like buddies, the platoon has become a *cohesive* unit. In science class you may learn the difference between *cohesion* (the tendency of a chemical's molecules to stick together) and *adhesion* (the tendency of the molecules of two different substances to stick together). Water molecules tend to cohere, so water falls from the sky in drops, not as separate molecules. But water molecules also *adhere* to molecules of other substances, so raindrops will often cling to the underside of a clothesline for a while before gravity pulls them down.

incoherent \ˌin-kō-ˈhir-ənt\ (1) Unclear or difficult to understand. (2) Loosely organized or inconsistent.

- The police had found him in an abandoned warehouse, and they reported that he was dirty, hungry, and incoherent.

Incoherent is the opposite of *coherent,* and both commonly refer to words and thoughts. Just as *coherent* means well ordered and clear, *incoherent* means disordered and hard to follow. *Incoherence* in speech may result from emotional stress, especially anxiety or anger. Incoherence in writing may simply result from poor planning; a twelve-page term paper that isn't written until the night before it's due will generally suffer from incoherence.

inherent \in-ˈhir-ənt\ Part of something by nature or habit.

- A guiding belief behind our Constitution is that individuals have certain inherent rights that can't be taken away.

Inherent literally refers to something that is "stuck in" something else so firmly that they can't be separated. A plan may have an inherent flaw that will cause it to fail; a person may have inherent virtues that everyone admires. Since the flaw and the virtues can't be removed, the plan may simply have to be thrown out and the person will remain virtuous forever.

FUG comes from the Latin verb *fugere,* meaning "to flee or escape." Thus, a *refugee* flees from some threat or danger, while a *fugitive* is usually fleeing from the law.

---

centrifugal \sen-ˈtri-fyu̇-gəl\ Moving outward from a center or central focus.

- Their favorite carnival ride was the Round-up, in which centrifugal force flattened them against the outer wall of a rapidly spinning cage.

Centrifugal force is what keeps a string with a ball on the end taut when you whirl it around. A *centrifuge* is a machine that uses centrifugal force. At the end of a washing machine's cycle, it becomes a weak and simple centrifuge as it whirls the water out of your clothes. Centrifuges hundreds of thousands of times as powerful are essential to nuclear technology and drug manufacturing. Part of an astronaut's training occurs in a centrifuge that generates force equal to several times the force of gravity (about like a washing machine) to get them used to the forces they'll encounter in a real space mission.

refuge \\'re-ˌfyüj\\ Shelter or protection from danger or distress, or a place that provides shelter or protection.

• Caught in a storm by surprise, they took refuge in an abandoned barn.

The *re-* in *refuge* means basically "back" or "backward" rather than "again" (see RE, p. 635); thus, a *refugee* is someone who is "fleeing backward." *Refuge* tends to appear with certain other words: you generally "seek refuge," "take refuge," or "find refuge." Religion may be a refuge from the woes of your life; a beautiful park may be a refuge from the noise of the city; and your bedroom may be a refuge from the madness of your family.

fugue \\'fyüg\\ A musical form in which a theme is echoed and imitated by voices or instruments that enter one after another and interweave as the piece proceeds.

• For his debut on the church's new organ, the organist chose a fugue by J. S. Bach.

Bach and Handel composed many fugues for harpsichord and organ in which the various parts (or voices) seem to flee from and chase each other in an intricate dance. Each part, after it has stated the theme or melody, apparently flees from the next part, which takes up the same theme and sets off in pursuit. Simple rounds such as "Three Blind Mice" or "Row, Row, Row Your Boat" could be called fugues for children, but a true fugue can be long and extremely complex.

subterfuge \\'səb-tər-ˌfyüj\\ (1) A trick designed to help conceal, escape, or evade. (2) A deceptive trick.

• The conservatives' subterfuge of funding a liberal third-party candidate in order to take votes away from the main liberal candidate almost worked that year.

With its "flee" root, the Latin verb *subterfugere* meant "to escape or avoid." Thus, a subterfuge is a way of escaping blame, embarrassment, inconvenience—or even prison—by tricky means. The life of spies consists of an endless series of subterfuges. In the more everyday world, putting words like "heart-healthy" on junk-food packaging is a subterfuge to trick unwary shoppers. And getting a friend to call about an "emergency" in order to get out of an evening engagement is about the oldest subterfuge in the book.

Quizzes

A. Fill in each blank with the correct letter:

a. cohere	e. centrifugal
b. refuge	f. adherent
c. incoherent	g. subterfuge
d. fugue	h. inherent

1. The author tries to take on so many different subjects that the book really doesn't _____ very well.
2. All the plans for the surprise party were in place except the _____ for keeping her out of the house until 6:30.
3. She had left Scientology and was now an _____ of the Unification Church.
4. Fleeing the Nazis, he had found _____ in the barn of a wealthy family in northern Italy.
5. By the time his fever reached 105°, the boy was mumbling _____ sentences.
6. A rock tied to a string and whirled about exerts _____ force on the string.
7. Mahatma Gandhi believed goodness was _____ in humans.
8. As the last piece in the recital, she had chosen a particularly difficult _____ by Bach.

B. Choose the closest definition:

1. inherent   a. built-in   b. inherited   c. confused   d. loyal
2. fugue   a. mathematical formula   b. musical form
     c. marginal figure   d. masonry foundation
3. adherent   a. sticker   b. stinker   c. follower   d. flower
4. centrifugal   a. moving upward   b. moving backward
     c. moving downward   d. moving outward

5. cohere   a. control   b. react   c. pause   d. unite
6. subterfuge   a. overhead serve   b. underhanded plot
    c. powerful force   d. secret supporter
7. incoherent   a. attached   b. constant   c. controlled
    d. confused
8. refuge   a. starting point   b. hideout   c. goal   d. return

---

COSM comes from the Greek word for "order." Since the Greeks believed the universe was an orderly place, words in this group usually relate to the universe. So *cosmonaut* was the word for a space traveler from the former Soviet Union. (The roots of our own word, *astronaut*, suggest "star traveler" instead.) Oddly enough, *cosmetics* comes from the same root, since putting things in order is similar to decorating something—such as your face.

---

cosmos \\'käz-ˌmōs\\ (1) The universe, especially when it is viewed as orderly and systematic. (2) Any orderly system that is complete in itself.

• The astronomer, the biologist, and the philosopher all try in their own ways to make sense of the cosmos.

Cosmos often simply means "universe." But the word is generally used to suggest an orderly or harmonious universe, as it was originally used by Pythagoras in the 6th century B.C. Thus, a religious mystic may help put us in touch with the cosmos, and so may a physicist. The same is often true of the adjective *cosmic*: Cosmic rays (really particles rather than rays) bombard us from outer space, but cosmic questions come from human attempts to find order in the universe.

cosmology \\käz-'mä-lə-jē\\ (1) A theory that describes the nature of the universe. (2) A branch of astronomy that deals with the origin and structure of the universe.

• New Age teachers propose a cosmology quite unlike the traditional Jewish, Christian, or Islamic ways of viewing the universe.

Most religions and cultures include some kind of cosmology to explain the nature of the universe. In modern astronomy, the leading cosmology is still the Big Bang theory, which claims that the universe began with a huge explosion that sent matter and energy spreading out in all directions. One reason why fans watch *Star Trek* is for the various cosmologies depicted in the show, including different conceptions of space, time, and the meaning of life.

microcosm \\'mī-krǝ-ˌkä-zǝm\\ Something (such as a place or an event) that is seen as a small version of something much larger.

* The large hippie communes of the 1960s and '70s were microcosms of socialist systems, with most of socialism's advantages and disadvantages.

A troubled urban school can look like a microcosm of America's educational system. A company's problems may be so typical that they can represent an entire small country's economic woes "in microcosm." *Microcosm,* and especially its synonym *microcosmos,* are also sometimes used when talking about the microscopic world. The documentary film *Microcosmos* is devoted to the remarkable insect life in an ordinary meadow on a single summer's day.

cosmopolitan \\ˌkäz-mǝ-'pä-lǝ-tǝn\\ (1) Having international sophistication and experience. (2) Made up of persons, elements, or influences from many different parts of the world.

* New York, like most cosmopolitan cities, offers a wonderful array of restaurants featuring foods from around the world.

Since *cosmopolitan* includes the root *polit-,* from the Greek word for "citizen," someone who is cosmopolitan is a "citizen of the world." She may be able to read the morning paper in Rio de Janeiro, attend a lecture in Madrid, and assist at a refugee camp in Uganda with equal ease—and maybe all in the same week. And a city or a country that is cosmopolitan has aspects and elements that come from various countries.

SCI comes from the Latin verb *scire,* "to know" or "to understand." The root appears in such common words as *science,* which originally meant simply "knowledge," and *conscience,* meaning "moral knowledge." And to be *conscious* is to be in a state where you are able to know or understand.

---

conscientious \ˌkän-shē-ˈen-shəs\ (1) Governed by morality; scrupulous. (2) Resulting from painstaking or exact attention.

• New employees should be especially conscientious about turning in all their assignments on time.

Conscience and its adjective *conscientious* both come from a Latin verb meaning "to be aware of guilt." *Conscientious* indicates extreme care, either in observing moral laws or in performing assigned duties. A conscientious person is someone with a strong moral sense, who has feelings of guilt when he or she violates it. A conscientious worker has a sense of duty that forces him or her to do a careful job. A conscientious report shows painstaking work on the part of the writer. And a *conscientious objector* is someone who, for reasons of conscience, refuses to fight in an army.

nescience \ˈne-shəns\ Lack of knowledge or awareness: ignorance.

• About once every class period, my political-science professor would angrily denounce the nescience of the American public.

This word, which means literally "non-knowledge," is only used by intellectuals, and the same is true of its adjective, *nescient*. We all have heard the remarkable facts: 40% of us believe that humans and dinosaurs lived on earth at the same time; 49% believe that the President can ignore the Constitution; 60% can't name the three branches of government; 75% can't find Israel on a map; and so on. Is it any wonder we Americans are sometimes called nescient?

prescient \ˈpre-shənt\ Having or showing advance knowledge of what is going to happen.

• For years she had read the *Wall Street Journal* every morning, looking for prescient warnings about crashes, crises, and catastrophes on the horizon.

Being truly prescient would require supernatural powers. But well-informed people may have such good judgment as to appear prescient, and *prescient* is often used to mean "having good foresight." Some newspaper columnists may seem prescient in their predictions, but we can't help suspecting that any apparent *prescience* is usually the result of leaks from people with inside knowledge.

unconscionable \ən-'kän-shə-nə-bəl\ (1) Not guided by any moral sense; unscrupulous. (2) Shockingly excessive, unreasonable, or unfair.

• When the facts about how the cigarette industry had lied about its practices for decades finally came out, most Americans found the behavior unconscionable.

Something that can't be done in good *conscience* is unconscionable, and such acts can range from betraying a confidence to mass murder. For a five-syllable word, *unconscionable* is actually quite common. This is partly because it isn't always used very seriously; so, for example, a critic is free to call a fat new book "an unconscionable waste of trees." In law, an unconscionable contract is one that, even though it was signed by both parties, is so ridiculous that a judge will just throw it out.

Quizzes

A. Complete the analogy:

1. clever : brainy :: prescient : _____
    a. evil b. wise c. existing d. painstaking
2. village : city :: microcosm : _____
    a. flea circus b. universe c. scale model d. bacteria
3. bold : shy :: cosmopolitan : _____
    a. planetary b. naive c. unique d. nearby
4. informed : ignorant :: conscientious : _____
    a. careful b. all-seeing c. well-informed d. scientific
5. geology : earth :: cosmology : _____
    a. sophistication b. universe c. explanation d. appearance
6. data : information :: nescience : _____
    a. wisdom b. ignorance c. judgment d. learning
7. forest : trees :: cosmos : _____
    a. stars b. earth c. orbits d. universe
8. corrupt : honest :: unconscionable : _____
    a. orderly b. attractive c. universal d. moral

B. Match the definition on the right to the correct word on the left:

1. cosmopolitan
2. nescience
3. microcosm
4. conscientious
5. unconscionable
6. cosmology
7. prescient
8. cosmos

a. having foresight
b. universe
c. lack of knowledge
d. well-traveled
e. small world
f. scrupulous
g. inexcusable
h. description of the universe

JUNCT comes from the Latin verb *jungere,* meaning "to join." A *junction* is a place where roads or railways come together. A *conjunction* is a word that joins two other words or groups of words: "this *and* that," "to be *or* not to be."

---

juncture \\'jəŋk-chər\\ (1) An important point in a process or activity. (2) A place where things join: junction.

• The architect claims his design for the new Islamic Museum represents a juncture of Muslim and Western culture.

The meaning of *juncture* can be entirely physical; thus, you can speak of the juncture of the turnpike and Route 116, or the juncture of the Shenandoah and Potomac Rivers. But it more often means something nonphysical. This may be a moment in time, especially a moment when important events are "crossing" ("At this critical juncture, the President called together his top security advisers"). But *juncture* also often refers to the coming together of two or more ideas, systems, styles, or fields ("These churches seem to operate at the juncture of religion and patriotism," "Her job is at the juncture of product design and marketing," etc.).

adjunct \\'a-ˌjəŋkt\\ Something joined or added to another thing of which it is not a part.

• All technical-school students learn that classroom instruction can be a valuable adjunct to hands-on training.

With its prefix, *ad-,* meaning "to or toward," *adjunct* implies that one thing is "joined to" another. A car wash may be operated as an adjunct to a gas station. An *adjunct* professor is one who's attached to the college without being a full member of the salaried faculty. And anyone trying to expand his or her vocabulary will find that daily reading of a newspaper is a worthwhile adjunct to actual vocabulary study.

disjunction \dis-'jəŋk-shən\ A break, separation, or sharp difference between two things.

- By now she realized there was a serious disjunction between the accounts of his personal life that his two best friends were giving her.

A disjunction may be a mere lack of connection between two things, or a large gulf. There's often a huge disjunction between what people expect from computers and what they know about them, and the disjunction between a star's public image and her actual character may be just as big. We may speak of the disjunction between science and morality, between doing and telling, or between knowing and explaining. In recent years, *disjunction* seem to have been losing out to a newer synonym, the noun *disconnect*.

conjunct \kən-'jəŋkt\ Bound together; joined, united.

- Politics and religion were conjunct in 18th-century England, and the American colonists were intent on separating the two.

With its prefix *con-*, meaning "with, together," *conjunct* means basically "joined together." A rather intellectual word, it has special meanings in music (referring to a smooth melodic line that doesn't skip up or down) and astronomy (referring to two stars or planets that appear next to each other), but its more general "bound together" meaning is rarer. A *conjunction* is a word (particularly *and, or,* or *but*) that joins together words or groups of words, and an adverb that joins two clauses or sentences (such as *so, however, meanwhile, therefore,* or *also*) is called a *conjunctive adverb*—or simply a *conjunct*.

PART, from the Latin word *pars,* meaning "part," comes into English most obviously in our word *part*. An *apartment* or *compartment* is part of a larger whole. The same is usually true of a *particle*.

---

bipartite \bī-'pär-₁tīt\ (1) Being in two parts. (2) Shared by two.

- The report is a bipartite document, and all the important findings are in the second section.

Usually a technical word, *bipartite* is common in medicine and biology. A bipartite patella, for example, is a split kneecap; many people are born with them. Many creatures have a bipartite life cycle, living life in two very distinct forms. As one example, the velella begins life as a creature that travels with thousands of others in the form of a kind of sailboat, blown across the ocean's surface with the wind; only later does each velella turn into a tiny jellyfish.

impartial \im-ˈpär-shəl\ Fair and not biased; treating or affecting all equally.

- Representatives of labor and management agreed to have the matter decided by an impartial third party.

To be "partial to" or "partial toward" someone or something is to be somewhat biased or prejudiced, which means that a person who is partial really only sees part of the whole picture. To be impartial is the opposite. The United Nations sends impartial observers to monitor elections in troubled countries. We hope judges and juries will be impartial when they hand down verdicts. But grandparents aren't expected to be impartial when describing their new grandchild.

participle \ˈpär-tə-ˌsi-pəl\ A word that is formed from a verb but used like an adjective.

- In the phrase "the crying child," "crying" is a present participle; in "satisfaction guaranteed," "guaranteed" is a past participle.

English verbs can take several basic forms, which we call their *principal parts*: the infinitive ("to move," "to speak," etc.), the past tense ("moved," "spoke"), the past participle ("moved," "spoken"), and the present participle ("moving," "speaking"). The participles are words that "take part" in two different word classes: that is, verb forms that can also act like adjectives ("the spoken word," "a moving experience"). A grammatical error called a *dangling participle* occurs when a sentence begins with a participle that doesn't modify the subject; in the sentence "Climbing the mountain, the cabin came in view," for example, "climbing" is a dangling participle since it doesn't modify "cabin."

partisan \ˈpär-tə-zən\ (1) A person who is strongly devoted to a particular cause or group. (2) A guerrilla fighter.

• Throughout his career on the Supreme Court, he had been a forthright partisan of the cause of free speech.

A partisan is someone who supports one *part* or *party*. Sometimes the support takes the form of military action, as when guerrilla fighters take on government forces. But *partisan* is actually most often used as an adjective, usually referring to support of a political party. so if you're accused of being too partisan, or of practicing partisan politics, it means you're mainly interested in boosting your own party and attacking the other one.

Quizzes

A. Choose the closest definition:

1. juncture   a. opening b. crossroads c. end
        d. combination
2. impartial   a. fair b. biased c. accurate d. opinionated
3. adjunct   a. warning b. addition c. disclosure
        d. difference
4. participle   a. verb part b. warning c. supplement
        d. guerrilla fighter
5. conjunct   a. joined b. difficult c. spread out
        d. simplified
6. bipartite   a. double-edged b. twice-married
        c. two-part d. having two parties
7. disjunction   a. prohibition b. break c. requirement
        d. intersection
8. partisan   a. judge b. teacher c. supporter d. leader

B. Indicate whether the following pairs of words have the same or different meanings:

1. impart / give   same ___ / different ___
2. conjunct / split   same ___ / different ___
3. participle / verb part   same ___ / different ___
4. impartial / supportive   same ___ / different ___
5. adjunct / supplement   same ___ / different ___
6. juncture / train station same ___ / different ___
7. partisan / fighter   same ___ / different ___
8. disjunction / connection same ___ / different ___

MIS comes from the Latin verb *mittere*, "to send." A *missile* is something sent speeding through the air or water. And when your class is *dismissed* at the end of the day, you're sent home.

mission \\'mi-shən\\ (1) A task that someone is given to do, especially a military task. (2) A task that someone considers an important duty.

• She considers it her mission to prevent unwanted puppies and kittens from being born.

Your own *mission* in life can be anything you pursue with almost religious enthusiasm. People with a mission—whether it's stopping drunk driving, keeping the town's public areas clean, increasing local recycling, or building a community center—very often succeed in really changing things.

missionary \\'mi-shə-ˌner-ē\\ A person undertaking a mission, and especially a religious missionary.

• North American missionaries have been working in Central America for decades, and you can find their churches in even the most remote jungle regions.

Beginning around 1540, an order of Catholic priests known as the Jesuits began to send its members to many parts of the world to convert peoples who believed in other gods to Christianity. Wherever they went, the Catholic missionaries built central buildings for their religious work, and the buildings themselves became known as *missions*; many 17th-century missions in the American West and Southwest are now preserved as museums. Their foes, the Protestants, soon began sending out their own missionaries, and today Protestant missionaries are probably far more numerous.

emissary \\'e-mə-ˌser-ē\\ Someone sent out to represent another; an agent.

• Now in his 70s, he had served over many years as a presidential emissary to many troubled regions of the world.

Like *missionaries,* emissaries are sent on missions. However, emissaries are more likely to be representing governments, political leaders, and nonreligious institutions, and an emissary's mission is usually to negotiate or to gather information. So a president may send a trusted emissary to a war-torn region to discuss peace terms.

A company's CEO may send an emissary to check out another company that they may be thinking of buying. And a politician may send out an emissary to persuade a wealthy individual to become a supporter.

transmission \trans-¹mi-shən\ (1) The act or process of sending something from one point to another, especially sending electrical signals to a radio, television, computer, etc. (2) The gears by which the power is passed from the engine to the axle in a motor vehicle.

• Even in the Middle Ages, transmission of news of a ruler's death across the Asian continent could be accomplished by sun reflectors within 24 hours.

Since *trans-* means "across" (see TRANS, p. 626), it's not hard to see the meaning of *transmission.* Disease transmission occurs when an infection passes from one living thing to another. TV signal transmission can be interrupted by tree leaves, including moving leaves and branches during a storm. Your car's transmission *transmits* the engine's power to the axle, changing the gears to keep the engine working with maximum efficiency at various speeds.

PEL comes from the Latin verb *pellere,* meaning "to move or drive." So a *propeller* moves a small airplane forward. And if you *dispel* someone's fears, you "drive them away."

---

compel \kəm-¹pel\ (1) To force (someone) to do something. (2) To make (something) happen.

• After returning from the lecture, they felt compelled to contribute to one of the refugee relief agencies.

The prefix *com-* acts as a strengthener in this word; thus, to compel is to drive powerfully, or force. So you may feel compelled to speak to a friend about his drinking, or compelled to reveal a secret in order to prevent something from happening. A *compulsion* is usually a powerful inner urge; a *compulsive* shopper or a compulsive gambler usually can't hold onto money for long. You might not want to do something unless there's a *compelling* reason; however, a compelling film is simply one that seems serious and important.

expel \ik-'spel\ (1) To drive or force out. (2) To force to leave, usually by official action.

- For repeatedly ignoring important agreements over several years, the two countries were eventually expelled from the trade organization.

To expel is to drive out, and its usual noun is *expulsion. Expel* is similar to *eject,* but *expel* suggests pushing out while *eject* suggests throwing out. Also, ejecting may only be temporary: the player ejected from a game may be back tomorrow, but the student expelled from school is probably out forever.

impel \im-'pel\ To urge or drive forward by strong moral force.

- As the meeting wore on without any real progress being made, she felt impelled to stand and speak.

Impel is very similar in meaning to *compel,* and often a perfect synonym, though it tends to suggest even more strongly an inner drive to do something and a greater urgency to act, especially for moral reasons. But when *impel* takes its noun and adjective forms, it changes slightly. So an *impulse*—such as "impulse buying," when you suddenly see something cool and know you've got to have it— often isn't based on anything very serious. And *impulsive* behavior in general, such as blurting out something stupid on the spur of the moment, is the kind of thing you're supposed to get over when you grow up.

repel \ri-'pel\ (1) To keep (something) out or away. (2) To drive back.

- Her son, knowing how she was repelled by rats and snakes, had started keeping them in his bedroom.

Since *re-* can mean not just "again" but also "back" (see RE-, p. 635), *repel* means "drive back." *Repel* has two common adjective forms; thus, a *repellent* or *repulsive* odor may drive us into the other room. Its main noun form is *repulsion*. Magnets exhibit both attraction and repulsion, and the goal of an armed defense is the repulsion of an enemy; but we generally use *repulsion* to mean "strong dislike." In recent years, *repulse* has been increasingly used as a synonym for *repel* ("That guy repulses me").

Quizzes

A. Fill in each blank with the correct letter:

a. mission   e. expel
b. missionary   f. impel
c. emissary   g. repel
d. transmission   h. compel

1. They knew that hunger would eventually _____ the grizzly to wake up.
2. An _____ was sent to the Duke with a new offer.
3. Men like him normally _____ her, so I'm surprised that she seems interested.
4. _____ of the bacteria usually occurs through close personal contact.
5. Though the Senate can _____ a member for certain crimes, it's almost never been done.
6. The only people in the village who could speak English were a Peace Corps volunteer and a _____ at the little church.
7. Don't count on conscience to _____ most people to make the right choice under such difficult circumstances.
8. Their _____ on this occasion was to convince their elderly father to surrender his driver's license.

B. Match the definition on the left to the correct word on the right:

1. force by moral pressure   a. transmission
2. evangelist   b. compel
3. drive irresistibly   c. repel
4. disgust   d. mission
5. agent   e. expel
6. sending   f. missionary
7. drive out   g. impel
8. errand   h. emissary

Words from Mythology

arachnid \ə-'rak-ˌnid\ A member of the class Arachnida, which principally includes animals with four pairs of legs and no antennae, such as spiders, scorpions, mites, and ticks.

* His interest in arachnids began when, as a child, he would watch spiders build their gorgeous webs in the corners of the porch.

The Greek word for "spider" is *arachne*, and, according to Greek mythology, the original arachnid was a girl named Arachne. A marvelous weaver, she made the mistake of claiming she was better at her craft than the goddess Athena. In a contest between the two, she angered the goddess by weaving a remarkable tapestry showing the gods behaving badly. As punishment, Athena changed Arachne into a spider, fated to spend her life weaving. With their eight legs, arachnids are easily distinguished from the six-legged insects, on which they feed by injecting digesting juices and then sucking up the liquefied remains.

calliope \kə-'lī-ə-pē\ A musical instrument similar to an organ in which whistles are sounded by steam or compressed air.

* The town's old calliope, with its unmistakable sound, summoned them to the fair every summer.

To the ancient Greeks, the Muses were nine goddesses, each of whom was the spirit of one or more of the arts and sciences. Calliope was the Muse of heroic or epic poetry, who inspired poets to write such epics as the *Iliad* and the *Odyssey*. Since the lengthy epics were generally sung from beginning to end, she was responsible for a great deal of musical reciting. But she wouldn't necessarily have approved of having her name used for the hooting organlike instrument that was invented in America around 1855. Calliopes gave a festive air to the great showboats that floated up and down the Mississippi and Ohio Rivers giving theatrical performances; the loudest could supposedly be heard eight miles away, attracting customers from all around. Today they are mostly heard on merry-go-rounds and at circuses.

dryad \'drī-əd\ A wood nymph.

* The ancient Greeks' love of trees can be seen in their belief that every tree contained a dryad, which died when the tree was cut.

The term *dryad* comes from the Greek word for "oak tree." As the Greeks saw it, every tree (not only oaks) had a spirit. The best known of the dryads was Daphne. The beautiful daughter of a river god, she was desired by the god Apollo; as he was about to capture her, she prayed to her father to save her, and he transformed her into a laurel tree. In her honor, Apollo commanded that the poet who won the highest prize every year be crowned with a laurel wreath. The Greeks' respect for trees unfortunately failed to keep Greece's forests from shrinking greatly over the centuries, and those that remain produce little wood of good quality.

fauna \ˈfȯ-nə\ Animal life, especially the animals that live naturally in a given area or environment.

• The larger fauna of the county include coyotes, black bear, deer, moose, wild turkey, hawks, and vultures.

Faunus and Fauna were the Roman woodland god and goddess for whom animals were a particular concern. Faunus was the Roman equivalent of the Greek god Pan, and like Pan, he had goats' legs. Their goat-legged helpers, called *fauns,* were known for their love of pleasure and mischief. The fauna of a continent are often very similar across a broad east-west band; from north to south, however, they may vary greatly.

flora \ˈflȯr-ə\ Plant life, especially the flowering plants that live naturally in a specific area or environment.

• Scientists are busily identifying the flora of the Amazon rain forest before the rapid expansion of commercial interests consumes it.

Flora means "flower" in Latin, and Flora was the Roman goddess of spring and flowering plants, especially wildflowers and plants not raised for food. She was shown as a beautiful young woman in a long, flowing dress with flowers in her hair, strewing flowers over the earth. English preserves her name in such words as *floral, floret,* and *flourish*. A region's flora may range from tiny violets to towering trees. The common phrase "flora and fauna" covers just about every visible living thing.

herculean \ˌhər-kyu̇-ˈlē-ən\ (1) Extremely strong. (2) Extremely extensive, intense, or difficult.

• Accomplishing all the things he promised during the presidential campaign will be a herculean task.

The hero Hercules, son of the god Zeus by a human mother, was famous for his superhuman strength. To pacify the wrath of the god Apollo, he was forced to perform twelve enormously difficult tasks, or "labors." These ranged from descending into the underworld to bring back the terrifying dog that guarded its entrance to destroying the many-headed monster called the Hydra. Any job or task that's extremely difficult or calls for enormous strength is therefore called herculean.

Pandora's box \pan-ˈdȯr-əz-ˈbäks\ A source of many troubles.

• In a thundering speech, he predicted that, if the bill was passed, the new policy would open a Pandora's box of economic problems.

The god Prometheus stole fire from heaven to give to the human race, which originally consisted only of men. To punish humanity, the other gods created the first woman, the beautiful Pandora. As a gift, Zeus gave her a box, which she was told never to open. However, as soon as he was out of sight she took off the lid, and out swarmed all the troubles of the world, never to be recaptured. Only Hope was left in the box, stuck under the lid. Anything that looks ordinary but may produce unpredictable harmful results can thus be called a Pandora's box.

Scylla and Charybdis \ˈsi-lə-and-kə-ˈrib-dəs\ Two equally dangerous alternatives.

• Doctors and patients who need to calculate the ideal dosage of the medication, knowing how it can trigger a different dangerous condition, often feel caught between Scylla and Charybdis.

The Strait of Messina is the narrow passage between the island of Sicily and the "toe" of Italy's "boot." In Greek mythology, two monsters hovered on either side of the strait. Scylla, a female monster with six snake-like heads, each with pointed teeth, barked like a dog from the rocks on the Italian side. Charybdis, on the Sicilian side, caused a whirlpool by swallowing the waters of the sea three times a day. When Odysseus attempted to sail between them, he encountered disaster on both sides. Being caught between Scylla and Charybdis is a lot like being between a rock and a hard place.

Quiz

Complete the analogy:

1. hobgoblin : imp :: dryad : _____
   a. moth b. oak tree c. nymph d. dragonfly
2. difficult : simple :: herculean : _____
   a. intense b. easy c. mammoth d. strong
3. wrath : anger :: Scylla and Charybdis : _____
   a. rage b. double peril c. ferocity d. whirlpools
4. piano : nightclub :: calliope : _____
   a. organ b. circus c. church d. steam
5. canine : dog :: flora : _____
   a. oak trees b. wood nymphs c. plants d. animals
6. reptile : snake :: arachnid : _____
   a. toad b. salamander c. bird d. scorpion
7. cabinet : china :: Pandora's box : _____
   a. pleasures b. troubles c. taxes d. music
8. cattle : livestock :: fauna : _____
   a. meadows b. flowers c. wildlife d. trees

Review Quizzes

A. Choose the correct synonym:

1. impartial   a. fair b. biased c. cautious d. undecided
2. cosmopolitan   a. bored b. intelligent
   c. inexperienced d. well-traveled
3. incoherent   a. clear b. uncertain c. confused
   d. unknown
4. mission   a. greeting b. assignment c. support
   d. departure
5. compel   a. drive b. prevent c. eject d. compare
6. inherent   a. local b. inherited c. acquired d. built-in
7. cosmos   a. chaos b. order c. universe d. beauty
8. impart   a. grant b. stick c. combine d. withhold
9. adjunct   a. addition b. neighbor c. connection
   d. acquaintance
10. repel   a. attract b. greet c. offend d. send

B. Match the definition on the right to the correct word on the left:

1.	emissary	a.	verb part
2.	conscientious	b.	cause to act
3.	participle	c.	equal perils
4.	impel	d.	agent
5.	dryad	e.	foresighted
6.	prescient	f.	attachment
7.	Scylla and Charybdis	g.	careful
8.	subterfuge	h.	very difficult
9.	herculean	i.	trick
10.	adjunct	j.	tree spirit

C. Fill in each blank with the correct letter:

a.	adherent	f.	flora
b.	centrifugal	g.	expel
c.	conscientious	h.	prescient
d.	arachnid	i.	disjunction
e.	transmission	j.	subterfuge

1. He's no longer really an _____ of that economic philosophy.
2. The most successful stockbrokers have the reputation of being almost eerily _____.
3. Most philosophers see no _____ between science and morality.
4. _____ force keeps roller-coaster cars from crashing to the ground.
5. _____ of electric power over long distances always involves considerable losses.
6. Unlike the spiders, the _____ we call the daddy longlegs has no waist.
7. The archerfish can _____ sudden jets of water at insects, knocking them into the lake or river.
8. She won praise for her _____ handling of details.
9. He always used to be able to get hold of Grateful Dead tickets by some kind of _____.
10. The _____ of the West Creek Valley includes at least a dozen rare species.

UNIT

10

PUT comes from the Latin verb *putare,* meaning "to think, consider, or believe." So, for example, a *reputation* is what others think of you. But when the root shows up in such words as *compute, dispute,* and *deputy,* its meaning is harder to trace.

reputed \ri-'pyü-təd\ Believed to be a certain way by popular opinion.

• The 15th-century prince Vlad the Impaler is reputed to have inspired the character Dracula, though in fact, evil though Vlad was, Dracula's creator only borrowed his nickname.

Reputed is used constantly today by reporters, and almost always to describe suspected criminals—"the reputed mobster," "the reputed drug kingpin," "the reputed gang leader," etc. But the word shouldn't be left to journalists; your elderly aunt may, for instance, be reputed to have made a large fortune in oil, or to have had four husbands who all died mysteriously. *Reputed* is easy to confuse with *reputable,* and they used to mean the same thing—that is, "having a good reputation"—but it's become rare to hear *reputed* used with that meaning today.

disrepute \ˌdis-ri-'pyüt\ Loss or lack of good reputation; disgrace.

• The family had fallen into disrepute after the conviction and imprisonment of his father and uncle.

A *reputation* can be easy to lose, and someone who is no longer respectable may eventually find he's become genuinely *disreputable*—the kind of person that almost no one wants to be seen with. Disrepute isn't only for individuals: A company may fall into disrepute as a result of news stories about its products' defects; drug scandals have brought entire sports into disrepute; and a scientific theory may fall into disrepute as a result of new discoveries.

impute \im-'pyüt\ To attribute.

• The British imputed motives of piracy to American ships trying to prevent them from interfering with American trade during the War of 1812.

Imputing something to someone (or something) usually means observing something invisible in that person (or thing). We may impute meaning to a play or novel, or to a casual remark by a friend, that was never intended. Many of us like to impute bad motives to others, while always regarding our own motives as pure. In tax law, imputed income is something that isn't actual money but might as well be—for example, the free use of a car lent to you by your employer.

putative \'pyü-tə-tiv\ Generally supposed; assumed to exist.

• To strengthen the case for the defense, a putative expert took the stand.

Putative is almost always used to express doubt or skepticism about a common belief. Thus, Tintagel Castle in Cornwall, a picturesque ruin, is the putative fortress of the medieval King Arthur. The residents of New York City are *putatively* chic, neurotic, rude, and dangerous. And cable TV is full of putative experts, who often turn out not to have much knowledge of the subjects they're talking about.

LOG, from the Greek word *logos,* meaning "word," "speech," or "reason," is found particularly in English words that end in *-logy* and *-logue*. The ending *-logy* often means "the study of"; so, for instance, *biology* is the study of life, and *anthropology* is the study of humans. And *-logue* usually indicates a type of discussion; thus, *dialogue* is conversation between two people or groups, and an *epilogue* is an author's last words on a subject. But exceptions aren't hard to find.

physiology \ˌfi-zē-ˈä-lə-jē\ (1) A branch of biology dealing with the processes and activities by which living things, tissues, and cells function. (2) The life processes and activities of a living thing or any of its parts.

• For students planning to go to medical school, the university's most popular major is Human Physiology.

The Latin root *physio-* generally means "physical," so human physiology deals with just about everything that keeps us alive and working, and other physiology specialties do the same for other animals and for plants. To do anything serious in the field of health, you've obviously got to know how the body's organs and cells function normally. Physiology used to be considered separately from anatomy, which focuses on the body's structures; however, it's now known that structure and function can't easily be separated in a scientific way, so "anatomy and physiology" are often spoken of in the same breath.

methodology \ˌme-thə-ˈdä-lə-jē\ A set of methods or rules followed in a science or field.

• Some researchers claimed that Dr. Keller's methodology was sloppy and had led to unreliable conclusions.

The methodology employed in an experiment is essential to its success, and bad methodology has spoiled thousands of research projects. So whenever a piece of research is published in a scientific or medical journal, the researchers always carefully describe their methodology; otherwise, other scientists couldn't possibly judge the quality of what they've done.

ideology \ˌī-dē-ˈä-lə-jē\ The set of ideas and beliefs of a group or political party.

• By the time she turned 19, she realized she no longer believed in her family's political ideology.

The root *ideo-*, as you might guess, means "idea." Ideas and theories about human behavior can always be carried too far, since such behavior is very hard to pin down. So *ideological* thinkers—people who come up with large theories about how the world works and try to explain everything (and maybe even predict the future) according to those theories—are almost always disappointed, sooner or later, to find that it doesn't really work out. A person intensely devoted to a set of political ideas or theories can be called an *ideologue*—

a translation of the French *idéologue*, a word actually coined by Napoleon as a label for those political thinkers full of ideas he had no use for.

cardiology \ˌkär-dē-ˈä-lə-jē\ The study of the heart and its action and diseases.

* After his heart attack, he actually bought himself a cardiology textbook and set about learning everything he could about his unreliable organ.

The root *card-* (closely related to *cord*—see CORD, p. 269) shows up in many heart-related words. *Cardiologists* frequently find themselves studying *cardiograms*, the charts of heart activity, made by machines called *cardiographs*. Heart attacks, and deaths caused by them, have both declined as a result of better medical emergency procedures, cholesterol-lowering drugs, and a decline in smoking. But the factors likely to actually improve heart health, such as better diets and more *cardiovascular* exercise (exercise, such as running, that improves the heart and blood vessels), haven't made any progress at all. So we should all be prepared to perform *cardiopulmonary resuscitation* (an emergency procedure done on someone whose heart has stopped, to get the heart and lungs working again).

Quizzes

A. Indicate whether the following pairs of words have the same or different meanings:

1. putative / supposed   same ___ / different ___
2. ideology / beliefs   same ___ / different ___
3. reputed / questioned   same ___ / different ___
4. cardiology / game theory   same ___ / different ___
5. disrepute / shame   same ___ / different ___
6. methodology / carefulness   same ___ / different ___
7. impute / compute   same ___ / different ___
8. physiology / bodybuilding   same ___ / different ___

B. Choose the closest definition:

1. methodology   a. endurance b. patience c. authority
   d. system
2. impute   a. imply b. revise c. attribute d. defy

3. reputed   a. famous   b. accused   c. determined
    d. supposed
4. ideology   a. notion   b. philosophy   c. standard
    d. concept
5. putative   a. assumed   b. appointed   c. solved   d. ignored
6. cardiology   a. ear specialty   b. heart specialty   c. brain
    specialty   d. nerve specialty
7. disrepute   a. argument   b. violence   c. untruth
    d. disgrace
8. physiology   a. sports medicine   b. body language
    c. study of medicine   d. study of organisms

TERR comes from the Latin *terra,* "earth." A *territory* is a large expanse of land. *Terra firma* is Latin for "firm ground" as opposed to the swaying seas. A *terrace* is a leveled area, often one created for farming on a sloping hill. And the French word for potato, *pomme de terre,* means literally "apple of the earth."

---

parterre \pär-'ter\ (1) A decorative garden with paths between the beds of plants. (2) The back area of the ground floor of a theater, often under the balcony.

• The city's park boasts a beautiful parterre with many varieties of roses.

Parterre comes to English by way of French, where it means "on the ground." And in the early years of the theater, the parterre was truly on the ground. In Shakespeare's day, an English theater's parterre was the cheap standing-room area right in front of the stage, normally filled with rowdy spectators. The original idea of the French parterre garden, with its carefully designed plots and walkways, was to present an artistic pattern when seen from above—from a balcony, a raised terrace, or the top of an outdoor staircase. English gardeners responded with garden designs that tried to make their viewers half-forget that they were seeing something created by humans rather than untamed nature itself.

subterranean \ˌsəb-tə-'rā-nē-ən\ Underground.

• In Carlsbad Caverns National Park there is an astonishing subterranean chamber over half a mile long.

A tunnel is a subterranean road or pathway, and a subway is a subterranean railway. The subterranean vaults at Fort Knox hold billions of dollars of gold reserves. Subterranean reservoirs called *aquifers* are tapped for water; in places where the pressure on the subterranean water is great enough, a hole drilled in the ground will bring it bubbling to the surface.

terrarium \tə-ˈrer-ē-əm\ An enclosure, usually transparent, with a layer of dirt in the bottom in which plants and sometimes small animals are kept indoors.

• When no one was watching, they dropped their snake in the fifth-grade terrarium, and then waited in the hall to hear the screams.

The turtle exhibit at a zoo is often in the form of a terrarium, as are some of the exhibits at a plant conservatory. In an ant terrarium, elementary-school students watch the ants dig their network of tunnels as if no one were watching. Terrariums try to create conditions as close as possible to a natural habitat. A covered terrarium can often sustain itself for months on the moisture trapped inside. But creating a good terrarium requires careful control not only of humidity but also of temperature, as well as good ventilation; the lighting should include the full spectrum of sunlight as well as a day-night regulator.

terrestrial \tə-ˈres-trē-əl\ (1) Having to do with Earth or its inhabitants. (2) Living or growing on land instead of in water or air.

• The roadrunner, although a largely terrestrial bird, can take flight for short periods when necessary.

Everything on or having to do with Earth can be called terrestrial. Mercury, Venus, and Mars are often called the terrestrial planets, since they are rocky balls somewhat like Earth rather than great globes of gas like Jupiter, Saturn, Uranus, and Neptune. Something *extraterrestrial* comes from beyond the earth and its atmosphere; the word can be used to describe anything "out of this world," from moon rocks to meteors. Turning to the second sense of *terrestrial*, animals are often divided into the terrestrial (land-living) and the aquatic (water-living). And sometimes terrestrial animals are contrasted with *arboreal* animals, those that live in trees.

MAR, from the Latin word *mare,* meaning "sea," brings its salty tang to several English words. A *submarine* is an undersea ship. *Marine* means basically "relating to the sea," so when the Continental Marines were established back in 1775, their job was to provide on-board security on naval ships; but they immediately began to be used on land as well, and the marines have continued to operate on both land and sea ever since.

marina \mə-ˈrē-nə\ A dock or harbor where pleasure boats can be moored securely, often with facilities offering supplies or repairs.

• The coast of Florida has marinas all along it for the use of anything from flimsy sailboats to enormous yachts.

Marina comes straight from Latin, where it means simply "of the sea." At a modern marina, sailors can acquire whatever they need for their next excursion, or they can tie up their boats until the next weekend comes along. Some even imitate John D. MacDonald's famous detective hero Travis McGee, who lives on his boat in Miami and rarely leaves the marina.

aquamarine \ˌä-kwə-mə-ˈrēn\ (1) A transparent blue or blue-green gem. (2) A pale blue or greenish blue that is the color of clear seawater in sunlight.

• Many of the houses on the Italian Riviera are painted aquamarine to match the Mediterranean.

Aqua marina is Latin for "seawater," so when a lovely blue-green form of the semiprecious gem known as beryl was given an English name several centuries ago, *aquamarine* seemed appropriate. Aquamarine is the ideal color that most of us carry around in our heads when we imagine the waters that lap the shores of the Greek and Caribbean islands on a sunny day. But even the Mediterranean and the Caribbean can take on lots of other colors depending on weather conditions.

mariner \ˈmer-ə-nər\ A seaman or sailor.

• When he signed on as a mariner, the young Ishmael never suspected that the ship would be pursuing a great white whale.

In Coleridge's *Rime of the Ancient Mariner,* an old seaman tells of how, by shooting a friendly albatross, he had brought storms and disaster to his ship, and how as punishment his shipmates hung the great seabird around the mariner's neck and made him wear it until it rotted. The word *mariner* has occasionally been used to mean simply "explorer," as in the famous Mariner spaceflights in the 1960s and '70s, the first to fly close to Mars, Venus, and Mercury.

maritime \\'mer-ə-ˌtīm\\ (1) Bordering on or having to do with the sea. (2) Having to do with navigation or commerce on the sea.

• As a result of the ocean, Canada's Maritime Provinces—New Brunswick, Nova Scotia, and Prince Edward Island—have a late spring but a mild winter.

The maritime countries of Portugal and England produced many seafaring explorers during the 16th and 17th centuries, many of whom sailed under the flags of other countries. Sailing for the Spanish, Ferdinand Magellan captained the ship that was the first to circle the world, charting many new maritime routes as it went. Henry Hudson, funded by the Dutch, sailed up what we call today the Hudson River, claiming the maritime area that now includes New York City for the Netherlands.

Quizzes

A. Complete the analogy:

1. crepe : pancake :: parterre : _____
   a. balcony b. planet c. garden d. parachute
2. motel : motorist :: marina : _____
   a. dock b. pier c. sailor d. boat
3. aquarium : water :: terrarium : _____
   a. plants b. turtles c. rocks d. earth
4. urban : city :: maritime : _____
   a. beach b. dock c. sea d. harbor
5. aquatic : water :: terrestrial : _____
   a. sea b. land c. forest d. mountain
6. pink : red :: aquamarine : _____
   a. blue b. watery c. turquoise d. yellow
7. submarine : underwater :: subterranean : _____
   a. blue b. belowground c. hollow d. rumbling
8. logger : lumberjack :: mariner : _____
   a. doctor b. lawyer c. chief d. sailor

B. Match the definition on the left to the correct word on the right:

1.	theater area	a.	mariner
2.	blue-green gem	b.	terrestrial
3.	under the ground	c.	marina
4.	near the sea	d.	terrarium
5.	contained habitat	e.	maritime
6.	seaman	f.	parterre
7.	small harbor	g.	subterranean
8.	earthly	h.	aquamarine

PATH comes from the Greek word *pathos,* which means "feeling" or "suffering." So a *pathetic* sight moves us to pity, and a *sympathetic* friend "feels with" you when you yourself are suffering.

---

pathos \\'pā-ˌthäs\\ (1) An element in life or drama that produces sympathetic pity. (2) An emotion of sympathetic pity.

• The pathos of the blind child beggars she had seen in India could still keep her awake at night.

Pathos comes directly from Greek. According to Aristotle, the persuasive power of public speaking relies on three elements: the speaker's authority, the logic of the speech, and the speech's pathos. Aristotle claims that pathos is the appeal to the audience's sense of right and wrong, and that it is this (unlike authority and logic) that moves the audience's emotions. Today we usually speak of pathos as an element in fiction, film, drama, music, or even painting, or the real-life pathos of a situation or personality. Since *pathos* is closely related to *pathetic*, it's not surprising that, like *pathetic*, *pathos* may occasionally be used a bit sarcastically.

apathetic \\ˌa-pə-'the-tik\\ (1) Showing or feeling little or no emotion. (2) Having no interest.

• His apathetic response to the victory bewildered his friends.

Apathy, or lack of emotion, is central to Albert Camus's famous novel *The Stranger,* in which the main character's indifference toward almost everything, including his mother's death, results in his imprisonment. We feel little *sympathy* for him, and may even feel *antipathy,* or dislike. The American voter is often called apathetic; of all the industrial democracies, only in America does half the adult population fail to vote in major elections. As you can see, *apathetic* isn't the opposite of *pathetic,* even though the *a-* that it begins with means "not" or "without."

empathy \\'em-pə-thē\\ The feeling of, or the ability to feel, the emotions and sensations of another.

• Her maternal empathy was so strong that she often seemed to be living her son's life emotionally.

In the 19th century, Charles Dickens counted on producing an *empathetic* response in his readers strong enough to make them buy the next newspaper installment of each novel. Today, when reading a novel such as *A Tale of Two Cities,* only the most hard-hearted reader could fail to feel empathy for Sidney Carton as he approaches the guillotine. One who *empathizes* suffers along with the one who feels the sensations directly. *Empathy* is similar to *sympathy,* but empathy usually suggests stronger, more instinctive feeling. So a person who feels sympathy, or pity, for victims of a war in Asia may feel empathy for a close friend going through the much smaller disaster of a divorce.

telepathic \\ˌte-lə-'pa-thik\\ Involving apparent communication from one mind to another without speech or signs.

• After ten years of marriage, their communication is virtually telepathic, and each always seems to know what the other is thinking.

Since *tele-* means "distant" (see TELE, p. 417), you can see how *telepathy* means basically "feeling communicated from a distance." The word was coined around 1880, when odd psychic phenomena were being widely discussed by people hoping that researchers might find a scientific basis for what they believed they themselves were experiencing. Today, when people talk about extrasensory perception, or ESP, telepathy is usually what they're talking about. In recent years, the notion of *memes*—ideas that might somehow physically fly from brain to brain so that people all over the world might have the same idea at about the same time without any obvious communication—has been widely discussed. Even though scientists haven't been able to establish the existence of telepathy, about 30% of Americans continue to believe in it.

PEN/PUN comes from the Latin words *poena,* "penalty," and *punire,* "to punish." A *penalty* is, of course, a *punishment.*

---

penal \\'pē-nəl\\ Having to do with punishment or penalties, or institutions where punishment is given.

* The classic novels *Les Misérables* and *The Count of Monte Cristo* portray the terrible conditions in French penal institutions in the 19th century.

A state or country's *penal code* defines its crimes and describes its punishments. During the 18th and 19th centuries, many countries established penal colonies, where criminals were sent as punishment. Often these were unbearably severe; but it was to such colonies that some of Australia's and the United States' early white inhabitants came, and the convicts provided labor for the European settlement of these lands.

impunity \\im-'pyü-nə-tē\\ Freedom from punishment, harm, or loss.

* Under the flag of truce, the soldiers crossed the field with impunity.

Impunity is protection from punishment, just as immunity is protection from disease. Tom Sawyer, in Mark Twain's novel, broke his Aunt Polly's rules with near impunity because he could usually sweet-talk her into forgiving him; if that failed, he had enjoyed himself so much he didn't care what *punishment* she gave him.

penance \\'pe-nəns\\ An act of self-punishment or religious devotion to show sorrow or regret for sin or wrongdoing.

* In the Middle Ages bands of pilgrims would trudge to distant holy sites as penance for their sins.

Penance as a form of apology for a mistake can be either voluntary or ordered by someone else. Many religions include penance among the ways in which believers can show *repentance* or regret for a misdeed. The Christian season of Lent, 40 days long, is traditionally a time for doing penance.

punitive \\'pyü-nə-tiv\\ Giving, involving, or aiming at punishment.

- The least popular teachers are usually the ones with punitive attitudes, those who seem to enjoy punishing more than teaching.

Punitive is an important word in the law. When you sue a person or company for having wronged you in some way, you normally ask for something of value equal to what you were deprived of by the other party. But when the defendant has done something particularly bad, you may also ask for *punitive damages,* money over and above the actual cost of the harm done, intended to teach the defendant a lesson. Punitive damages are fairly rare, but when they're actually granted they may be as much as four times the size of the basic damages.

Quizzes

A. Fill in each blank with the correct letter:

a.	impunity	e.	empathy
b.	apathetic	f.	penal
c.	punitive	g.	pathos
d.	telepathic	h.	penance

1. You can't go on breaking the speed limit with _____ forever.
2. He had covered disasters before, but the _____ of the situation in Haiti was beyond description.
3. In some households, grounding is a severe form of _____ action.
4. The mildest of the federal _____ institutions are the so-called "country club" prisons.
5. The public's response to studies predicting dangerous climate change was _____ for many years.
6. As _____ during the period of Lent, Christians may give up a favorite food.
7. Almost everyone feels some _____ for a child's misery.
8. Identical twins have claimed to experience _____ communication about important events.

B. Complete the analogy:

1. passionate : emotional :: apathetic : _____
   a. caring b. unjust c. indifferent d. dominant

2. fine : speeding :: penance : _____
   a. misdeed b. credit card c. fee d. behavior
3. humor : laughter :: pathos : _____
   a. comedy b. ridicule c. death d. pity
4. immunity : sickness :: impunity : _____
   a. death b. flood c. punishment d. sleep
5. kindness : cruelty :: empathy : _____
   a. pity b. heartlessness c. emotion d. tears
6. educational : school :: penal : _____
   a. judge b. police c. prison d. sentence
7. telephonic : electric :: telepathic : _____
   a. extrasensory b. superhuman c. airborne d. sci-fi
8. encouraging : reward :: punitive : _____
   a. damage b. penalty c. praise d. jury

MATR/MATER comes from the Greek and Latin words for "mother." A *matron* is a mature woman with children. And *matrimony* is marriage itself, the traditional first step toward motherhood.

maternity \mə-ˈtər-nə-tē\ The state of being a mother; motherhood.

• It's quite possible that the *Mona Lisa* is a portrait of maternity, and that the painting marks the recent birth of her child Andrea.

Maternity is used as both a noun and an adjective. *Maternity benefits* are benefits specially provided by employers for women having babies, and usually include *maternity leave,* time off work. With maternity come *maternal* feelings, which are shown by all species of warm-blooded animals as well as a few reptiles such as crocodiles and alligators.

matriarch \ˈmā-trē-ˌärk\ A woman who controls a family, group, or government.

• Every August all the grown children and their families are summoned to the estate by the matriarch.

A *matriarchy* is a social unit governed by a woman or group of women. It isn't certain that a true *matriarchal* society has ever existed, so matriarchy is usually treated as an imaginative concept. But there are societies in which relatedness through women rather than men is stressed, and elements of matriarchy may be stronger in certain societies than they are in most of the Western world. And most of us can point to families in which a woman has become the dominant figure, or grande dame, or matriarch.

matrilineal \ˌma-trə-ˈli-nē-əl\ Based on or tracing the family through the mother.

• Many of the peoples of Ghana in Africa trace their family through matrilineal connections.

A person's *lineage* is his or her *line* of ancestors. So *matrilineal* means basically "through the mother's line," just as *patrilineal* means "through the father's line." *Matrilineality* is an important concept in anthropology; among other things, it usually determines who will inherit property on a person's death. Though families that follow the European model take the father's name and are therefore patrilineal, matrilineal societies have existed around the world, including among various American Indian tribes.

matrix \ˈmā-triks\ (1) Something (such as a situation or a set of conditions) in which something else develops or forms. (2) Something shaped like a pattern of lines and spaces.

• The country's political matrix is so complex that no one who hasn't lived there could possibly understand it.

In ancient Rome, a *matrix* was a female animal kept for breeding, or a plant (sometimes called a "parent plant" or "mother plant") whose seeds were used for producing other plants. In English the word has taken on many related meanings. Mathematicians use it for a rectangular organization of numbers or symbols that can be used to make various calculations; geologists use it for the soil or rock in which a fossil is discovered, like a baby in the womb. And *matrix* was a good choice as the name of the reality in which all humans find themselves living in a famous series of science-fiction films.

AQU comes from *aqua*, the Latin word for "water." We keep pet fish in an *aquarium* at home or visit larger sea animals in a building with that name. Water sports such as swimming, canoeing, and sailing are sometimes called *aquatics*. In Scandinavia there's a popular drink called *aquavit*, the name coming from the Latin *aqua vitae*, "water of life"—though instead of water it mostly consists of alcohol.

---

aquaculture \\'ä-kwə-ˌkəl-chər\ The farming of plants and animals (such as kelp, fish, and shellfish) that live in the water.

• The farming of oysters by the Romans was an early form of aquaculture that has continued to the present day.

For most of the modern history of aquaculture, only costly fish and shellfish like salmon and shrimp were harvested. But new technologies are allowing cheaper and more efficient cultivation of fish for food, and such common fish as cod are now being farmed. Seaweeds and other algae are also being grown—for food (mostly in Asia), cattle feed, fertilizer, and experimentally as a source of energy. Aquaculture is now the world's fastest-growing form of food production.

aquanaut \\'ä-kwə-ˌnȯt\ A scuba diver who lives and works both inside and outside an underwater shelter for an extended time.

• Each scientist at the laboratory spent two weeks a year as an aquanaut living in the deep-sea station.

Aquanaut combines *aqua* with the Greek *nautes*, meaning "sailor." Like *astronaut* and *aeronaut*, the word may remind you of those mythical Greek heroes known as the Argonauts, who sailed with Jason on his ship, the *Argo*, in quest of the Golden Fleece. Various underwater habitats for aquanauts, such as Conshelf, SEALAB, and MarineLab, have captured the public imagination since the 1960s.

aqueduct \\'a-kwə-ˌdəkt\ (1) A pipe or channel for water. (2) A bridgelike structure for carrying water over a valley.

• Roman aqueducts were built throughout the empire, and their spectacular arches can still be seen in Greece, France, Spain, and North Africa.

Based party on the Latin *ducere*, meaning "lead" or "conduct" (see DUC, p. 35), the word *aqueduct* named an ancient civil-engineering marvel. You may have seen photos of the great arches of ancient aqueducts spanning valleys in countries throughout the old Roman Empire, practical pipelines that are also regarded as works of timeless beauty. From the 20th century, the 242-mile Colorado River Aqueduct, the 336-mile Central Arizona Project, and the 444-mile California Aqueduct are considered wonders of American engineering, but they are not renowned for their beauty. Most aqueducts today either are riverlike channels or run underground, perhaps appearing simply as a long mound.

aquifer \\'a-kwə-fər\ A layer of rock, sand, or gravel that can absorb and hold water.

* Cities without access to a nearby lake or river must rely on underground aquifers to meet their water needs.

The vast but relatively shallow Ogallala Aquifer lies beneath the Great Plains, under portions of eight states. Its thickness ranges from a few feet to more than a thousand feet. The Ogallala yields about 30 percent of the nation's groundwater used for irrigation in agriculture, and provides drinking water for most of the people within the area. But for many years more water has been extracted from the Ogallala than has been returned, and the situation today is of great concern.

Quizzes

A. Choose the closest definition:

1. matriarch   a. goddess   b. mermaid   c. bride   d. grande dame
2. aquaculture   a. aquarium design   b. reef diving   c. pearl fishing   d. water farming
3. matrilineal   a. through the mother's family   b. graduating   c. adopted   d. female
4. aqueduct   a. channel   b. dam   c. dike   d. reservoir
5. matrix   a. formula   b. alternate reality   c. scheme   d. source
6. aquanaut   a. swimmer   b. diver   c. surfer   d. pilot
7. maternity   a. motherhood   b. nightgown   c. women's club   d. marriage
8. aquifer   a. waterway   b. fishpond   c. spring   d. underground reservoir

B. Fill in each blank with the correct letter:

a.	aquifer	e.	matrilineal
b.	aquaculture	f.	matriarch
c.	maternity	g.	aqueduct
d.	matrix	h.	aquanaut

1. Marriage didn't seem to affect her much, but _____ has changed her completely.

2. After five years living in the suburb, they felt they had become part of a complex social _____.
3. As an _____ she often lives underwater for several days at a time.
4. The _____ they depend on for irrigation is slowly being depleted, and the farmers are being forced to cut back on water use.
5. Wild salmon has become an expensive rarity, and _____ is the source of most of the salmon we now eat.
6. The tribe seemed to be _____, with all inheritances passing through the females rather than the males.
7. The _____ that runs through the city is an open concrete-lined river.
8. He'd been married to Cynthia for three years, but she hadn't yet dared to introduce him to her great-aunt, the family _____.

Words from Mythology

cereal \\'sir-ē-əl\\ (1) A plant that produces grain that can be eaten as food, or the grain it produces. (2) The food made from grain.

• Rice is the main food cereal of Asia, whereas wheat and corn are the main food cereals of the West.

The Roman goddess Ceres, the equivalent of the Greek Demeter, was a calm goddess who didn't take part in the quarrels of the other gods. Her particular responsibility was the food-giving plants, and for that reason the food grains came to carry her name. Cereals of the ancient Romans included wheat, barley, spelt, oats, and millet—but not corn (maize), which was a cereal of the Americas.

Junoesque \\,jü-nō-'esk\\ Having mature, poised, and dignified beauty.

• In 1876, as a centennial gift, the French sent to America a massive statue of a robed Junoesque figure representing Liberty, to be erected in New York Harbor.

Juno was the wife of Jupiter, the chief of the Roman gods. As the first among goddesses, her power gave her particular dignity; and as goddess of women and marriage, she was a mature matron. But such younger goddesses as Diana, goddess of the hunt, perhaps came closer to today's ideals of slim and athletic female beauty.

martial \\'mär-shǝl\\ Having to do with war and military life.

* The stirring, martial strains of "The British Grenadiers" echoed down the snowy street just as dawn was breaking.

Mars was the Roman god of war and one of the patron gods of Rome itself. He was responsible for everything military, from warriors to weapons to marching music. Thus, *martial arts* are skills of combat and self-defense also practiced as sport. When *martial law* is declared, a country's armed forces take over the functions of the police. And a *court-martial* is a military court or trial.

Promethean \\prǝ-'mē-thē-ǝn\\ New or creative in a daring way.

* The Promethean energy of Beethoven's symphonies was a revelation to European audiences in the early years of the 19th century.

Prometheus was a Titan, a generation older than Zeus. When Zeus overthrew his own father Cronus and seized power, Prometheus fought on the side of the gods and against his fellow Titans. But when Zeus later wanted to destroy the race of humans, Prometheus saved them by stealing fire for them from the gods. He also taught them how to write, farm, build houses, read the stars and weather, cure themselves when sick, and tame animals—in short, all the arts and skills that make humans unique. So inventive was he that anything of great creativity and originality can still be called Promethean. But Prometheus had taken a terrible risk; enraged by his disobedience, Zeus had him chained to a rocky cliff, where for many long centuries an eagle daily tore at his liver.

Sisyphean \\ˌsi-sǝ-'fē-ǝn\\ Endless and difficult, involving many disappointments.

* After twenty years, many researchers had begun to think that defeating the virus was a Sisyphean task that would never succeed.

Reputedly the cleverest man on earth, King Sisyphus of Corinth tricked the gods into bringing him back to life after he had died. For this they punished him by sending him back to the underworld, where he must eternally roll a huge rock up a long, steep hill, only to watch it roll back to where he started. Something Sisyphean demands the same kind of unending, thankless, and ultimately unsuccessful efforts.

titanic \tī-'ta-nik\ Having great size, strength, or power; colossal.

- The titanic floods of 1993 destroyed whole towns on the Mississippi River.

In Greek mythology, the Titans were the generation of giant creators that produced the younger, stronger, cleverer gods, who soon overpowered and replaced them (see *Promethean* above). In 1911 the largest ship that had ever been built was christened the *Titanic* for its unmatched size and strength. But the name may have proved unlucky; on its maiden voyage in 1912 a massive iceberg ripped a fatal hole in the great ship, and it sank in the icy waters off Newfoundland.

Triton \'trī-tən\ (1) A being with a human upper body and the lower body of a fish; a merman. (2) Any of various large mollusks with a heavy, conical shell.

- In one corner of the painting, a robust Triton emerges from the sea with his conch to announce the coming of the radiant queen.

Triton was originally the son of the sea god Poseidon (or Neptune). A guardian of the fish and other creatures of the sea, he is usually shown as hearty, muscular, and cheerful. Like his father, he often carries a trident (three-pronged fork) and may ride in a chariot drawn by seahorses. Blowing on his conch shell, he creates the roar of the ocean. As a decorative image, Tritons are simply the male version of mermaids. The handsome seashells that bear their name are the very conchs on which they blow. Triton has also given his name to the planet Neptune's largest moon.

vulcanize \'vəl-kə-ˌnīz\ To treat crude or synthetic rubber or plastic so that it becomes elastic and strong and resists decay.

- The native islanders had even discovered how to vulcanize the rubber from the local trees in a primitive way.

The Roman god Vulcan (the Greek Hephaestus) was in charge of fire and the skills that use fire, especially blacksmithing. When

Charles Goodyear almost accidentally discovered how to vulcanize rubber in 1839, he revolutionized the rubber industry. He called his process *vulcanization* because it used fire to heat a mix of rubber and sulfur. Vulcanized rubber was soon being used for shoes and other products, and in the Civil War balloons made of this new, stronger rubber carried Union spies over the Confederate armies. The material's importance increased greatly over the years, and today vulcanized rubber remains in use for automobile tires and numerous other products.

Quiz

Fill in each blank with the correct letter:

a.	Promethean	e.	Sisyphean
b.	titanic	f.	vulcanize
c.	Triton	g.	cereal
d.	Junoesque	h.	martial

1. For a mother of nine, laundry and ironing can seem _____ in their endlessness and drudgery.
2. One clear and beautiful morning, a series of _____ waves swept the entire village into the sea.
3. The aging jazz singer acquired a certain _____ quality in her mature years.
4. On each arm of the great candelabra was carved a _____ blowing on his conch.
5. Corn, unknown in ancient Europe, has become a staple _____ of the modern world.
6. When Goodyear discovered how to _____ rubber, he made Henry Ford's Model T possible.
7. In some ways, Edison's mind may have been the most _____ since Leonardo da Vinci's.
8. The _____ arts of the Far East have become popular in the West as means of self-defense.

Review Quizzes

A. Indicate whether the following pairs of words have the same or different meanings:

1. aquamarine / navy blue   same ___ / different ___
2. subterranean / underground   same ___ / different ___
3. physiology / sports medicine   same ___ / different ___
4. disrepute / disgrace   same ___ / different ___
5. empathy / sentimentality   same ___ / different ___
6. Junoesque / slender   same ___ / different ___
7. Promethean / creative   same ___ / different ___
8. penance / regret   same ___ / different ___
9. mariner / sailor   same ___ / different ___
10. pathos / anger   same ___ / different ___
11. titanic / powerful   same ___ / different ___
12. vulcanize / organize   same ___ / different ___
13. terrestrial / earthly   same ___ / different ___
14. impunity / freedom from harm   same ___ / different ___
15. penal / legal   same ___ / different ___
16. matrix / puzzle   same ___ / different ___
17. marina / dock   same ___ / different ___
18. putative / natural   same ___ / different ___
19. terrarium / garden   same ___ / different ___
20. apathetic / indifferent   same ___ / different ___

B. Choose the word that does not belong:

1. Sisyphean   a. difficult   b. unending   c. demanding
       d. rolling
2. maternity   a. femininity   b. parenthood
       c. motherliness   d. motherhood
3. mariner   a. sailor   b. seaman   c. crew member
       d. archer
4. cereal   a. corn   b. eggplant   c. rice   d. barley
5. reputed   a. known   b. reported   c. believed   d. thought
6. ideology   a. essay   b. philosophy   c. principles
       d. beliefs
7. punitive   a. disciplinary   b. punishing
       c. correctional   d. encouraging
8. empathy   a. fascination   b. pity   c. concern
       d. compassion

9. maritime   a. coastal b. nautical c. oceangoing
    d. lakeside
10. apathetic   a. unfortunate b. unconcerned
    c. uncaring d. uninterested

C. Match the definition on the right to the correct word on the left:

1. impute   a. fancy garden
2. martial   b. through the mother's line
3. parterre   c. assign
4. maritime   d. nautical
5. penal   e. related to war
6. matrilineal   f. disciplinary
7. terrestrial   g. procedure
8. methodology   h. earthly

UNIT

11

CANT, from the Latin verb *cantare,* meaning "sing," produces several words that come directly from Latin. But some others came to English by way of French, which added an *h* to the root, giving us such words as *chant* and *chantey.*

---

cantata \kən-ˈtä-tə\ A musical composition, particularly a religious work from the 17th or 18th century, for one or more voices accompanied by instruments.

• Composers of the 18th century composed sacred cantatas by the dozen, and Bach's friend G. P. Telemann actually wrote over a thousand.

A cantata is sung, unlike a sonata, which is played on instruments only. The most famous cantatas are by Johann Sebastian Bach, who wrote the music for about 200 religious cantatas, using hymns and new religious poems as his texts. His cantatas consisted of several different sections for different voices—solos, duets, and choruses. Some of his nonreligious cantatas have been performed like mini-operas.

incantation \ˌin-ˌkan-ˈtā-shən\ (1) A use of spells or verbal charms spoken or sung as part of a ritual of magic. (2) A formula of words used in, or as if in, such a ritual.

• He repeated the words slowly over and over like an incantation.

Incantation comes directly from the Latin word *incantare,* "enchant." *Incantare* itself has *cantare* as a root, which reminds us that magic and ritual have always been associated with chanting and music. Incantations have often been in strange languages; "Abracadabra" is a not-so-serious version of an incantation.

cantor \\'kan-tər\\ An official of a Jewish synagogue who sings or chants the music of the services and leads the congregation in prayer.

• The congregation waited for the cantor to begin the prayers before joining in.

The cantor is, after the rabbi, the most important figure in a Jewish worship service. A cantor not only must possess an excellent singing voice but also must know by heart long passages of Hebrew. Cantors such as Jan Peerce and Richard Tucker became international opera stars. The comedian and singer Edward Israel Iskowitz renamed himself Eddie Cantor for his original profession and became enormously popular on stage, screen, radio, and television for over 40 years.

descant \\'des-ˌkant\\ An additional melody sung above the principal melody.

• The soprano added a soaring descant to the final chorus that held the listeners spellbound.

The prefix *des-*, meaning "two" or "apart," indicates that the descant is a "second song" apart from the main melody. In popular songs a descant will often be sung at the very end to produce a thrilling climax.

LINGU comes from the Latin word that means both "tongue" and "language," and in English today *tongue* can still mean "language" (as in "her native tongue"). Our expression "slip of the tongue" is just a translation of the Latin phrase *lapsus linguae*. The root even shows up in a slangy-sounding word like *lingo*. And since *lingu-* changed to *langu-* in French, our word *language* is related as well.

---

linguistics \\liŋ-'gwi-ˌstiks\\ The study of human speech.

• The new speechwriter, who had majored in linguistics, was soon putting his knowledge of the deceptive tricks of language to good use.

Any analysis of language, including 8th-grade grammar, can be called linguistics. As recently as 200 years ago, ordinary grammar was about the only kind of linguistics there was. Today a *linguist* may be a person who learns foreign languages, but the term usually refers to people who devote themselves to analyzing the structure of language. Many linguists concentrate on the history of a language; others study the way children learn to speak; others analyze the sounds of a language—and still others just study English grammar, a subject so big that you could easily spend your entire life on it.

multilingual \məl-tē-ˈliŋ-gwəl\ Using or able to use several languages.

- She soon discovered that he was truly multilingual, fluent in not only the German and Polish he had grown up speaking but in English and Arabic as well.

The roots of *multilingual* come from Latin (see MULTI, p. 582). If you happen to prefer Greek, use the synonym *polyglot*, in which *poly-* has the same meaning as *multi-*, and *-glot* means the same thing as *-lingual*. The best way to become multilingual is probably to be born in a *bilingual* (two-language) household; learning those first two seems to give the mind the kind of exercise that makes later language-learning easy.

lingua franca \ˈliŋ-gwə-ˈfraŋ-kə\ A language used as a common or commercial language among peoples who speak different languages.

- That first evening in Tokyo, she heard English being spoken at the next table, and realized it was serving as a lingua franca for a party of Korean and Japanese businessmen.

In the Middle Ages, the Arabs of the eastern Mediterranean referred to all Europeans as Franks (the name of the tribe that once occupied the land we call France). Since there was plenty of Arab-European trade, the traders in the Mediterranean ports eventually developed a trading language combining Italian, Arabic, and other languages, which almost everyone could more or less understand, and it became known as the "Frankish language," or lingua franca. Some languages actually succeed in becoming lingua francas without changing much. So, when the Roman empire became vast and mighty, Latin became the important lingua franca; and at a meeting between Japanese and Vietnamese businesspeople today, English may well be the only language spoken.

linguine \liŋ-ˈgwē-ˈnē\ A narrow, flat pasta.

* As a test of her clients' table manners, she would serve them challenging dishes and watch to see how gracefully they could handle chopsticks or deal with long, slithery linguine.

The modern language closest to Latin is Italian, and the Italian word *linguine* means literally "little tongues." Linguine is only one of the types of pasta whose names describes their shapes. Others include *spaghetti* ("little strings"), *fettuccine* ("little ribbons"), *penne* ("little quills"), *orzo* ("barley"), *farfalle* ("butterflies"), *vermicelli* ("little worms"), *capellini* ("little hairs"), *fusilli* ("little spindles"), and *radiatori* ("little radiators"). If you're thinking about learning Italian, you could make a good start by just visiting an Italian restaurant.

Quizzes

A. Choose the closest definition:

1. descant   a. climb downward b. added melody
      c. supposed inability d. writing table
2. linguistics   a. language study b. reading
      c. mouth surgery d. tongue exercise
3. incantation   a. ritual chant b. ceremony
      c. solemn march d. recorded song
4. linguine   a. slang b. pasta c. Italian dessert
      d. common language
5. cantata   a. snack bar b. pasta dish
      c. sung composition d. farewell gesture
6. lingua franca   a. Old French b. common language
      c. Italian casserole d. French coin
7. cantor   a. singer b. refusal c. traitor d. gallop
8. multilingual   a. highly varied b. in separate parts
      c. born with multiple tongues d. fluent in several
      languages

B. Indicate whether the following pairs of words have the same or different meanings:

1. lingua franca / pasta dish   same ___ / different ___
2. incantation / sacred dance   same ___ / different ___
3. linguine / Italian language   same ___ / different ___
4. descant / enchant   same ___ / different ___

5. linguistics / science of singing　　same ___ / different ___
6. cantata / sonata　　　　　　　　　　same ___ / different ___
7. cantor / conductor　　　　　　　　　same ___ / different ___
8. multilingual / using
　 several fingers　　　　　　　　　　 same ___ / different ___

SPIR comes from the Latin words meaning "breath" and "breathe." When we *inspire* others—that is, give them *inspiration*—it's as though we're breathing new energy and imagination into them. When you *expire*, or die, you "breathe out" your soul in your last breath. A license, membership, credit card, or free offer may also expire, at a time indicated by its *expiration* date.

---

spirited \ˈspir-ə-təd\ Full of energy or courage; very lively or determined.

• The team put up a spirited defense, but they were doomed from the start.

You may see *spirited* used to describe a conversation, a debate, a horse, or a campaign. And it often shows up in such words as *high-spirited* ("bold and energetic"), *mean-spirited* ("spiteful"), and *public-spirited* ("generous to a community"), all of which reflect the original meaning of *spirit*, a notion much like "soul" or "personality."

dispiriting \di-ˈspir-ə-tiŋ\ Causing a loss of hope or enthusiasm.

• It was terribly dispiriting for them to lose yet another game, and he had to reassure his daughter that she'd actually done a great job as goalie.

Lots of things can be dispiriting: a bad job interview, an awful film, a relationship going sour. Maybe for that reason, *dispiriting* has lots of synonyms: *discouraging, disheartening, demoralizing, depressing,* etc.

respirator \ˈre-spə-ˌrā-tər\ (1) A device worn over the nose and mouth to filter out dangerous substances from the air. (2) A device for maintaining artificial respiration.

- His lungs had been terribly damaged by decades of heavy smoking, and he'd been living on a respirator for the last year.

Respiration means simply "breathing." We usually come across the word in *artificial respiration,* the lifesaving technique in which you force air into the lungs of someone who's stopped breathing. Respirators can take several different forms. Scuba-diving equipment always includes a respirator, though it doesn't actually do the breathing for the diver. Medical respirators, which are used especially for babies and for emergency care and actually take over the job of getting oxygen into the lungs, are today usually called ventilators, so as to distinguish them from simple oxygen systems (which merely provide a steady flow of oxygen into the nostrils) and face masks.

transpire \tran-ˈspīr\ (1) To happen. (2) To become known.

- We kept up our questioning, and it soon transpired that the boys had known about the murder all along.

Since the prefix *trans-* means "through" (see TRANS, p. 626), *transpire*'s most literal meaning is something like "breathe through." Thus, the original meaning of the English word—still used today—is to give off a watery vapor through a surface such as a leaf. From there, it came to mean also the gradual appearance of previously secret information, as if leaking out of the pores of a leaf (as in "It transpired that she was not only his employee but also his girlfriend"). And soon it was being used to mean simply "happen" (as in "I wondered what had transpired in the cafeteria at lunchtime").

VER comes from the Latin word for "truth." A *verdict* in a trial is "the truth spoken" (see DICT, p. 272). But a just verdict may depend on the *veracity,* or "truthfulness," of the witnesses.

---

verify \ˈver-ə-ˌfī\ (1) To prove to be true or correct. (2) To check or test the accuracy of.

- It is the bank teller's job to verify the signature on a check.

During talks between the United States and the former Soviet Union on nuclear weapons reduction, one big problem was how to verify that weapons had been eliminated. Since neither side wanted the other to know its secrets, *verification* of the facts became a difficult issue. Because of the distrust on both sides, many doubted that the real numbers would ever be *verifiable*.

aver \ə-'vər\ To state positively as true; declare.

• The defendant averred that she was nowhere near the scene of the crime on the night in question.

Since *aver* contains the "truth" root, it basically means "confirm as true." You may aver anything that you're sure of. In legal situations, *aver* means to state positively as a fact; thus, Perry Mason's clients aver that they are innocent, while the district attorney avers the opposite. If you make such a statement while under oath, and it turns out that you lied, you may have committed the crime of perjury.

verisimilitude \ˌver-ə-sə-'mi-lə-ˌtüd\ (1) The appearance of being true or probable. (2) The depiction of realism in art or literature.

• By the beginning of the 20th century, the leading European painters were losing interest in verisimilitude and beginning to experiment with abstraction.

From its roots, *verisimilitude* means basically "similarity to the truth." Most fiction writers and filmmakers aim at some kind of verisimilitude to give their stories an air of reality. They need not show something actually true, or even very common, but simply something believable. A mass of good details in a play, novel, painting, or film may add verisimilitude. A spy novel without some verisimilitude won't interest many readers, but a fantastical novel may not even attempt to seem true to life.

veracity \və-'ra-sə-tē\ (1) Truth or accuracy. (2) The quality of being truthful or honest.

• We haven't been able to check the veracity of most of his story, but we know he wasn't at the motel that night.

People often claim that a frog placed in cold water that then is gradually heated will let itself be boiled to death, but the story actually lacks veracity. We often hear that the Eskimo (Inuit) peoples have dozens of words for "snow," but the veracity of the statement is doubtful, since Eskimo languages seem to have no more snow words than English (with *flake, blizzard, powder, drift, freezing rain,* etc.). In 2009 millions accepted the veracity of the claim that, against all the evidence, the elected president wasn't a native-born American. Not all the "facts" we accept without thinking are harmless.

Quizzes

A. **Fill in each blank with the correct letter:**

a. transpire   e. spirited
b. aver   f. veracity
c. respirator   g. dispiriting
d. verify   h. verisimilitude

1. Maybe some new information will _____ when they question the family tomorrow.
2. The company was doing badly, and she'd been having problems with her boss, so all in all it had been a _____ week at work.
3. The prosecutor expected the witness to _____ that the suspect was guilty.
4. Critics complained about the lack of _____ in his crime writing, saying it sounded as if he'd never even been inside a police station.
5. There's always a _____ exchange of opinions around the Thanksgiving table, but nobody ever takes offense.
6. His father has been living on a _____ for the last two weeks, but now his lungs seem to be improving.
7. She was never able to _____ anything he had told her about his past.
8. The boys claim they never went near the river that afternoon, but we suspect their _____.

B. **Complete the analogy:**

1. believe : doubt :: aver : _____
    a. state b. mean c. deny d. subtract
2. transfer : hand over :: transpire : _____
    a. breathe out b. cross c. encourage d. come to light
3. illusion : fantasy :: verisimilitude : _____
    a. appearance b. realism c. style d. proof
4. gloomy : glum :: spirited : _____
    a. spiraling b. alcoholic c. lively d. complex
5. loyalty : treason :: veracity : _____
    a. dishonesty b. truthfulness c. ideals d. safekeeping
6. exciting : thrilling :: dispiriting : _____
    a. dreary b. calming c. relaxing d. soothing

7. praise : ridicule :: verify : _____
   a. testify   b. contradict   c. establish   d. foretell
8. pacemaker : heart :: respirator : _____
   a. kidneys   b. brain   c. liver   d. lungs

TURB comes from the Latin verb *turbare,* "to throw into confusion or upset," and the noun *turba,* "crowd" or "confusion." So a *disturbance,* for example, confuses and upsets normal order or routine.

---

turbid \\'tər-bid\ (1) Thick or murky, especially with churned-up sediment. (2) Unclear, confused, muddled.

• The mood of the crowd was restless and turbid, and any spark could have turned them into a mob.

The Colorado River in spring, swollen by melting snow from the high mountains, races through the Grand Canyon, turbid and churning. A chemical solution may be described as turbid rather than clear. And your emotions may be turbid as well, especially where love is involved: What did he mean by that glance? Why did she say it like that?

perturb \pər-'tərb\ To upset, confuse, or disarrange.

• News of the new peace accord was enough to perturb some radical opponents of any settlements.

With its *per-* prefix, *perturb* meant originally "thoroughly upset," though today the word has lost most of its intense edge. *Perturb* and *perturbation* are often used by scientists, usually when speaking of a change in their data indicating that something has affected some normal process. When someone is referred to as *imperturbable*, it means he or she manages to remain calm through the most trying experiences.

turbine \\'tər-ˌbīn\ A rotary engine with blades made to turn and generate power by a current of water, steam, or air under pressure.

• The power plant used huge turbines powered by water going over the dam to generate electricity.

The oldest and simplest form of turbine is the waterwheel, which is made to rotate by water falling across its blades and into buckets suspended from them. Hero of Alexandria invented the first steam-driven turbine in the 1st century A.D., but a commercially practical steam turbine wasn't developed until 1884; steam turbines are now the main elements of electric power stations. Jet engines are gas turbines. A *turbojet* engine uses a turbine to compress the incoming air that feeds the engine before being ejected to push the plane forward; a *turboprop* engine uses its exhaust to drive a turbine that spins a propeller. A wind turbine generates electricity by being turned by the wind; the largest now have vanes with a turning diameter of over 400 feet.

turbulent \\'tər-byu̇-lənt\ (1) Stirred up, agitated. (2) Stirring up unrest, violence, or disturbance.

• The huge ocean liner *Queen Elizabeth II* was never much troubled by turbulent seas that might have sunk smaller boats.

Some people lead turbulent lives, and some are constantly in the grip of turbulent emotions. The late 1960s are remembered as turbulent years of social revolution in America and Europe. Often the captain of an airplane will warn passengers to fasten their seatbelts because of upper-air *turbulence,* which can make for a bumpy ride. El Niño, a seasonal current of warm water in the Pacific Ocean, may create turbulence in the winds across the United States, affecting patterns of rainfall and temperature as well.

VOLU/VOLV comes from the Latin verb *volvere,* meaning "to roll, wind, turn around, or twist around." Thus, *revolve* simply means "turn in circles." And a *volume* was originally a scroll or roll of papyrus.

---

voluble \\'väl-yu̇-bəl\ Speaking readily and rapidly; talkative.

• He proved to be a voluble informer who would tell stories of bookies, smugglers, and hit men to the detectives for hours.

A voluble person has words "rolling" off his or her tongue. In O. Henry's famous story "The Ransom of Red Chief," the kidnappers nab a boy who turns out to be so unbearably voluble that they can hardly wait to turn him loose again.

devolve \di-'välv\ (1) To pass (responsibility, power, etc.) from one person or group to another person or group at a lower level of authority. (2) To gradually go from an advanced state to a less advanced state.

- Since 1998, considerable power has been devolving from the British government in London to the new Scottish Parliament in Edinburgh.

With its *de-* prefix (see DE-, p. 601), *devolution* implies moving backward. Once powers have been centralized in a unified government, giving any powers back—that is, devolving the power—to a smaller governmental unit can seem to be reversing a natural development. In a somewhat similar way, a job that your boss doesn't want to do may devolve upon you. But *devolve* and *devolution* are also treated nowadays as the opposites of *evolve* and *evolution*. So we may also speak of moral devolution, such as occurred in Germany in the 1930s, when a country with an extraordinary culture became a brutal dictatorship. And parents may watch their slacker teenager and wonder if devolution is occurring right in front of their eyes.

evolution \ˌe-və-ˈlü-shən\ A process of change from a lower, simpler, or worse state to one that is higher, more complex, or better.

- Thomas Jefferson and the other Founding Fathers believed that political evolution reached its highest form in democracy.

Part of the humor of the old *Flintstones* cartoon show is that it contradicts what is known about biological evolution, since humans actually *evolved* long after dinosaurs were extinct. *Evolution* can also be used more broadly to refer to technology, society, and other human creations. For example, an idea may evolve, even in your own mind, as the months or years pass. And though many people don't believe that human beings truly become better with the passing centuries, many will argue that our societies tend to evolve, producing more goods and providing more protection for more people.

convoluted \ˈkän-və-ˌlü-təd\ (1) Having a pattern of curved windings. (2) Involved, intricate.

- After 10 minutes, Mr. Collins's strange story had become so convoluted that none of us could follow it.

Convolution originally meant a complex winding pattern such as those visible on the surface of the brain. So a convoluted argument or a convoluted explanation is one that winds this way and that. An official document may have to wind its way through a convoluted process and be stamped by eight people before being approved. Convoluted language makes many people suspicious; as a great philosopher once said, "Anything that can be said can be said clearly."

Quizzes

A. Choose the closest definition:

1. convoluted   a. spinning b. babbling c. grinding
   d. winding
2. turbine   a. whirlpool b. engine c. headdress
   d. carousel
3. evolution   a. process of development b. process of
   democracy c. process of election d. process of
   elimination
4. perturb   a. reset b. inset c. preset d. upset
5. voluble   a. whirling b. unpleasant c. talkative
   d. garbled
6. turbulent   a. churning b. turning c. yearning
   d. burning
7. turbid   a. flat b. calm c. confused d. slow
8. devolve   a. hand down b. hand in c. turn up
   d. turn around

B. Match the word on the left to the correct definition on the right:

1. voluble   a. murky
2. turbine   b. chatty
3. evolution   c. seething
4. turbid   d. complicated
5. devolve   e. turning engine
6. perturb   f. degenerate
7. convoluted   g. disturb
8. turbulent   h. progress

FAC comes from the Latin verb *facere,* meaning "to make or do." Thus, a *fact* was originally simply "something done." A *benefactor* is someone who does good. And to *manufacture* is to make, usually in a *factory.*

factor \\'fak-tər\ Something that contributes to producing a result: ingredient.

• The most important factor in the success of the treaty talks was the physical presence of the two presidents.

In Latin *factor* means simply "doer." So in English a factor is an "actor" or element or ingredient in some situation or quantity. Charm can be a factor in someone's success, and lack of exercise can be a factor in producing a poor physique. In math we use *factor* to mean a number that can be multiplied or divided to produce a given number (for example, 5 and 8 are factors of 40). And in biology a gene may be called a factor, since genes are ingredients in the total organism.

factotum \fak-'tō-təm\ A person whose job involves doing many different kinds of work.

• Over the years she had become the office factotum, who might be doing legal research one day and organizing the company picnic the next.

This odd word doesn't come from ancient Latin, but it was coined to look as if it did. The term *Johannes factotum*, meaning "Jack-of-all-trades," first shows up in writing in 1592 to describe none other than Shakespeare himself. The word *gofer* is similar to *factotum* but a bit less dignified. In other words, a factotum is an assistant, but one who may have taken over some fairly important functions.

facile \\'fa-səl\ (1) Easily accomplished. (2) Shallow, superficial.

• The principal made a facile argument for the school's policy, but no one was convinced.

A facile suggestion doesn't deal with the issue in any depth, and a facile solution may be only temporarily effective. A facile writer is one who seems to write too quickly and easily, and a careful reader may discover that the writer hasn't really said very much.

facilitate \fə-'si-lə-ˌtāt\ To make (something) easier; to make (something) run more smoothly.

• Her uncle hadn't exactly gotten her the job, but he had certainly facilitated the process.

Facilitating is about getting things done. Clever employees are quietly facilitating all kinds of useful activity within their organizations all the time. People who lead therapy groups or workshops are often called *facilitators*, since their job isn't to teach or to order but rather to make the meetings as productive as possible. Even businesses now use facilitators in meetings where they don't want any person's particular desires to outweigh anyone else's. The *facilitation* of a rewarding discussion should be a facilitator's only goal. Today, in recognition of the many different situations that may call for a facilitator, there is even an International Association of Facilitators.

LUM comes from the Latin noun *lumen*, meaning "light." Thus, our word *illuminate* means "to supply with light" or "make clear," and *illumination* is light that shines on something.

---

lumen \ˈlü-mən\ In physics, the standard unit for measuring the rate of the flow of light.

• The lumen is a measure of the perceived power of light.

There are two common units for measuring light, the candela and the lumen. Both are recognized as standard international units, which also include the second (for time), the kilogram (for weight), and the meter (for length). The *candela* is a measure of intensity; an ordinary candle gives off light with the intensity of about one candela. The lumen is a measure of "luminous flux"; a standard 100-watt lightbulb gives off 1500–1700 lumens. Luminous flux indicates how much light is actually perceived by the human eye. Technologies vary in how efficiently they turn electricity into light; halogen lights produce about 12 lumens per watt, ordinary incandescent lightbulbs produce about 15 lumens per watt, and compact fluorescent bulbs produce about 50 lumens per watt.

luminous \ˈlü-mə-nəs\ (1) Producing or seeming to produce light. (2) Filled with light.

• She ended her recital with a luminous performance of Ravel's song cycle, and the crowd called her back for repeated encores.

Luminous, like its synonyms *radiant, shining, glowing,* and *lustrous*, is generally a positive adjective, especially when it describes something that doesn't literally glow, such as a face, a performance, or a poem. Luminous signs depend on a gas such as neon, krypton, argon, xenon, or radon—and you can use luminous (DayGlo) paint to make your own signs. New technologies have now given us luminous fabrics, which are being used to produce striking or creepy effects in clothing, upholstery, and interior surfaces.

bioluminescent \ˌbī-ō-ˌlü-mə-ˈne-sᵊnt\ Relating to light given off by living organisms.

• Most of the light emitted by bioluminescent marine organisms is blue or blue-green.

Bio- comes from the Greek word for "life" (see BIO, p. 407). On land, fireflies, glowworms, and the fox-fire fungus are all known for their *bioluminescence*. In the sea, bioluminescent life-forms include plankton, squid, and comb jellies, as well as some unusual fish. Most deep-sea animals are bioluminescent, but single-celled algae living at or near the surface can also create a remarkable show, as they often do in Bioluminescent Bay on the Puerto Rican island of Vieques. But bioluminescence is unknown in true plants, and mammals, birds, reptiles, and amphibians never got the knack of it either.

luminary \ˈlü-mə-ˌner-ē\ A very famous or distinguished person.

• Entering the glittering reception room, she immediately spotted several luminaries of the art world.

The Latin word *luminaria* could mean either "lamps" or "heavenly bodies." For medieval astrologers, the luminaries were the sun and the moon, the brightest objects in the heavens. Today a luminary is usually a person of "brilliant" achievement: a celebrity, a "leading light," or a "star."

Quizzes

A. Fill in each blank with the correct letter:

a.	lumen	e.	facile
b.	bioluminescent	f.	factor
c.	luminary	g.	factotum
d.	luminous	h.	facilitate

1. The light output of an ordinary candle provided the basis for the light unit called the _____ .
2. Her _____ voice was all the critics could talk about in their reviews of the musical's opening night.

3. She was quick-witted, but her reasoning was often _____ and not deeply thoughtful.

4. The _____ insects that he studies use their light for mating.

5. The support of the financial industry would greatly _____ the passage of the bill.

6. He had just been introduced to another _____ of the literary world and was feeling rather dazzled.

7. The main _____ in their decision to build was their desire for a completely "green" home.

8. As the company's _____, she often felt overworked and underappreciated.

B. Indicate whether the following pairs of words have the same or different meanings:

1. facilitate / ease   same ___ / different ___
2. lumen / lighting   same ___ / different ___
3. factor / element   same ___ / different ___
4. luminary / star   same ___ / different ___
5. factotum / expert   same ___ / different ___
6. luminous / glowing   same ___ / different ___
7. facile / practical   same ___ / different ___
8. bioluminescent / brilliant   same ___ / different ___

Words from Mythology and History

muse \\'myüz\ A source of inspiration; a guiding spirit.

• At 8:00 each morning he sat down at his desk and summoned his muse, and she almost always responded.

The Muses were the nine Greek goddesses who presided over the arts (including *music*) and literature. A shrine to the Muses was called in Latin a *museum*. An artist or poet about to begin work would call on his particular Muse to inspire him, and a poem itself might begin with such a call; thus, Homer's *Odyssey* begins, "Sing to me of the man, Muse" (that is, of Odysseus). Today a muse may be one's special creative spirit, but some artists and writers have also chosen living human beings to serve as their muses.

iridescent \\,ir-ə-'de-sənt\ Having a glowing, rainbowlike play of color that seems to change as the light shifts.

- The children shrieked with glee as the iridescent soap bubbles floated away in the gentle breeze.

Iris, the Greek goddess of the rainbow, took messages from Mount Olympus to earth, and from gods to mortals or other gods, using the rainbow as her stairway. *Iridescence* is thus the glowing, shifting, colorful quality of a rainbow, also seen in an opal, a light oil slick, a butterfly wing, or the mother-of-pearl that lines an oyster shell.

mausoleum \ˌmȯ-zə-ˈlē-əm\ (1) A large tomb, especially one built aboveground with shelves for the dead. (2) A large, gloomy building or room.

- The family's grand mausoleum occupied a prominent spot in the cemetery, for all the good it did the silent dead within.

Mausolus was ruler of a kingdom in Asia Minor in the 4th century B.C. He beautified the capital, Halicarnassus, with all sorts of fine public buildings, but he is best known for the magnificent monument, the Mausoleum, that was built by his wife Artemisia after his death. With its great height (perhaps 140 feet) and many beautiful sculptures, the Mausoleum was declared one of the Seven Wonders of the Ancient World. Though Halicarnassus was repeatedly attacked, the Mausoleum would survive for well over 1,000 years.

mentor \ˈmen-ˌtȯr\ A trusted counselor, guide, tutor, or coach.

- This pleasant old gentleman had served as friend and mentor to a series of young lawyers in the firm.

Odysseus was away from home fighting and journeying for 20 years, according to Homer. During that time, the son he left as a babe in arms grew up under the supervision of Mentor, an old and trusted friend. When the goddess Athena decided it was time to complete young Telemachus's education by sending him off to learn about his father, she visited him disguised as Mentor and they set out together. Today, anyone such as a coach or tutor who gives another (usually younger) person help and advice on how to achieve success in the larger world is called a mentor. And in recent years we've even been using the word as a verb, and now in business we often speak of an experienced employee *mentoring* someone who has just arrived.

narcissism \ˈnär-si-ˌsi-zəm\ (1) Extreme self-centeredness or fascination with oneself. (2) Love or desire for one's own body.

- His girlfriend would complain about his narcissism, saying he spent more time looking at himself in the mirror than at her.

Narcissus was a handsome youth in Greek mythology who inspired love in many who saw him. One was the nymph Echo, who could only repeat the last thing that anyone said. When Narcissus cruelly rejected her, she wasted away to nothing but her voice. Though he played with the affections of others, Narcissus became a victim of his own attractiveness. When he caught sight of his own reflection in a pool, he sat gazing at it in fascination, wasting away without food or drink, unable to touch or kiss the image he saw. When he finally died, the gods turned him into the flower we call the *narcissus*, which stands with its head bent as though gazing at its reflection. People with "*narcissistic* personality disorder" have a somewhat serious mental condition, according to psychologists, but the rest of us are free to call anyone who seems vain and self-centered a *narcissist*.

tantalize \\'tan-tə-ˌlīz\\ To tease or torment by offering something desirable but keeping it out of reach.

- The sight of a warm fire through the window tantalized the little match girl almost unbearably.

King Tantalus, according to Greek mythology, killed his son Pelops and served him to the gods in a stew for dinner. Almost all the gods realized what was happening and refused the meal, though only after Demeter had taken a nibble out of Pelops's shoulder. After they had reconstructed him, replacing the missing shoulder with a piece of ivory, they turned to punishing Tantalus. In Hades he stands in water up to his neck under a tree laden with fruit. Each time he stoops to drink, the water moves out of reach; each time he reaches up to pick something, the branches move beyond his grasp. He is thus eternally tantalized by the water and fruit. Today anything or anyone that tempts but is unobtainable is tantalizing.

thespian \\'thes-pē-ən\\ An actor.

- In summer the towns of New England welcome troupes of thespians dedicated to presenting plays of all kinds.

Greek drama was originally entirely performed by choruses. According to tradition, the Greek dramatist Thespis, of the 6th century B.C., was the inventor of tragedy and the first to write roles for the individual actor as distinct from the chorus, and the actor's exchanges with the chorus were the first dramatic dialogue. Since

Thespis himself performed the individual parts in his own plays, he was also the first true actor. Ever since choruses disappeared from drama, thespians have filled all the roles in plays. *Thespian* is also an adjective; thus, we can speak of "thespian ambitions" and "thespian traditions," for example.

zephyr \\'ze-fər\ (1) A breeze from the west. (2) A gentle breeze.

* Columbus left Genoa sailing against the zephyrs that continually blow across the Mediterranean.

The ancient Greeks called the west wind Zephyrus and regarded him and his fellows—Boreas (god of the north wind), Eurus (god of the east wind), and Notus (god of the south wind)—as gods. A zephyr is a kind wind, bringer of clear skies and beautiful weather.

Quiz

Fill in each blank with the correct letter:

a.	mausoleum	e.	muse
b.	thespian	f.	mentor
c.	iridescent	g.	zephyr
d.	tantalize	h.	narcissism

1. At the middle of the cemetery stood the grand ＿＿＿ of the city's wealthiest family.
2. On fair days a gentle ＿＿＿ would blow from morning until night.
3. The company president took the new recruit under her wing and acted as her ＿＿＿ for the next several years.
4. He would often ＿＿＿ her with talk of traveling to Brazil or India, but nothing ever came of it.
5. The oil slick on the puddle's surface became beautifully ＿＿＿ in the slanting light.
6. After his last book of poetry was published, his ＿＿＿ seemed to have abandoned him.
7. In everyone there is a bit of the ＿＿＿ yearning for a stage.
8. By working as a model, she could satisfy her ＿＿＿ while getting paid for it.

Review Quizzes

A. Choose the correct definition:

1. voluble   a. argumentative b. mumbly c. speechless
    d. talkative
2. facilitate   a. guide b. build   c. order d. obstruct
3. verify   a. reverse b. mislead c. prove d. test
4. zephyr   a. stormy blast b. icy rain c. light shower
    d. gentle breeze
5. aver   a. reject b. detract c. deny d. assert
6. turbulent   a. unending b. swirling c. muddy d. angry
7. facile   a. tough b. quiet c. familiar d. easy
8. perturb   a. soothe b. restore c. park d. upset
9. devolve   a. decay b. turn into c. suggest d. improve
10. convoluted   a. disorderly b. complex c. discouraged
    d. superior
11. muse   a. singer b. poetry c. inspiration d. philosopher
12. tantalize   a. visit b. satisfy c. tease d. watch
13. iridescent   a. shimmering b. drab c. striped d. watery
14. mentor   a. translator b. interpreter c. guide d. student
15. factotum   a. manufacturer b. untruth c. dilemma
    d. assistant

**B. Indicate whether the following pairs of terms have
the same or different meanings:**

1. thespian / teacher   same ___ / different ___
2. facile / handy   same ___ / different ___
3. evolution / extinction   same ___ / different ___
4. verify / prove   same ___ / different ___
5. turbine / plow   same ___ / different ___
6. spirited / energetic   same ___ / different ___
7. incantation / chant   same ___ / different ___
8. turbid / muddy   same ___ / different ___
9. transpire / ooze   same ___ / different ___
10. aver / claim   same ___ / different ___

C. Fill in each blank with the correct letter:

a. lingua franca
b. narcissism
c. descant
d. verisimilitude
e. cantata
f. veracity
g. facilitate
h. linguistics
i. cantor
j. devolve
k. turbine
l. mausoleum

1. The defense lawyers knew the jury might be doubtful about the next witness's _____.
2. They were a very attractive couple, but their _____ often annoyed other people.
3. The university chorus was going to perform a Bach _____ along with the Mozart *Requiem*.
4. They finally realized they would need a real-estate agent to _____ the sale of the property.
5. He began his singing career as a _____ in Brooklyn and ended it as an international opera star.
6. She had hired a highly experienced deputy, hoping to _____ many of her responsibilities onto him.
7. One day in the cemetery the _____ door was open, and he peered in with horrified fascination.
8. Never having studied _____, he didn't feel able to discuss word histories in much depth.
9. The Spaniards and Germans at the next table were using English as a _____.
10. Her films showed her own reality, and she had no interest in _____.
11. The roar of the _____ was so loud they couldn't hear each other.
12. As part of their musical training, she always encouraged them to sing their own _____ over the main melody.

UNIT

12

UMBR comes from the Latin *umbra,* meaning "shadow." Thus, the familiar *umbrella,* with its ending meaning "little," casts a "little shadow" to keep off the sun or the rain.

---

umber \\'əm-bər\\ (1) A darkish brown mineral containing manganese and iron oxides used for coloring paint. (2) A color that is greenish brown to dark reddish brown.

- Van Dyke prized umber as a pigment and used it constantly in his oil paintings.

The mineral deposits of Italy provided sources of a number of natural pigments, among them umber. Since the late Renaissance, umber has been in great demand as a coloring agent. When crushed and mixed with paint, it produces an olive color known as *raw umber*; when crushed and burnt, it produces a darker tone known as *burnt umber.*

adumbrate \\'a-dəm-brāt\\ (1) To give a sketchy outline or disclose in part. (2) To hint at or foretell.

- The Secretary of State would only adumbrate his ideas for bringing peace to Bosnia.

A synonym for *adumbrate* is *foreshadow,* which means to present a shadowy version of something before it becomes reality or is provided in full. Tough questioning by a Supreme Court justice may adumbrate the way he or she is planning to rule on a case. A bad review by a critic may adumbrate the failure of a new film. And rats scurrying off a ship were believed to adumbrate a coming disaster at sea.

penumbra \pə-ˈnəm-brə\ (1) The partial shadow surrounding a complete shadow, as in an eclipse. (2) The fringe or surrounding area where something exists less fully.

• This area of the investigation was the penumbra where both the FBI and the CIA wanted to pursue their leads.

Every solar eclipse casts an *umbra,* the darker central area in which almost no light reaches the earth, and a penumbra, the area of partial shadow where part of the sun is still visible. *Penumbra* can thus be used to describe any "gray area" where things aren't all black and white. For example, the right to privacy falls under the penumbra of the U.S. Constitution; though it isn't specifically guaranteed there, the Supreme Court has held that it is implied, and thus that the government may not intrude into certain areas of a citizen's private life. Because its existence is still shadowy, however, the Court is still determining how much of an individual's life is protected by the right to privacy.

umbrage \ˈəm-brij\ A feeling of resentment at some slight or insult, often one that is imagined rather than real.

• She often took umbrage at his treatment of her, without being able to pinpoint what was offensive about it.

An umbrage was originally a shadow, and soon the word also began to mean "a shadowy suspicion." Then it came to mean "displeasure" as well—that is, a kind of shadow blocking the sunlight. *Umbrage* is now generally used in the phrase "take umbrage at." An overly sensitive person may take umbrage at something as small as having his or her name pronounced wrong.

VEST comes from the Latin verb *vestire,* "to clothe" or "to dress," and the noun *vestis,* "clothing" or "garment." *Vest* is the shortest English word we have from this root, and is the name of a rather small piece of clothing.

---

divest \dī-ˈvest\ (1) To get rid of or free oneself of property, authority, or title. (2) To strip of clothing, ornaments, or equipment.

- In protest against apartheid, many universities in the 1980s divested themselves of all stock in South African companies.

If you decide to enter a monastery, you may divest yourself of most of your possessions. When a church is officially abandoned, it's usually divested of its ornaments and furnishings. A company that's going through hard times may divest itself of several stores, and investors are constantly divesting themselves of stocks that aren't performing well enough. And when it turns out that athletes have been using steroids, they're usually divested of any awards they may have won.

investiture \in-'ves-tə-ˌchùr\ The formal placing of someone in office.

- At an English monarch's investiture, he or she is presented with the crown, scepter, and sword, the symbols of power.

In its original meaning, an *investiture* was the clothing of a new officeholder in garments that symbolized power. The Middle Ages saw much debate over the investiture of bishops by kings and emperors. These rulers felt that high religious offices were theirs to give as rewards for someone's loyal service or as bribes for someone's future support; the popes, on the other hand, regarded these investitures as the improper buying and selling of church offices. The investiture struggle caused tension between popes and monarchs and even led to wars.

transvestite \tranz-'ves-ˌtīt\ A person, especially a male, who wears clothes designed for the opposite sex.

- In Handel's operas, the heroic male leading roles are today often sung by female transvestites, since he originally wrote them for the soprano range.

Transvestite includes the prefix *trans-*, "across," and thus means literally "cross-dresser" (and the word *cross-dresser* is in fact now commonly used in place of *transvestite*). In the theater, from ancient Greece to Elizabethan England, *transvestism* was common because all parts—even Juliet—were played by men. Traditional Japanese Kabuki and Noh drama still employ transvestism of this sort. In everyday life, women's clothing includes fashions so similar to men's fashions that both *transvestite* and *cross-dresser* are generally applied only to men. The much newer word *transgender* describes people whose gender identity differs from the sex they had or were identified as having at birth.

travesty \\'tra-vəs-tē\ (1) An inferior or distorted imitation. (2) A broadly comic imitation in drama, literature, or art that is usually grotesque and ridiculous.

* The senator was shouting that the new tax bill represented a travesty of tax reform.

The word *travesty* comes from the same prefix and root as *transvestite*. Since cross-dressing often isn't very convincing, the word has usually referred to something absurd. So a verdict that angers people may be denounced as a "travesty of justice." *Saturday Night Live* specializes in dramatic travesties mocking everything from political figures and issues to popular culture—"disguised" versions intended for entertainment. *Travesty* may also be a verb; thus, Mel Brooks has travestied movie genres of all kinds—westerns, thrillers, and silent films, among others.

Quizzes

A. Fill in the blank with the correct letter:

a. penumbra   e. divest
b. transvestite   f. umber
c. investiture   g. umbrage
d. travesty   h. adumbrate

1. All the pigments—crimson, russet, _____, cobalt blue, and the rest—were mixed by his assistants.
2. The _____ of the prime minister was an occasion of pomp and ceremony.
3. Some people are quick to take _____ the moment they think someone might have been disrespectful.
4. Since all the judges were cronies of the dictator, the court proceedings were a _____ of justice.
5. The new director planned to _____ the museum of two of its Picassos.
6. The farther away a source of light is from the object casting a shadow, the wider will be that shadow's _____.

7. The young model became a notorious success when she was discovered to be a _____.
8. The increasing cloudiness and the damp wind seemed to _____ a stormy night.

B. Match the definition on the left to the correct word on the right:

1. resentment   a. penumbra
2. brownish color   b. travesty
3. installing in office   c. transvestite
4. cross-dresser   d. adumbrate
5. bad imitation   e. divest
6. get rid of   f. umbrage
7. near shadow   g. investiture
8. partially disclose   h. umber

THE/THEO comes from the Greek word meaning "god." *Theology,* the study of religion, is practiced by *theologians. Monotheism* is the worship of a single god; Christianity, Islam, and Judaism are *monotheistic* religions, and all three worship the same god. *Polytheistic* religions such as those of ancient Greece and Rome, on the other hand, worship many gods.

---

apotheosis \ə-ˌpä-thē-ˈō-səs\ (1) Transformation into a god. (2) The perfect example.

• Abraham Lincoln's apotheosis after his assassination transformed the controversial politician into the saintly savior of his country.

In ancient Greece, historical figures were sometimes worshipped as gods. In Rome, apotheosis was rare until the emperor Augustus declared the dead Julius Caesar to be a god, and soon other dead emperors were being *apotheosized* as well. In older paintings you may see a heroic figure—Napoleon, George Washington, or Shakespeare, for example—being raised into the clouds, symbolizing his or her apotheosis. But today any great classic example of something can be called its apotheosis. You might hear it said, for example, that Baroque music reached its apotheosis in the works of J. S. Bach, or that the Duesenberg Phaeton was the apotheosis of the touring car.

atheistic \ˌā-thē-ˈis-tik\ Denying the existence of God or divine power.

* The atheistic Madalyn Murray O'Hair successfully sought the removal of prayer from American public schools in the 1960s.

In the Roman Empire, early Christians were called atheistic because they denied the existence of the Roman gods. And once the Christian church was firmly established, it condemned the Romans as *atheists* because they didn't believe in the Christian God. In later centuries, English-speaking Christians would often use the words *pagan* and *heathen* to describe such non-Christians, while *atheist* would be reserved for those who actually denied the existence of any god. *Atheism* is different from *agnosticism,* which claims that the existence of any higher power is unknowable; and lots of people who simply don't think much about religion often call themselves *agnostics* as well.

pantheon \ˈpan-thē-än\ (1) A building serving as the burial place of or containing memorials to the famous dead of a nation. (2) A group of notable persons or things.

* A Hall of Fame serves as a kind of pantheon for its field, and those admitted in the early years are often the greatest of all.

Each of the important Roman gods and goddesses had many temples erected in their name. But in 27 B.C. a temple to all the gods together was completed in Rome; twice destroyed, it was ultimately replaced by a third temple around A.D. 126. This extraordinary domed structure is still one of the important sights of Rome, and the burial place for the painters Raphael and Carracci and two kings. In Paris, a great church was completed in 1789–90; named the Panthéon, it was announced as the future resting place of France's great figures, and the bodies of Victor Hugo, Louis Pasteur, Marie Curie, and many others now rest within its walls.

theocracy \thē-ˈä-krə-sē\ (1) Government by officials who are regarded as divinely inspired. (2) A state governed by a theocracy.

* The ancient Aztecs lived in a theocracy in which guidance came directly from the gods through the priests.

In the Middle Ages, the Muslim empires stretching around much of the Mediterranean were theocracies, and the pope ruled most of modern-day Italy. But theocracies are rare today. Modern Iran and Saudi Arabia (and perhaps half a dozen others) are usually regarded as *theocratic* governments, since, even though Iran's president is elected by popular vote and Saudi Arabia is ruled by a royal family, the countries' laws are religious laws. But when a government tries to follow all the teachings of a single religion, things usually don't work out terribly well, so U.S. Constitution and Bill of Rights forbid using religion as the principal basis for democracy.

ICON comes from the Greek *eikon*, which led to the Latin *icon*, both meaning "image." Though the *icon-* root hasn't produced many English words, the words that is does appear in tend to be interesting.

---

icon \\'ī-ˌkän\\ (1) A religious image usually painted on a small wooden panel: idol. (2) Emblem, symbol.

* Henry Ford's assembly line captured the imagination of the world, and he and his company became icons of industrial capitalism.

In the Eastern Orthodox church, much importance is given to icons, usually small portraits on wood—sometimes with gold-leaf paint— of Jesus, Mary, or a saint, which hang in churches and in the houses of the faithful. The Orthodox church favors icons partly because they communicate directly and forcefully even to uneducated people. They are regarded as sacred; some believers actually pray to them, and many believe that icons have carried out miracles. The common modern uses of *icon* grew out of this original sense. The fact that Orthodox icons have a symbolic role led to *icon* being used to mean simply "symbol." Because of the icon's sacredness, the term also came to mean "idol." And once we began to use *idol* to refer to pop-culture stars, it wasn't long before we began using *icon* the same way. But for the little computer-desktop images that you click on, the older meaning of "symbol" is the one we're thinking of.

iconic \\ī-'kä-nik\\ (1) Symbolic. (2) Relating to a greatly admired and successful person or thing.

* The 1963 March on Washington was the iconic event in the history of the civil-rights movement, now familiar to all American schoolchildren.

The original meaning of *iconic* was essentially "resembling an icon," but today it more often seems to mean "so admired that it could be the subject of an icon." And with that meaning, *iconic* has become part of the language of advertising and publicity; today companies and magazines and TV hosts are constantly encouraging us to think of some consumer item or pop star or show as first-rate or immortal or flawless—absolutely "iconic"—when he or she or it is actually nothing of the kind.

iconoclast \ī-'kä-nə-ˌklast\ (1) A person who destroys religious images or opposes their use. (2) A person who attacks settled beliefs or institutions.

• She's always rattling her friends by saying outrageous things, and she enjoys her reputation as an iconoclast.

When the early books of the Bible were being written, most of the other Middle Eastern religions had more than one god; these religions generally encouraged the worship of idols of the various gods, which were often regarded as magical objects. But in the Ten Commandments given to Moses in the Old Testament, God prohibits the making of "graven images" or "idols" for worship, proclaiming that the Jews are to worship only one God, who is too great to be represented in an idol. However, by the 6th century A.D., Christians had begun to create religious images in order to focus the prayers of the faithful. Opposition to icons led to the *Iconoclastic* Controversy in A.D. 726, when, supported by the pope, iconoclasts began smashing and burning the images in churches and monasteries (*clast*- comes from the Greek word meaning "to break"). In time, peace was restored, and almost all Christians have since accepted depictions of Jesus, Mary, and the saints. Today an iconoclast is someone who constantly argues with conventional thinking, refusing to "worship" the objects of everyone else's "faith."

iconography \ˌī-kə-'nä-grə-fē\ (1) The imagery and symbolism of a work of art or an artist. (2) The study of artistic symbolism.

• Today scholars pore over the advertisements in glossy magazines, studying the iconography for clues to the ads' hidden meanings.

If you saw a 17th-century painting of a man writing at a desk with a lion at his feet, would you know you were looking at St. Jerome, translator of the Bible, who, according to legend, once pulled a thorn from the paw of a lion, which thereafter became his devoted friend? And if a painting showed a young woman reclining on a bed with a shower of gold descending on her, would you recognize her as Danaë, locked up in a tower to keep her away from the lustful Zeus, who then managed to gain access to her by transforming himself into golden light (or golden coins)? An *iconographic* approach to art can make museum-going a lot of fun—and amateur *iconographers* know there are also plenty of symbols lurking in the images that advertisers bombard us with daily.

Quizzes

A. Fill in each blank with the correct letter:

a. pantheon	e. icon
b. iconic	f. apotheosis
c. atheistic	g. iconoclast
d. iconography	h. theocracy

1. Her personal _____ of actresses included Vanessa Redgrave, Helen Mirren, Emma Thompson, and Maggie Smith.
2. He enjoyed being an _____, since he had a lot of odd ideas and arguing suited his personality well.
3. His well-known _____ beliefs meant that he couldn't hope for great success in politics.
4. Thirty years later, his great speech was viewed as an _____ moment in modern American history.
5. Being inducted into the Hall of Fame is as close as a modern ballplayer can come to _____.
6. The strange _____ of the painting had caught her attention years ago, and she continued to puzzle over the obviously symbolic appearance of various odd objects.
7. They had come back from Russia with a beautiful _____ of Mary and another of St. Basil.
8. The high priest in this medieval _____ was equivalent to a dictator.

B. Match the word on the left to its definition on the right:

1. icon
2. pantheon
3. apotheosis
4. iconography
5. atheistic
6. iconoclast
7. theocracy
8. iconic

a. state ruled by religion
b. symbolic
c. symbol
d. nonbelieving
e. artistic symbolism
f. hall of fame
g. dissenter
h. perfect example

URB comes from the Latin noun for "city." Our word *urban* describes cities and the people who live in them. With its *sub-* prefix (see SUB, p. 455), a *suburb* is a town "near" or "under" a larger city, and *suburban* houses are home to *suburbanites*.

urbane \ˌər-ˈbān\ Sophisticated and with polished manners.

• He was remembered as a gentlemanly and urbane host of elegant dinner parties.

Urbane's synonyms include *suave, debonair,* and especially *cosmopolitan*. *Urbanity* was a trait of such classic movie stars as Fred Astaire, Cary Grant, William Powell, Leslie Howard, Charles Boyer, and George Sanders. (Notice that, for some reason, *urbane* is almost always used to describe men rather than women.) Teenagers in the 1960s read James Bond novels and watched his character onscreen to get tips about acquiring an urbane identity. But it's hard to acquire urbanity without actually having had wide social experience in sophisticated cities. And, since times have changed, the whole notion doesn't seem to attract young people quite the way it used to.

exurban \ek-ˈsər-bən\ Relating to a region or settlement that lies outside a city and usually beyond its suburbs and often is inhabited chiefly by well-to-do families.

• Exurban areas typically show much higher education and income levels than closer-in suburbs or nearby rural counties.

With its prefix *ex-*, ("outside of," the noun *exurb* was coined around 1955 to describe the ring of well-off communities beyond the suburbs that were becoming commuter towns for an urban area. Most exurbs were probably quiet little towns before being discovered by young city dwellers with good incomes looking for a pleasant place to raise their children. Planners, advertisers, and political strategists today often talk about such topics as exurban development, exurban trends, exurban migration, and exurban voters.

interurban \ˌin-tər-ˈər-bən\ Going between or connecting cities or towns.

• Businesspeople in the two cities have been waiting for decades for a true high-speed interurban railway on the Japanese model.

Interurban is generally used to describe transportation. As a noun (as in "In those days you could take the interurban from Seattle to Tacoma"), *interurban* has meant a fairly heavy but fast electric train, something between an urban trolley and a full-fledged long-distance train, that offers more frequent service than an ordinary railway. Interurban transit today may include bus, ferry, and limousine— and, in a few lucky areas, a regional railway. With oil supplies dwindling, there's hope that interurban railways will be coming back into wider use.

urbanization \ˌər-bə-nə-ˈzā-shən\ The process by which towns and cities are formed and become larger as more and more people begin living and working in central areas.

• The area has been undergoing rapid urbanization, and six or seven of the old small towns are now genuine suburbs.

The word *urbanization* started appearing in print way back in the 1880s, which says something about the growth of American cities. The expansion of Los Angeles was an early example of uncontrolled urbanization. Urbanization is often seen as a negative trend, with bad effects on quality of life and the environment. But apartments require much less heat than houses, and commuting by mass transit rather than cars can reduce pollution and energy use, and cities offer improved opportunities for jobs (and often for education and housing as well), so city growth doesn't make everyone unhappy.

CULT comes from the Latin *cultus*, meaning "care." So *cultivation* is care of something, such as a garden, in a way that encourages its growth. And *culture* is what is produced by cultivating human knowledge, skills, beliefs, manners, science, and art over many years.

---

acculturation \ə-ˌkəl-chə-ˈrā-shən\ (1) Modification of the culture of an individual, group, or people by adapting to or borrowing traits from another culture. (2) The process by which a human being acquires the culture of a particular society from infancy.

• The old Eastern European bagel has gone through an acculturation in America, where it has acquired a soft texture, a white interior, and fillers like eggs and peanut butter.

Whenever people come in close contact with a population that's more powerful, they're generally forced to *acculturate* in order to survive. Learning a new language is usually part of the acculturation process, which may also include adopting new clothing, a new diet, new occupations, and even a new religion. An older generation often fails to acculturate thoroughly, but their children often pick up the new ways quickly.

cross-cultural \ˈkrȯs-ˈkəlch-rəl\ Dealing with or offering comparison between two or more different cultures or cultural areas.

• A cross-cultural study of 49 tribes revealed a tight relationship between the closeness of mother-infant bonding in a given tribe and that tribe's peacefulness toward its neighbors.

If you've ever traveled in a foreign country, you've found yourself making some cross-cultural comparisons: Why are huge family dinners so much more common in Italy than back home? Why do Mexican teenagers seem to play with their little relatives so much more than teenagers in the U.S.? Cross-cultural analysis has produced extremely interesting data about such things as the effects of various nations' diets on their populations' health. Though *cross-cultural* was originally used by anthropologists to refer to research comparing aspects of different cultures, it's also often used to describe the reality that lots of us face daily while simply walking the streets of a big American city.

horticulture \ˈhȯr-tə-ˌkəl-chər\ The science and art of growing fruits, vegetables, flowers, or ornamental plants.

- He considered majoring in botany, but has decided instead on horticulture, hoping he can spend more time in a greenhouse than in the library or the lab.

Hortus is Latin for "garden," and the first gardens were planted about 10,000 years ago in what is often called the Fertile Crescent—the crescent-shaped area stretching from Israel north through Syria and down Iraq's two great rivers to the Persian Gulf. Probably more fertile in previous centuries than it is today, it was the original home of such food plants as wheat, barley, peas, and lentils or their ancient ancestors (not to mention the ancestors of cows, pigs, sheep, and goats as well). Many *horticulturists* today work as researchers or plant breeders or tend orchards and greenhouses—but most American households contain at least one amateur horticulturist.

subculture \\'səb-ˌkəl-chər\\ A group whose beliefs and behaviors are different from the main groups within a culture or society.

- Members of the emo subculture at her high school recognized each other by their skinny jeans, dyed hair, and canvas sneakers.

This common meaning of *subculture* (it has an older biological meaning) only appeared in the 1930s, and for about 20 years it was used mostly by sociologists, psychologists, and anthropologists. But in the 1950s, as America's wealth led to more and more teenagers getting their own cars and thus their independence, not to mention the arrival of rock 'n' roll, people noticed something unusual happening among young people, and began to speak of the "youth subculture." As the country's wealth and freedom of movement continued to increase, we realized that the U.S. had become home to a large number of subcultures. Today the Web makes possible more than anyone could have dreamed of back in the 1950s. When we happen to stumble on a subculture—bodybuilders, Trekkies, hackers, Airstreamers, anime lovers, motocross enthusiasts—we may realize with astonishment that we had never even imagined that it might exist.

Quizzes

A. Choose the closest definition:

1. cross-cultural   a. combining art and music   b. between two or more cultures   c. combining fruits and vegetables   d. intensively cultivated

2. interurban   a. densely populated   b. between cities   c. from the inner city   d. within the city

3. urbanization   a. moving to cities   b. street construction   c. becoming citylike   d. mass transit

4. horticulture   a. intellectual knowledge   b. science of growing plants   c. animal science   d. horse breeding

5. acculturation   a. developing cultural institutions   b. turning woods into farmland   c. acquiring aspects of another culture   d. appreciation of music and dance

6. urbane   a. foolish   b. old-fashioned   c. dependable   d. sophisticated

7. subculture   a. group within a culture   b. cultivation below ground   c. goth kids   d. small garden

8. exurban   a. high-rise   b. crowded   c. above the city   d. beyond the suburbs

B. Fill in each blank with the correct letter:

a. exurban	e. interurban
b. urbane	f. urbanization
c. acculturation	g. horticulture
d. cross-cultural	h. subculture

1. In their _____ home, 25 miles from the city, they looked out on a small field and woods.

2. _____ had proceeded swiftly over the previous ten years, and shopping malls had replaced the cozy streets of the old suburb.

3. A _____ study had revealed far greater levels of anxiety in middle-class Americans than in middle-class Scandinavians.

4. Their next-door neighbors were an _____ couple who threw lively parties where you could meet writers, artists, designers, and media people.

5. His wife's background in _____ led them to plant a large fruit orchard and build a huge greenhouse for flower cultivation.

6. After the island was acquired by Japan around 1910, the population began undergoing rapid ____, eventually giving up its native language.
7. In his teens he became part of a Web-based ____ whose members were devoted to raising poisonous reptiles.
8. ____ railways have begun making a comeback as city dwellers have become increasingly concerned about climate change.

DEM/DEMO comes from the Greek word meaning "people." "Government by the people" was invented by the ancient Greeks, so it's appropriate that they were the first to come up with a word for it: *demokratia*, or *democracy*.

---

demographic \ˌde-mə-ˈgra-fik\ Having to do with the study of human populations, especially their size, growth, density, and patterns of living.

• Each year the state government uses the most current demographic figures to determine how to distribute its funding for education.

Demographic analysis, the statistical description of human populations, is a tool used by government agencies, political parties, and manufacturers of consumer goods. Polls conducted on every topic imaginable, from age to toothpaste preference, give the government and corporations an idea of who the public is and what it needs and wants. The government's census, which is conducted every ten years, is the largest demographic survey of all. Today *demographic* is also being used as a noun; so, for example, TV advertisers are constantly worrying about how to appeal to "the 18-to-24-year-old demographic."

endemic \en-ˈde-mik\ (1) Found only in a given place or region. (2) Often found in a given occupation, area, or environment.

• Malaria remains endemic in tropical regions around the world.

With its *en-* prefix, *endemic* means literally "in the population." Since the Tasmanian devil is found in the wild exclusively in Tasmania, scientists say it is "endemic to" that island. But the word can also mean simply "common" or "typical"; so we can say that corruption is endemic in the government of a country, that colds are "endemic in" nursery school, or that love of Barbie dolls is "endemic among" young American girls. Don't confuse *endemic* with *epidemic*; something can be endemic in a region for centuries without ever "exploding."

demagogue \\'de-mə-ˌgäg\\ A political leader who appeals to the emotions and prejudices of people in order to arouse discontent and to advance his or her own political purposes.

• His supporters called him a "man of the people"; his enemies called him a lying demagogue.

Demagogue was once defined by the writer H. L. Mencken as "one who will preach doctrines he knows to be untrue to men he knows to be idiots," and Mencken's definition still works quite well. The "doctrines" (ideas) preached by demagogues will naturally always be the kind that appeal directly to the ordinary voter, the "common man" or "little guy." Appealing to the common people is not itself a bad thing, but it has often been used by those who calculate that *demagoguery* (or *demagogy*) is the easiest way to power. In most countries, fear of *demagogic* leaders is so strong that voters aren't even permitted to vote directly for the nation's leader, but instead vote only for a local representative.

demotic \\di-'mä-tik\\ Popular or common.

• Partly because of television, the demotic language and accents of America's various regions have become more and more similar.

For many years *demotic* was used only to describe the writing of ancient Egypt, as the name of the script used by ordinary Egyptians rather than by their priests. *Demotic* is still an intellectual word, but it can now be used to describe any popular style in contrast to a style associated with a higher class, especially a style of speech or writing. So, for example, demotic Californian is different from demotic Texan. The most demotic dress today is probably blue jeans and sneakers, and those who wear them have demotic taste in fashion. The problem is, in American society it can sometimes be hard to find a style that *can't* be described as demotic.

POPUL comes from the Latin word meaning "people," and in fact forms the basis of the word *people* itself. So the *population* is the people of an area, and *popular* means not only "liked by many people" but also (as in *popular culture*) "relating to the general public."

populist \\'pä-pyə-list\\ A believer in the rights, wisdom, or virtues of the common people.

• He knew he would have to campaign as a populist in order to appeal to the working-class voters.

The word *populist* first appeared in the 1890s with the founding of the Populist Party, which stood for the interests of the farmers against the big-money interests. In later years *populism* came to be associated with the blue-collar class in the cities as well. Populism can be hard to predict. It sometimes has a religious tendency; it usually isn't very interested in international affairs; it has sometimes been unfriendly to immigrants and blacks; and it's often anti-intellectual. So populism often switches between liberal and conservative. But the *populist* style always shows its concern with Americans with average incomes as opposed to the rich and powerful.

populace \\'pä-pyủ-ləs\\ (1) The common people or masses. (2) Population.

• Perhaps Henry Ford's major achievement was to manufacture a car that practically the entire populace could afford—the Model T.

Populace is usually used to refer to all the people of a country. Thus, we're often told that an educated and informed populace is essential for a healthy American democracy. Franklin D. Roosevelt's famous radio "Fireside Chats" informed and reassured the American populace in the 1930s as we struggled through the Great Depression. We often hear about what "the general populace" is thinking or doing, but generalizing about something so huge can be tricky.

populous \\'pä-pyủ-ləs\\ Numerous, densely settled, or having a large population.

• Most Americans can't locate Indonesia, the fourth most populous country in the world, on a map.

With a metropolitan area of more than 20 million people, Mexico City could be called the world's second or third most populous city. And the nearby Aztec city of Tenochtitlán was one of the largest cities in the world even when Hernán Cortés arrived there in 1519. But by the time Cortés conquered the city in 1521 it wasn't nearly so populous, since European diseases had greatly reduced the population. Avoid confusing *populous* and *populace,* which are pronounced exactly the same.

vox populi \\'väks-'pä-pyü-,lī\ Popular sentiment or opinion.

• Successful politicians are always listening to the vox populi and adjusting their opinions or language accordingly.

Dating from at least the time of Charlemagne, the Latin saying "Vox populi, vox Dei" means literally "The voice of the people is the voice of God"—in other words, the people's voice is sacred, or the people are always right. Today, by means of modern opinion polls, we seem to hear the vox populi (or *vox pop* for short) year-round on every possible issue. But maybe we should occasionally keep in mind that full Charlemagne-era quotation: "Those people should not be listened to who keep saying the voice of the people is the voice of God, since the riotousness of the crowd is always very close to madness."

Quizzes

A.   Choose the closest definition:

1. demagogue   a. medium-sized city b. fiery politician
    c. democratic socialist d. new democracy
2. populace   a. politics b. numerous c. masses
    d. popularity
3. endemic   a. common b. absent c. infectious
    d. occasional
4. demotic   a. devilish b. common c. cultural d. useful
5. populous   a. well-liked b. foreign c. numerous
    d. obscure
6. demographic   a. describing politics b. describing
    populations c. describing policies d. describing
    epidemics
7. populist   a: communist b. campaigner c. socialist
    d. believer in the people
8. vox populi   a. public policy b. public survey c. public
    opinion d. public outrage

B. Indicate whether the following pairs of words have the same or different meanings:

1. demotic / common   same ___ / different ___
2. populist / politician   same ___ / different ___
3. endemic / locally common   same ___ / different ___
4. populace / popularity   same ___ / different ___
5. demographic / phonetic   same ___ / different ___
6. vox populi / mass sentiment   same ___ / different ___
7. demagogue / prophet   same ___ / different ___
8. populous / well-loved   same ___ / different ___

Animal Words

aquiline \\'a-kwə-ˌlīn\\ (1) Relating to eagles. (2) Curving like an eagle's beak.

* The surviving busts of noble Romans show that many of the men had strong aquiline noses.

Aquiline, from the Latin word meaning "eagle," is most often used to describe a nose that has a broad curve and is slightly hooked, like a beak. The aquiline figure on the U.S. seal brandishes the arrows of war and the olive branch of peace. The word for eagle itself, *Aquila,* has been given to a constellation in the northern hemisphere.

asinine \\'a-sə-ˌnīn\\ Foolish, brainless.

* He's not so great when he's sober, but when he's drunk he gets truly asinine.

The donkey, or *ass,* has often been accused of stubborn, willful, and stupid behavior lacking in logic and common sense. Asinine behavior exhibits similar qualities. Idiotic or rude remarks, aggressive stupidity, and general immaturity can all earn someone (usually a man) this description. If you call him this to his face, however, he might behave even worse.

bovine \\'bō-ˌvīn\\ (1) Relating to cows and oxen. (2) Placid, dull, unemotional.

* In that part of Texas, many of the veterinarians specialize in bovine conditions and won't even deal with dogs or cats.

Bovine comes from the Latin word for "cow," though the biological family called the Bovidae actually includes not only cows and oxen but also goats, sheep, bison, and buffalo. So *bovine* is often used technically, when discussing "bovine diseases," "bovine anatomy," and so on. It can also describe a human personality, though it can be a rather unkind way to describe someone. When Hera, the wife of Zeus, is called "cow-eyed," though, it's definitely a compliment, and Zeus fairly melts when she turns those big bovine eyes on him.

canine \ˈkā-ˌnīn\ Relating to dogs or the dog family; doglike.

• Pleasure in getting their tummies rubbed must be a basic canine trait, since all our dogs have loved it.

Dogs are prized for their talents and intelligence but aren't always given credit for their independence. Instead, tales of canine devotion and attachment are legendary; the old *Lassie* and *Rin-Tin-Tin* television series featured at least one heroic act of devotion per show. So we often hear people described as having "doglike devotion" or "doglike loyalty." But *canine* itself, unlike *doglike*, usually refers to four-legged creatures. *Canine* is not only an adjective but also a noun. Dogs and their relatives in the Canidae family—the wolves, jackals, foxes, and coyotes—are often called canines. And so are those two slightly pointed teeth a bit to the right and left of your front teeth.

feline \ˈfē-ˌlīn\ (1) Relating to cats or the cat family. (2) Like a cat in being sleek, graceful, sly, treacherous, or stealthy.

• The performers moved across the high wire with feline grace and agility.

Cats have always provoked a strong reaction from humans. The Egyptians worshipped them, leaving thousands of feline mummies and idols as evidence. In the Middle Ages, *felines* were feared as agents of the devil, and were thought to creep around silently at night doing evil. (Notice that *feline* is also a noun.) The fascinating family called the Felidae includes about 40 species of superb hunters, including the lions, tigers, jaguars, cheetahs, cougars, bobcats, and lynxes, and almost all of them are smooth, silent, and independent.

leonine \ˈlē-ə-ˌnīn\ Relating to lions; lionlike.

- As he conducted, Leonard Bernstein would fling his leonine mane wildly about.

The Latin word for "lion" is *leon,* so the names Leon, Leo, and Leona all mean "lion" as well. A leonine head usually has magnificent hair, like a male lion's mane. The leonine strength of Heracles (Hercules) is symbolized by the lion's pelt that he wears, the pelt of the fabled Nemean Lion which he had slain as one of his Twelve Labors. But leonine courage is what is so notably lacking in *The Wizard of Oz*'s Cowardly Lion.

porcine \\'pȯr-ˌsīn\\ Relating to pigs or swine; piglike.

- She describes her landlord's shape as porcine, and claims he has manners to match.

Pigs are rarely given credit for their high intelligence or their friendliness as pets, but instead are mocked for their habit of cooling themselves in mud puddles and the aggressive way they often go after food. While *porcine* isn't as negative a term as *swinish,* it may describe things that are fat, greedy, pushy, or generally piggish—but primarily fat. Porky Pig and Miss Piggy aren't particularly porcine in their behavior, only in their appearance—that is, pink and pudgy.

vulpine \\'vəl-ˌpīn\\ (1) Relating to foxes; foxlike. (2) Sneaky, clever, or crafty; foxy.

- She'd already decided she didn't like anything about him, especially the twitchiness, that vulpine face, and those darting eyes.

Foxes may be sleek and graceful runners with beautiful coats and tails, but they're almost impossible to keep out of the henhouse. Over the centuries they have "outfoxed" countless farmers. Because of the quick intelligence in their faces and their cunning nighttime raids, *vulpine* today almost always describes a face or manner that suggests a person capable of the same kind of sly scheming.

Quiz

Fill in each blank with the correct letter:

a. leonine   e. canine
b. aquiline   f. feline
c. porcine   g. vulpine
d. asinine   h. bovine

1. Collies and chow chows often have splendid _____ neck ruffs.
2. The dancers, in their black leotards, performed the piece with slinky, _____ grace.
3. Proud of the _____ curve of his nose, the star presents his profile to the camera in old silent films at every opportunity.
4. The slick fellow offering his services as guide had a disturbingly _____ air about him.
5. Some of the most beloved _____ traits, such as loyalty and playfulness, are often lacking in humans.
6. The last applicant she had interviewed struck her as passive and _____ and completely lacking in ambition.
7. Jeff and his crowd were in the balcony, catcalling, throwing down cans, and being generally _____.
8. She peeked out to see her _____ landlord climbing the stairs slowly, gasping for breath, with the eviction notice in his hand.

Review Quizzes

A. Choose the closest definition:

1. vulpine   a. reddish b. sly c. trustworthy d. furry
2. atheistic   a. boring b. godless c. roundabout
         d. contagious
3. adumbrate   a. revise b. punish c. advertise d. outline
4. populous   a. numerous b. populated c. popular
         d. common
5. iconoclast   a. icon painter b. dictator c. dissident
         d. tycoon

6. endemic   a. local b. neighborly c. sensational
   d. foreign
7. iconic   a. wealthy b. famous c. indirect d. symbolic
8. feline   a. sleek b. clumsy c. crazy d. fancy
9. pantheon   a. mall b. road race c. trouser store
   d. hall of fame
10. icon   a. psychic b. leader c. symbol d. prophet
11. urbane   a. calm b. elegant c. excited d. secure
12. horticulture   a. interior decoration b. food science
    c. horse breeding d. plant growing
13. demotic   a. reduced b. common c. upper-class
    d. demented
14. luminary   a. ruler b. lantern c. lighting designer
    d. celebrity
15. travesty   a. farce b. outfit c. transportation d. success
16. divest   a. add on b. take off c. take in d. add up

B. Fill in each blank with the correct letter:

a. populist   f. apotheosis
b. demographic   g. bovine
c. theocracy   h. populace
d. investiture   i. vulpine
e. aquiline   j. cross-cultural

1. The _____ of the great Albert Einstein seemed to occur
   while he was still living.
2. _____ surveys often divide the U.S. population by
   income and education.
3. Nothing ever seemed to disturb her pleasant but _____
   manner.
4. He was interested in _____ studies that showed that
   these kinds of cancers don't appear in African tribal
   populations.
5. The _____ of the society's new leader was a secret and
   solemn event.
6. With his _____ nose, he looked like a member of the
   ancient Roman senate.
7. He had a nervous, _____ manner, with a tense alertness
   and shifty eyes.
8. She ran her campaigns as a _____, a champion of the
   common man, though she herself had a great deal of
   money.

9. The general ____ has never cared much about foreign policy except when the country goes to war.

10. In a true ____, the legal punishments are often those called for in the holy books.

C. Match the word on the left to the correct definition on the right:

1.	porcine	a.	half-shadow
2.	divest	b.	doglike
3.	asinine	c.	brown
4.	penumbra	d.	public opinion
5.	leonine	e.	cross-dresser
6.	umber	f.	symbolic
7.	vox populi	g.	foolish
8.	iconic	h.	plump
9.	transvestite	i.	lionlike
10.	canine	j.	get rid of

UNIT

13

CORD, from the Latin word for "heart," turns up in several common English words. So does its Greek relative *card-*, which is familiar to us in words such as *cardiac*, "relating to the heart."

accord \ə-'kȯrd\ (1) To grant. (2) To be in harmony; agree.

- What she told police under questioning didn't accord with the accounts of the other witnesses.

A new federal law may accord with—or be in *accordance* with— the guidelines that a company has already established. The rowdy behavior of the hero Beowulf accords with Norse ideals of the early Middle Ages; but such behavior wouldn't have been in accordance with the ideals of a later young lord from the same general region, Shakespeare's Prince Hamlet. *Accord* is also a noun, meaning "agreement." Thus, we often hear of two countries signing a peace accord; and we also frequently hear of two things or people being "in accord with" each other.

concord \'kän-ˌkȯrd\ (1) A state of agreement: harmony. (2) A formal agreement.

- In 1801 Napoleon signed a concord with the pope reestablishing the Catholic Church in France.

The roots of *concord* suggest the meaning "hearts together." At the very outset of the American Revolution, the town of Concord, Massachusetts, was the site of a famous battle—obviously not exactly in keeping with its name. It shares that name with the capital of New Hampshire and a few other towns and cities, and *Concordia*, the original Latin word for "concord," is the name of several Lutheran universities. Today *concord* is a rather formal term, probably most often used to mean a specific agreement; thus, two countries may sign a concord on matters that have led to trouble in the past.

cordial \\ˈkȯr-jəl\\ Warm, friendly, gracious.

• After the meeting, the president extended a cordial invitation to everyone for coffee at her own house.

Anything that is cordial comes from the heart. Cordial greetings to friends on the street, or cordial relations between two countries, are warm without being passionate. *Cordial* is also a noun, which originally meant any stimulating medicine or drink that was thought to be good for the heart. Today a cordial is a liqueur, a sweetened alcoholic drink with interesting flavoring. Cordials such as crème de menthe, Drambuie, or Benedictine are alcoholic enough to warm the spirits and the heart.

discordant \\dis-ˈkȯr-dənt\\ Being at odds, conflicting, not in harmony.

• The first discordant note at dinner was struck by my cousin, when he claimed the president was only interested in taking away our guns.

Discord, a word more common in earlier centuries than today, means basically "conflict," so *discordant* often means "conflicting." The opinions of Supreme Court justices are frequently discordant; justices who disagree with the Court's decision usually write a dissenting opinion. *Discordant* is often used with a somewhat musical meaning, suggesting that a single wrong note or harmony has been heard in the middle of a performance—even though musical words such as *chord* actually come from a different Latin word, meaning "cord" or "string" (a reference to the strings of ancient instruments such as the lyre).

CULP comes from the Latin word for "guilt." Its best-known appearance in English is probably in *culprit,* meaning someone who is guilty of a crime.

---

culpable \\ˈkəl-pə-bəl\\ Deserving to be condemned or blamed.

- The company was found guilty of culpable negligence in allowing the chemical waste to leak into the groundwater.

Culpable normally means simply "guilty." To a lawyer, "culpable negligence" is carelessness so serious that it becomes a crime—for instance, building a swimming pool in your suburban yard with no fence around it, so that a neighbor's child could fall in and drown. But degrees of *culpability* are important in the law; someone who intended to do harm always faces a more serious challenge in court than someone who was merely careless.

exculpate \\'ek-skəl-ˌpāt\\ To clear from accusations of fault or guilt.

- The girls aren't proud of what they did that night, but they've been exculpated by witnesses and won't be facing criminal charges.

Exculpate gets its meaning from the prefix *ex-*, which here means "out of" or "away from." A suspected murderer may be exculpated by the confession of another person. And *exculpatory* evidence is the kind that defense lawyers are always looking for.

inculpate \\in-'kəl-ˌpāt\\ To accuse or incriminate; to show evidence of someone's involvement in a fault or crime.

- It was his own father who finally inculpated him, though without intending to.

Inculpate is the opposite of *exculpate*, just as *inculpatory* evidence is the opposite of *exculpatory* evidence. By inculpating someone else, an accused person may manage to exculpate himself. Through plea bargaining, the prosecution can often encourage a defendant to inculpate his friends in return for a lighter sentence.

mea culpa \\ˌmā-ə-'kùl-pə\\ An admission of personal fault or error.

- The principal said his mea culpa at the school board meeting, but not all the parents were satisfied.

Mea culpa, Latin for "through my fault," comes from the prayer in the Catholic mass in which, back when Latin was still the language of the mass, one would confess to having sinned "mea culpa, mea culpa, mea maxima culpa" ("through my fault, through my fault, through my most grievous fault"). When we say "Mea culpa" today, it means "I apologize" or "It was my fault." But *mea culpa* is also common as a noun. So, for instance, a book may be a long mea culpa for the author's past treatment of women, or an oil company may issue a mea culpa after a tanker runs aground.

Quizzes

A. Choose the closest definition:

1. exculpate   a. convict b. prove innocent c. suspect
     d. prove absent
2. discordant   a. insulting b. relieved c. unlimited
     d. conflicting
3. culpable   a. disposable b. refundable c. guilty
     d. harmless
4. cordial   a. hateful b. friendly c. fiendish d. cool
5. inculpate   a. incorporate b. resist c. accuse
     d. offend
6. concord   a. generosity b. straightness c. agreement
     d. pleasure
7. mea culpa   a. rejection b. apology c. excuse
     d. forgiveness
8. accord   a. harmonize b. accept c. distress d. convince

B. Match the definition on the left to the correct word on the right:

1. accuse   a. accord
2. excuse   b. concord
3. goodwill   c. mea culpa
4. heartfelt   d. discordant
5. grant   e. culpable
6. blamable   f. cordial
7. disagreeing   g. inculpate
8. confession   h. exculpate

DICT comes from *dicere,* the Latin word meaning "to speak." So a *dictionary* is a treasury of words for speaking. And a *contradiction* (with its prefix *contra-,* "against") speaks against or denies something.

diction \\'dik-shən\ (1) Choice of words, especially with regard to correctness, clearness, or effectiveness. (2) Clarity of speech.

• Our CEO is determined to appear in some TV ads, but he first needs to work on his diction with a vocal coach.

When your English teacher complains about some of the words you chose to use in an essay, she's talking about your diction. She may also use the term when commenting on the word choices made by a poet, and why a particular word was the best one possible in a particular line. (Compare *syntax*, p. 660.) But the second meaning of *diction* is just as common, and your English teacher might use that one on you as well, especially when she's asked you to read something aloud and you mumble your way through it.

edict \\'ē-ˌdikt\ (1) An official announcement that has the force of a law. (2) An order or command.

• In 1989 an edict by the leader of Iran pronouncing a death sentence on a British novelist stunned the world.

Edicts are few and far between in a democracy, since very few important laws can be made by a president or prime minister acting alone. But when a crisis arose in the Roman Republic, the senate would appoint a *dictator,* who would have the power to rule by edict. The idea was that the dictator could make decisions quickly, issuing his edicts faster than the senate could act. When the crisis was over, the edicts were canceled and the dictator usually retired from public life. Things are different today: dictators almost always install themselves in power, and they never give it up.

jurisdiction \ˌjùr-is-'dik-shən\ (1) The power or right to control or exercise authority. (2) The territory where power may be exercised.

• Unluckily for the defendants, the case fell within the jurisdiction of the federal court rather than the more tolerant state court.

Questions of jurisdiction are generally technical legal matters. The most important ones include which court will hear a given case and which law-enforcement agency can get involved. But although they may seem like mere technicalities, *jurisdictional* matters sometimes turn out to be all-important in the final outcome. Jurisdiction may depend on where you are (for example, in which state), on who you are (if you're a juvenile, for example, you may only be tried in juvenile court), and on what the subject is (for example, cases involving the estate left by someone who has died are dealt with in probate court).

dictum \\'dik-təm\ A formal and authoritative statement.

• It has long been a dictum of American foreign policy that the government doesn't negotiate with kidnappers and terrorists.

The word *dictum* is frequently used in philosophy, but also in economics, political science, and other fields. Almost any condensed piece of wisdom—"The perfect is the enemy of the good," "Buy low, sell high," "All politics is local," etc.—can be called a dictum. In the law, judges may often add to a written opinion an *obiter dictum,* or "statement made in passing"—a strong statement that isn't directly relevant to the case being decided. If they're well thought out and eloquent, *obiter dicta* (notice the plural form) may be referred to by later judges and lawyers for years afterward.

GNI/GNO comes from a Greek and Latin verb meaning "to know," and can be found at the root of *know* itself. Among other words built from this root, you may *recognize* ("know again") some and be *ignorant* of ("not know") others. But only an *ignoramus* would know absolutely none of them.

---

cognitive \\'käg-nə-tiv\ (1) Having to do with the process of knowing, including awareness, judgment, and understanding. (2) Based on factual knowledge that has been or can be gained by experience.

• A child isn't a computer; a third-grader's cognitive abilities are highly dependent on his or her upbringing and happiness.

Cognitive skills and knowledge involve the ability to acquire factual information, often the kind of knowledge that can easily be tested. So *cognition* should be distinguished from social, emotional, and creative development and ability. *Cognitive science* is a growing field of study that deals with human perception, thinking, and learning.

agnostic \ag-'nä-stik\ A person who believes that whether God exists is not known and probably cannot be known.

• Both of them were always agnostics, but after they had children they started attending church again.

The words *agnostic* and *agnosticism* were coined around 1870 by the great English biologist T. H. Huxley, who had just spent a decade defending the works of Charles Darwin against the attacks of the church. Scientists often put a high value on evidence when arguing about religion, and many *agnostic* thinkers believe that human minds simply aren't equipped to grasp the nature of God. But agnostics differ from *atheists*, who actually claim that no God exists and may even think they can prove it. You may have seen the similar word *gnostic*, the name for followers of certain religious sects from around the time of Christ that sought spiritual knowledge and rejected the material world. An increasing interest in *gnosticism* today can be seen in the popular novels of Philip Pullman, Dan Brown, and Neil Gaiman.

incognito \ˌin-ˌkäg-ˈnē-tō\ In disguise, or with one's identity concealed.

* Years after her reign as a top Hollywood star, she was discovered working incognito as a bartender in Manhattan while living in cheap hotels.

In a famous myth, Zeus and Hermes visit a village incognito to test the villagers. The seemingly poor travelers are turned away from every household except that of Baucis and Philemon. This elderly couple, though very poor themselves, provide the disguised gods with a feast. When the gods finally reveal themselves, they reward the couple generously for their hospitality, but destroy the rest of the village.

prognosis \präg-ˈnō-səs\ (1) The chance of recovery from a given disease or condition. (2) A forecast or prophecy.

* The prognosis for a patient with chicken pox is usually excellent; the prognosis for someone with liver cancer is terrible.

With its prefix *pro-*, meaning "before," *prognosis* means basically "knowledge beforehand" of how a situation is likely to turn out. *Prognosis* was originally a strictly medical term, but it soon broadened to include predictions made by experts of all kinds. Thus, for example, economists are constantly offering prognoses (notice the irregular plural form) about where the economy is going, and climate scientists regularly *prognosticate* about how quickly the earth's atmosphere is warming.

Quizzes

A. Fill in each blank with the correct letter:

a. agnostic   e. diction
b. dictum   f. incognito
c. cognitive   g. edict
d. jurisdiction   h. prognosis

1. Psychology is not entirely a ____ science, since it deals with behavior as well as the mind.
2. He often repeated Balzac's famous ____: "Behind every great fortune is a great crime."
3. Movie stars often go out in public ____, in faded sweatshirts, worn-out pants, and sunglasses.
4. When their dictatorial grandfather issued an ____, everyone obeyed it.
5. She has strong opinions about lots of public issues, but she's an ____ about foreign policy.
6. The ____ for the world's climate in the next century is uncertain.
7. He complains about his students' ____, saying they mumble so much that he often can't understand them.
8. The judge refused to consider two elements in the case, saying that they lay outside his ____.

B. Indicate whether the following pairs of words have the same or different meanings:

1. agnostic / complex   same ___ / different ___
2. cognitive / digestive   same ___ / different ___
3. diction / wordiness   same ___ / different ___
4. dictum / declaration   same ___ / different ___
5. incognito / hospitable   same ___ / different ___
6. jurisdiction / authority   same ___ / different ___
7. prognosis / outlook   same ___ / different ___
8. edict / order   same ___ / different ___

GRAPH comes from the Greek verb *graphein*, "to write." Thus, a *biography* is a written account of someone's life (see BIO, p. 407), a *discography* is a written list of recordings on disc (records or CDs), and a *filmography* is a list of motion pictures. But lots of uses of *-graph* and *-graphy* don't mean literally "writing" (as in *autograph* or *paragraph*), but instead something more like "recording," as in *photography*, *seismograph*, or *graph* itself.

calligraphy \kə-ˈli-grə-fē\ The art of producing beautiful hand-writing.

• Calligraphy can be seen today in event invitations, logo designs, and stone inscriptions.

Kalli- is a Greek root meaning "beautiful," and "beautiful" in the case of *calligraphy* means artistic, stylized, and elegant. Calligraphy has existed in many cultures, including Indian, Persian, and Islamic cultures; Arabic puts a particularly high value on beautiful script, and in East Asia calligraphy has long been considered a major art. Calligraphers in the West use pens with wide nibs, with which they produce strokes of widely differing width within a single letter.

hagiography \ˌha-gē-ˈä-grə-fē\ (1) Biography of saints. (2) Biography that idealizes or idolizes.

• According to the new biography, which should really be called a hagiography, the former prime minister doesn't seem to have done anything small-minded or improper in his entire life.

For those able to read, reading stories of the lives of the saints was a popular pastime for centuries, and books collecting short saints' biographies were best sellers. These often included terrifically colorful stories (about slaying dragons, magically traveling through space, etc.) that were perhaps a bit too good to be strictly true, and after finding God not one of them ever did a single thing that wasn't saintly—and some of them may not have actually existed. Still today, *hagiographic* accounts of the lives of politicians and pop-culture stars are being written, though there now seems to be a bigger audience for biographies that seek out the not-so-wholesome secrets of the person's life, sometimes even making up a few of them.

choreography \ˌkȯr-ē-ˈä-grə-fē\ (1) The art of composing and arranging dances and of representing them in symbolic notation. (2) The movements by dancers in a performance.

- The reviews praised the show for its eye-catching choreography, calling it the best element of the whole musical.

In ancient Greece, a *choreia* was a circular dance accompanied by a singing *chorus*. But the actual notating of dances by means of symbols didn't begin until the 17th or 18th century, when ballet developed into a complex art form in France. The *choreographer* of a major ballet, which might run to an hour or more, will always record his or her work in notation, though *choreographing* a five-minute segment for a TV talent show usually doesn't require any record at all.

lithograph \\'li-thə-ˌgraf\\ A picture made by printing from a flat surface (such as a smooth stone) prepared so that the ink will only stick to the design that will be printed.

- To make a lithograph, the artist first draws an image, in reverse, on a fine-grained limestone or aluminum plate.

Lithos is Greek for "stone," and a stone surface has traditionally been involved in lithography, though a metal plate may take its place today. The *lithographic* process was invented around 1796 and soon became the main method of printing books and newspapers. Artists use *lithography* to produce prints (works intended to be sold in many copies), and art lithographs sometimes resemble older types of prints, including etchings, engravings, and woodcuts. Pablo Picasso, Marc Chagall, Joan Miró, and M. C. Escher are among the many artists who have used lithography to produce important original works. Today lithographic printing accounts for over 40% of all printing, packaging, and publishing.

ART comes from the Latin word for "skill." This reminds us that, until a few centuries ago, almost no one made a strong distinction between skilled craftsmanship and what we would now call "art." And the word *art* itself could also mean simply "cleverness." The result is that this root appears in some words where we might not expect it.

---

artful \\'ärt-fəl\\ (1) Skillful. (2) Wily, crafty, sly.

- It was an artful solution: each side was pleased with the agreement, but it was the lawyer himself who stood to make the most money off of it.

A writer may produce an artful piece of prose, one that's clearly and elegantly written. The same writer might also make an artful argument, one that cleverly leaves out certain details and plays up others so as to make a stronger case. In the first instance, the prose is well crafted; in the second, the argument might instead be called crafty. But even though both uses are correct, most of us still use *artful* somewhat differently from *artistic*.

artifact \ˈär-ti-ˌfakt\ A usually simple object made by human workmanship, such as a tool or ornament, that represents a culture or a stage in a culture's development.

* Through the artifacts found by archaeologists, we now know a considerable amount about how the early Anasazi people of the Southwest lived.

One of the things that make humans unique is their ability to make and use tools, and ever since the first rough stone axes began to appear about 700,000 years ago, human cultures have left behind artifacts from which we've tried to draw a picture of their everyday life. The roots of artifact mean basically "something made with skill"; thus, a mere stone that was used for pounding isn't an artifact, since it wasn't shaped by humans for its purpose—unlike a ram's horn that was polished and given a brass mouthpiece and was blown as part of a religious ritual.

artifice \ˈär-tə-fəs\ (1) Clever skill. (2) A clever trick.

* By his cunning and artifice, Iago convinces Othello that Desdemona has been unfaithful.

Artifice can be a tricky word to use. It combines the same roots as *artifact,* so it's sometimes seen in descriptions of craftsmanship ("The artifice that went into this jewelry can still astound us," "The chef had used all his artifice to disguise the nature of the meat"). But it can also be used for many situations that don't involve physical materials ("They had gotten around the rules by a clever artifice," "The artifice of the plot is ingenious"). Like its adjective, *artificial*, *artifice* isn't necessarily either positive nor negative. But both words can make us slightly uncomfortable if we like to think of simplicity and naturalness as important values.

artisan \ˈär-tə-zən\ A skilled worker or craftsperson.

- At the fair, they saw examples of the best carving, pottery, and jewelry by local artisans.

Artisans aren't the same as *artists*, but it can sometimes be hard to tell the difference. In the Middle Ages, artisans organized themselves into guilds. In every city each group of artisans—weavers, carpenters, shoemakers, and so on—had its own guild, which set wages and prices, kept standards high, and protected its members from outside competitors. In America, however, most artisans have always been fiercely independent. Today, when factories produce almost all of our goods, artisans usually make only fine objects for those who can afford them. And we now even include food among the artisan's crafts, so you can buy *artisanal* cheeses, breads, and chocolates—but probably not if you're watching your budget.

Quizzes

A. **Fill in each blank with the correct letter:**

a. choreography	e. calligraphy
b. lithograph	f. hagiography
c. artful	g. artifact
d. artisan	h. artifice

1. The strangest _____ they had dug up was a bowl on which an extremely odd animal was painted.
2. A signed _____ by Picasso wouldn't be valued nearly as highly as one of his paintings.
3. She admired the _____, but the dancers didn't seem to have practiced enough.
4. He'd done an _____ job of writing the proposal so as to appeal to each board member who would have to approve it.
5. In his spare time he practiced _____, using special pens to write short quotations suitable for framing.
6. Each room in the palace was a masterpiece of _____, from its wall paintings to its chandeliers to its delicate furniture.
7. Each worker at the tiny textile workshop thought of himself or herself as an _____.

8. The book was pure _____, painting its statesman hero as not only brilliant but saintly.

B. Match the definition on the left to the correct word on the right:

1. craftsperson   a. artful
2. saint's biography   b. artifice
3. ingenious   c. lithograph
4. print   d. choreography
5. clever skill   e. artisan
6. beautiful handwriting f. hagiography
7. man-made object   g. calligraphy
8. dance design   h. artifact

FORT comes from *fortis*, Latin for "strong." The familiar noun *fort*, meaning a building strengthened against possible attacks, comes directly from it. And our verb *comfort* actually means "to give strength and hope to."

---

fortify \ˈfȯr-tə-ˌfī\ To strengthen.

• Fortified by a good night's sleep and a big breakfast, they set off for the final 20 miles of their journey.

Medieval cities were fortified against attack by high walls, and volunteers may fortify a levee against an overflowing river by means of sandbags. Foods can be fortified by adding vitamins, but "fortified wines," such as sherry and port, have brandy (a "stronger" drink) rather than vitamins added to them. By adopting good exercise habits, you can fortify your body against illness. And fortifying needn't always be physical. An author's reputation may be fortified by the success of his new book, or a prosecutor can fortify a case against a suspect by finding more evidence.

fortification \ˌfȯr-tə-fə-ˈkā-shən\ (1) The building of military defenses to protect a place against attack. (2) A structure built to protect a place.

• The city's fortifications had withstood powerful assaults by catapults, battering rams, and tall siege towers that rolled up to release soldiers onto the top of the walls.

In the Middle Ages, many European cities were entirely enclosed by sturdy walls, with walkways along the top and towers at intervals, designed to make an invasion impossible. A water-filled ditch, or moat, might run alongside the wall for added defense. Such defenses turned the entire city into a *fort*, or *fortress*. Over the centuries, fortifications changed steadily with the development of new weaponry. In World War II, the German fortification of the French coast included antitank barriers, bunkers, minefields, and underwater obstacles, but it wasn't enough to turn back the immense force of the Allied invasion on D-day.

forte \\ˈfȯrt, ˈfȯr-ˌtā, fȯr-ˈtā\\ Something that a person does particularly well; one's strong point.

• Her forte was statistics, and she was always at a disadvantage when the discussion turned to public policy.

In the Middle Ages, swords were often known to break in battle, so the strongest part of a sword's blade—the part between the handle (or hilt) and the middle of the blade—was given a name, the *forte*. Today a forte is usually a special strength. But no one can agree on how to pronounce it: all three pronunciations shown above are heard frequently. Part of the problem is confusion with the Italian musical term *forte* (always pronounced /ˈfȯr-ˌtā/), meaning "loud."

fortitude \\ˈfȯr-tə-ˌtüd\\ Mental strength that allows one to face danger, pain, or hardship with courage.

• He's just too nice, and we worry that he won't have the fortitude to deal with the monsters in that office.

How many people know that the famous marble lions that guard the steps of the New York Public Library in Manhattan are named Patience and Fortitude? In Latin, the quality of *fortitudo* combines physical strength, vigor, courage, and boldness, but the English *fortitude* usually means simply firmness and steadiness of will, or "backbone." The philosopher Plato long ago listed four essential human virtues—prudence (i.e., good judgment), justice (i.e., ability to be fair in balancing between one's own interests and others'), temperance (i.e., moderation or restraint), and fortitude, and in Christian tradition these became known as the four "cardinal virtues."

CIS comes from the Latin verb meaning "to cut, cut down, or slay." An *incisor* is one of the big front biting teeth; beavers and woodchucks have especially large ones. A *decision* "cuts off" previous discussion and uncertainty.

concise \kən-'sīs\ Brief and condensed, especially in expression or statement.

• Professor Childs's exam asked for a concise, one-page summary of the causes of the American Revolution.

Many students think that adding unnecessary sentences with long words will make their writing more impressive. But in fact almost every reader values *concision*, since concise writing is usually easier to read, better thought out, and better organized—that is, simply better writing. Words such as *short* don't have the full meaning of *concise*, which usually means not just "brief" but "packed with information."

excise \'ek-ˌsīz\ To cut out, especially surgically.

• The ancient Minoans from the island of Crete apparently excised the hearts of their human sacrifices.

Excise takes part of its meaning from the prefix *ex-*, "out." A writer may excise long passages of a novel to reduce it to a reasonable length, or a film director may excise a scene that might give offense. A surgeon may excise a large cancerous tumor, or make a tiny *excision* to examine an organ's tissue. *Excise* is also a noun, meaning a tax paid on something manufactured and sold in the U.S. Much of what consumers pay for tobacco or alcohol products go to cover the excise taxes that the state and federal government charge the manufacturers. But it's only accidental that this noun is spelled like the verb, since it comes from a completely different source.

incisive \in-'sī-siv\ Impressively direct and decisive.

• A few incisive questions were all that was needed to expose the weakness in the prosecutor's case.

From its roots, *incise* means basically "to cut into." So just as a doctor uses a scalpel to make an *incision* in the skin, an incisive remark cuts into the matter at hand. A good analyst makes incisive comments about a news story, cutting through the unimportant details, and a good critic *incisively* identifies a book's strengths and weaknesses.

precision \pri-ˈsi-zhən\ Exactness and accuracy.

* By junior year she was speaking with greater precision, searching for exact words in place of the crude, awkward language of her friends.

Many of us often use *precision* and *accuracy* as synonyms, but not scientists and engineers. For them, accuracy describes a particular measurement—that is, how close it is to the truth. But precision describes a measurement system—that is, how good it is at giving the same result every time it measures the same thing. This may be why even nonscientists now often speak of "precision instruments" for measuring, "precision landings" made by airplanes, "precision drilling" for natural gas, and so on.

Quizzes

A. Fill in each blank with the correct letter:

a.	forte	e.	concise
b.	fortify	f.	excise
c.	fortification	g.	incisive
d.	precision	h.	fortitude

1. Ms. Raymond's report was _____ but managed to discuss all the issues.
2. Carpentry isn't his _____, but he could probably build something simple like a bed.
3. They could _____ their theory by positive results from some more experiments.
4. The judge was deeply knowledgeable about the case, and his questions to both lawyers were _____.
5. The last Spanish _____ along the river proved to be the most difficult one for the French forces to take.
6. Whenever she was on the verge of despair, she remembered her grandfather's words about _____ being the character trait most important for success.
7. Before eating an apple, some people carefully _____ the brown spots.

8. What the tipsy darts players lacked in _____ they made up for in enthusiasm.

B. Choose the closest definition:

1. precision   a. accuracy   b. beauty   c. brilliance   d. dependence
2. fortitude   a. armor   b. endurance   c. skill   d. weapon
3. excise   a. add   b. examine   c. refuse   d. cut out
4. forte   a. discipline   b. force   c. castle   d. special strength
5. incisive   a. damaging   b. sharp   c. lengthy   d. definite
6. fortification   a. diet   b. exercise   c. stronghold   d. belief
7. concise   a. concentrated   b. sure   c. shifting   d. blunt
8. fortify   a. attack   b. strengthen   c. struggle   d. excite

Animal Words

apiary \ˈā-pē-ˌer-ē\ A place where bees are kept for their honey.

- Apple orchards are excellent sites for apiaries, since the bees keep the apple trees productive by pollinating them.

Beekeeping, or *apiculture*, is the care of honeybees that ensures that they produce more honey than they can use. An apiary usually consists of many separate beehives. The social life of a hive is strange and marvelous. The queen bee, who will become the mother of an entire colony, is actually created by being fed "royal jelly" while she is still only a larva. The tens of thousands of worker bees are underdeveloped females; only a handful of the bees are male, and they do no work at all. The workers defend the hive by kamikaze means, stinging any intruder and dying as they do so. There's more drama in a quiet-looking apiary than the casual observer might notice.

caper \ˈkā-pər\ (1) A playful leap. (2) A prank or mischievous adventure.

- For their caper in the girls' bathroom, all three seniors were suspended for a week.

Caper in Latin means "a male goat." Anyone who has watched a young goat frolic in a field or clamber onto the roof of a car knows the kind of crazy fun the English word *caper*—which is also a verb—

is referring to. A *capriole* is a backward kick done in midair by a trained horse. *Capricorn,* meaning "horned goat," is a constellation and one of the signs of the zodiac. And a *capricious* act is one that's done with as little thought as a frisky goat might give it.

equestrian \i-'kwes-trē-ən\ Of or relating to horseback riding.

- The circus's equestrian acts, in which bareback riders performed daring acrobatic feats atop prancing horses, were her favorites.

Equestrian comes from *equus,* Latin for "horse." Old statues of military heroes, like the famous one of General Sherman on New York's Fifth Avenue, are frequently equestrian. In these sculptures the man always sits nobly upright on a horse, but the horse's stance varies; depending on whether the rider was killed in battle or survived, was victorious or defeated, the horse traditionally stands with four, three, or two hooves on the ground. Equestrian statues have been popular through the centuries, because until the 20th century almost every officer in Europe and America was trained in equestrian skills and combat.

lupine \'lü-ˌpīn\ Like a wolf; wolfish.

- Doctors reported that the boy showed lupine behavior such as snarling and biting, and walked with his knees bent in a kind of crouch.

Lupine comes from *lupus,* Latin for "wolf," and its related adjective *lupinus,* "wolfish." Lupine groups have a highly organized social structure, with leaders and followers clearly distinguished; dogs, since they're descended from wolves, often show these lupine patterns when living in groups. Stories of children raised by wolves (the most famous being Romulus, the legendary founder of Rome) have generally been hard to prove, partly because "wild" children lack human language abilities and can't describe their experiences. *Lupine* is also a noun, the name of a well-known garden flower, which was once thought to drain, or "wolf," the soil of its nutrients.

ovine \'ō-ˌvīn\ Of, relating to, or resembling sheep.

- In her veterinary practice she specialized in ovine medicine, but often treated cows and pigs as well.

Sheep belong to the same family of mammals as goats, antelope, bison, buffalo, and cows. The genus *Ovis* includes at least five species, including the domestic sheep. Some 12,000 years ago, in the area now known as Iraq, sheep became one of the first animals to be domesticated; only the dog is known to have been tamed earlier. At first, they were valued for their milk, skin, and meat (mutton and lamb); not until about 1500 B.C. did the weaving of wool begin. Today a billion sheep are being farmed worldwide. The term *ovine* (which is a noun as well as an adjective) is mostly used in scientific and medical writing—which means you could impress your friends by dropping it into a casual conversation.

ornithologist \ˌȯr-nə-ˈthä-lə-jist\ A person who studies birds.

• John James Audubon, the great painter of the birds of early America, was also a writing ornithologist of great importance.

The Greek root *ornith-* means "bird," so *ornithology* is the study of birds. Amateur ornithology, usually called *birding* or *birdwatching,* is an extraordinarily popular pastime in America, where over 40 million people pursue it. Roger Tory Peterson's many field guides have long been some of the amateur ornithologist's most useful tools. Amateurs often make essential contributions to serious ornithology, as in the annual Christmas Bird Count, when tens of thousands of birders fan out across North and South America to produce a kind of census of all the species in the New World.

serpentine \ˈsər-pən-ˌtīn\ Like a snake or serpent in shape or movement; winding.

• The Great Wall of China, the greatest construction of all time, wends its serpentine way for some 4,000 miles across the Chinese landscape.

A snake moves by curving and winding along the ground. Roads through the Pyrenees, the mountains that separate Spain from France, tend to be serpentine, curving back and forth on themselves up and down the steep slopes. *Serpentine* has other meanings as well. As a noun, it's the name for a soft green mineral, and also for the party streamers you might throw at midnight on New Year's Eve. The *serpentine belt* under the hood in your car is the long, looping belt that most of the car's accessories—the AC, the power steering, the alternator, and so on—depend on to get their power.

simian \ˈsi-mē-ən\ Having to do with monkeys or apes; monkey-like.

- Every afternoon the pale youth could be found watching the simian antics in the Monkey House with strange intensity.

The Latin word for "ape" is *simia,* which itself comes from *simus,* "snub-nosed." *Simian* is usually a scientific word; thus, for instance, biologists study simian viruses in the search for cures to AIDS and other diseases. But *simian* can be used by the rest of us to describe human behavior. Human babies often cling to their mothers in a simian way, and kids playing on a jungle gym may look like *simians.* But if you notice that a friend has a simian style of walking or eating bananas, it might be best not to tell him.

Quiz

Indicate whether the following pairs have the same or different meanings:

1. equestrian / horselike   same ___ / different ___
2. ornithologist / studier of birds   same ___ / different ___
3. lupine / apelike   same ___ / different ___
4. apiary / monkey colony   same ___ / different ___
5. ovine / goatlike   same ___ / different ___
6. caper / leap   same ___ / different ___
7. simian / catlike   same ___ / different ___
8. serpentine / winding   same ___ / different ___

Review Quizzes

A. Fill in each blank with the correct letter:

a.	artisan	i.	inculpate
b.	edict	j.	serpentine
c.	equestrian	k.	precision
d.	artifact	l.	artifice
e.	discordant	m.	prognosis
f.	cognitive	n.	simian
g.	apiary	o.	jurisdiction
h.	exculpate		

1. The farmer tended his ＿＿ lovingly and gathered delicious wildflower honey every year.
2. In trying to ＿＿ herself, she only made herself look guiltier.
3. They arrived in time to see the top riders compete in the championship ＿＿ event.
4. The doctor's ＿＿ is guarded, but she is cautiously optimistic that recovery will be complete.
5. It was a tall vase, with elaborate ＿＿ shapes winding around it from top to bottom.
6. Each side's anger at the other has set a sadly ＿＿ tone for the negotiations.
7. We set the clock with great ＿＿ on the first day of every new year.
8. He's trying hard to ＿＿ as many of his friends in the crime as he can.
9. These beautiful handblown goblets were obviously made by a talented ＿＿.
10. The final ＿＿ from the presidential palace commanded every citizen to wear a baseball cap at all times.
11. The child scrambled over the wall with ＿＿ agility.
12. They're worried about their son's mental health, though the doctors say his ＿＿ skills are fine.
13. She found a small clay ＿＿ in the shape of a bear at the site of the ancient temple.
14. He used every ＿＿ imaginable to hide his real age from the television cameras.
15. Firing local teachers falls outside the superintendant's actual ＿＿.

B. Choose the correct *antonym*:

1. accord   a. harmonize b. strengthen c. differ d. agree
2. incisive   a. dull b. noble c. faulty d. exceptional
3. artful   a. lovely b. sly c. talented d. awkward
4. forte   a. weak point b. sword c. quarrel d. pinnacle
5. cordial   a. lazy b. cool c. terrific d. heartfelt
6. incognito   a. indoors b. in disguise c. as oneself d. as you were
7. fortify   a. construct b. reinforce c. supply d. weaken
8. concise   a. lengthy b. wide c. dated d. brief

9. culpable   a. prisonlike b. misleading c. guilty
     d. innocent
10. concord   a. belief b. conflict c. deception d. peace

C. Choose the closest definition:

1. ornithologist   a. student of fish b. student of words
     c. student of birds d. student of wolves
2. mea culpa   a. through my eyes b. through my fault
     c. through my door d. through my work
3. lupine   a. foxy b. horselike c. sheepish d. wolfish
4. discordant   a. energetic b. temporary c. phony
     d. clashing
5. jurisdiction   a. area of power b. area of coverage
     c. area of damage d. area of target
6. excise   a. call out b. hold out c. cut out d. fold out
7. choreography   a. book design b. dance script c. choir
     practice d. bird study
8. ovine   a. oval b. egglike c. sheep-related d. birdlike
9. dictum   a. word b. statement c. update d. answer
10. caper   a. wolf b. goat c. character d. prank

UNIT

14

CRYPT comes from the Greek word for "hidden." To *encrypt* a message is to encode it—that is, to hide its meaning in code language. When a scientific term begins with *crypto-*, it always means that there's something hidden about it.

---

crypt \\\'kript\\ (1) A room completely or partly underground, especially under the main floor of a church. (2) A room or area in a large aboveground tomb.

• His old nightmare was of being locked in a crypt with corpses as his only companions.

Hidden under the main floor of a great church is often a large room, often with a tomb as its centerpiece. Many major European churches were built over the remains of a saint—the Vatican's great St. Peter's Basilica is an example—and instead of having the coffin buried, it was often given its spacious room below ground level. In a large aboveground tomb, or *mausoleum*, there may be several small chambers for individual coffins, also called crypts; when the comic book *Tales from the Crypt* made its first appearance in 1950, it was this meaning that the authors were referring to.

encrypt \\in-\'kript\\ (1) To convert into cipher. (2) To convert a message into code.

• Messages on the group's Web site are encrypted in code words to keep law-enforcement agents from understanding them.

Codes aren't always in another language; people have always been able to communicate in ways that conceal their real meaning. In countries ruled by dictators, novelists and playwrights have sometimes managed to encrypt their messages, conveying political ideas to their audiences so that the authorities never notice. But *encryption* today usually refers to a complex procedure performed on electronic text to make sure the wrong people—whether a nation's enemies or a business competitor (most businesses use encryption today)—can't read it. And sensitive data that merely resides on a company's own computers is often encrypted as well.

cryptic \\'krip-tik\\ (1) Mysterious; puzzlingly short. (2) Acting to hide or conceal.

• From across the room, Louisa threw Philip a cryptic look, and he puzzled over what she was trying to tell him.

Until the writing on the famous Rosetta Stone was finally translated in the early 19th century, Egyptian hieroglyphic writing was entirely cryptic, its meaning hidden from the modern world. In the same way, a cryptic comment is one whose meaning is unclear, and a cryptic note may leave you wondering. Cryptic coloring among plants and animals acts like camouflage; so, for example, some moths that are tasty to blue jays are *cryptically* colored to look like bugs that jays won't touch.

cryptography \\krip-'tä-grə-fē\\ (1) Secret writing. (2) The encoding and decoding of messages.

• As a graduate student in mathematics, she never dreamed she would end up working in cryptography for the Defense Department.

During World War II, cryptography became an extremely complex science for both the Allied and Axis powers. The Allies managed to secretly crack the code produced by the Nazis' Enigma machine, and thereby may have shortened the war by two years. The Axis *cryptographers,* on the other hand, never managed to crack the Americans' ultimate code—the spoken languages of the Navajo and other American Indians. In the age of computers, cryptography has become almost unbelievably complex; it's widely used in peacetime in such areas as banking telecommunications.

AB/ABS comes to us from Latin, and means "from," "away," or "off." *Abuse* is the use of something in the wrong way. To *abduct* is to "lead away from" or kidnap. *Aberrant* behavior is behavior that "wanders away from" what is acceptable. But there are so many words that include these roots that it would be *absurd* to try to list them all here.

abscond \ab-'skänd\ To depart in secret and hide.

- They discovered the next morning that their guest had absconded with most of the silverware during the night.

Wagner's massive four-part opera *The Ring of the Nibelung* begins with a dwarf absconding with gold which he turns into a magic ring. And in J. R. R. Tolkien's *The Hobbit,* Bilbo Baggins absconds from Gollum's caves with the ring he has found, the ring Gollum calls "my precious"; what follows is detailed in the three-volume *Lord of the Rings.* (Tolkien knew Wagner's opera well.) A young couple might abscond from their parents to get married, but sooner or later they must face those parents again.

abstemious \ab-'stē-mē-əs\ Restrained, especially in the consumption of food or alcohol.

- Her parents had left her two million dollars when they died, having been so abstemious for years that their neighbors all assumed they were poor.

Many 14th-century monks lived by the Rule of St. Benedict, which demands an abstemious life of obedience and poverty. But not all monks could maintain such abstemious habits. Chaucer's *Canterbury Tales* contains a portrait of a fat monk who is supposed to follow a vegetarian diet but instead is an enthusiastic hunter who loves a juicy swan best. He justifies breaking the Rule by saying that it's old-fashioned and that he's just keeping up with modern times. *Abstemious* itself has a slightly old-fashioned sound today, especially in a country where everyone is constantly encouraged to consume.

abstraction \ab-'strak-shən\ The consideration of a thing or idea without associating it with a particular example.

- All the ideas she came up with in class were abstractions, since she had no experience of actual nursing at all.

From its roots, *abstraction* should mean basically "something pulled or drawn away." So *abstract* art is art that has moved away from painting objects of the ordinary physical world in order to show something beyond it. Theories are often abstractions; so a theory about economics, for instance, may "pull back" to take a broad view that somehow explains all of economics (but maybe doesn't end up explaining any of it very successfully). An *abstract* of a medical or scientific article is a one-paragraph summary of its contents—that is, the basic findings "pulled out" of the article.

abstruse \ab-ˈstrüs\ Hard to understand; deep or complex.

• In every class he fills the blackboard with abstruse calculations, and we usually leave more confused than ever.

The original meaning of *abstruse,* coming almost straight from the Latin, was "concealed, hidden." It's easy to see how the word soon came to describe the kind of language used by those who possess certain kinds of expert knowledge (and don't necessarily want to share it with other people). Scientific writing is often filled with the kind of abstruse special vocabulary that's necessary for exact and precise descriptions. Unfortunately, the language of a science like quantum physics can make an already difficult subject even more abstruse to the average person.

Quizzes

A. Match the definition on the left to the correct word on the right:

1. mysterious   a. encrypt
2. code writing   b. abstraction
3. translate to code   c. abscond
4. difficult   d. cryptic
5. tomb   e. abstruse
6. generalization   f. crypt
7. self-controlled   g. cryptography
8. flee   h. abstemious

B. Fill in each blank with the correct letter:

a. cryptic   e. cryptography
b. abscond   f. abstemious
c. abstraction   g. encrypt
d. crypt   h. abstruse

1. She had failed to _____ the file when she put it on her hard drive, and her secretary had secretly copied it.
2. His answer was so short and _____ that I have no idea what he meant.
3. The great, echoing _____ of St. Stephen's Cathedral could have held hundreds of people.
4. That's a clever _____, but in the real world things work very differently.
5. The _____ vocabulary of the literature professor led many students to drop her class.
6. He's given up drinking and leads an _____ life these days, rarely thinking about his former high living.
7. Their _____ hasn't been revised in two years, and we've been worried about the security of the data.
8. The bride is so shy that her mother fears she'll _____ from the reception.

PED comes from the Greek word for "child." The same root also has the meaning "foot" (see p. 78), but in English words it usually isn't hard to tell the two apart.

---

pedagogy \\'pe-də-ˌgō-jē\ The art, science, or profession of teaching.

• His own pedagogy is extremely original; it sometimes alarms school officials but his students love it.

Since in Greek *agogos* means "leader," a *paidagogos* was a slave who led boys to school and back, but also taught them manners and tutored them after school. In time, *pedagogue* came to mean simply "teacher"; today the word has an old-fashioned ring to it, so it often means a stuffy, boring teacher. The word *pedagogy*, though, is still widely used, and often means simply "teaching." And *pedagogic* training is what everyone majoring in education receives.

pedant \\'pe-dənt\\ (1) A formal, unimaginative teacher. (2) A person who shows off his or her learning.

• At one time or another, every student encounters a pedant who can make even the most interesting subject tedious.

It isn't always easy to tell a *pedantic* teacher from one who is simply thorough. Some professors get an undeserved reputation for *pedantry* from students who just don't like the subject much. Regardless of that, a pedant need not be a teacher; anyone who goes around displaying his or her knowledge in a boring way can qualify.

pediatrician \\ˌpē-dē-ə-'tri-shən\\ A doctor who specializes in the diseases, development, and care of children.

• Children in the U.S. usually see a pediatrician until they turn at least 15 or 16.

Since *iatros* means "physician" in Greek (see IATR, p. 615), words such as *pediatric* naturally refer to "children's medicine." *Pediatrics* is a fairly new medical specialty; until about 1900, children were considered small adults and given the same medical treatment, only milder. Benjamin Spock was the most famous pediatrician of the 20th century, and his book *Baby and Child Care* changed the way millions of Americans raised their children.

encyclopedic \\in-ˌsī-klə-'pē-dik\\ (1) Of or relating to an encyclopedia. (2) Covering a wide range of subjects.

• Someone with the kind of encyclopedic knowledge she has should be competing on *Jeopardy*.

In Greek, *paidaea* meant not simply "child-rearing" but also "education," and *kyklios* meant "general"; thus, an encyclopedia is a work broad enough to provide a kind of general education. The world's most eminent general encyclopedia, the *Encyclopaedia Britannica,* is a huge work that covers every field of human knowledge. But *encyclopedic* doesn't have to refer to books; it's often used to describe the wide-ranging knowledge that certain types of minds just can't stop acquiring.

TROP comes from the Greek *tropos*, meaning "turn" or "change." The *troposphere* is the level of the atmosphere where most weather changes—or "turns in the weather"—occur. And the *Tropics* of Cancer and Capricorn are the lines of latitude where the sun is directly overhead when it reaches its northernmost and southernmost points, on about June 22 and December 22 every year—that is, the point where it seems to turn and go back the other way.

tropism \\'trō-,pi-zəm\\ Automatic movement by an organism unable to move about from place to place, especially a plant, that involves turning or growing toward or away from a stimulus.

• The new president was soon showing a tropism for bold action, a tendency that seemed more the result of instinct than of careful thought.

In *hydrotropism*, a plant's roots grow in the direction of increasing moisture, hoping to obtain water. In *phototropism*, a plant (or fungus) moves toward light, usually the sun—perhaps because, in the colder climates where such plants are usually found, concentrating the sun's warmth within the sun-seeking flower can create a warm and inviting environment for the insects that fertilize it. In *thigmotropism*, the organism moves in response to being touched; most climbing plants, for example, put out tiny tendrils that feel around for something solid and then attach themselves or curl around it. When microbiologists talk about tropism, however, they're often referring instead to the way a virus will seek out a particular type of cell to infect. And when intellectuals use the word, they usually mean a tendency shown by a person or group which they themselves might not even be aware of.

entropy \\'en-trə-pē\\ (1) The decomposition of the matter and energy in the universe to an ultimate state of inactive uniformity. (2) Chaos, randomness.

• The apartment had been reduced to an advanced state of entropy, as if a tiny tornado had torn through it, shattering its contents and mixing the pieces together in a crazy soup.

With its Greek prefix *en-*, meaning "within," and the *trop-* root here meaning "change," *entropy* basically means "change within (a closed system)." The closed system we usually think of when speaking of entropy (especially if we're not physicists) is the entire universe. But entropy applies to closed systems of any size. Entropy is seen when the ice in a glass of water in a warm room melts—that is, as the temperature of everything in the room evens out. In a slightly different type of entropy, a drop of food coloring in that glass of water soon spreads out evenly. However, when a nonphysicist uses the word, he or she is usually trying to describe a large-scale collapse.

heliotrope \\'hē-lē-ə-ˌtrōp\\ Any of a genus of herbs or shrubs having small white or purple flowers.

- A long bank of purple heliotrope lined the walkway, and her guests were always remarking on the flowers' glorious fragrance.

Helios was the god of the sun in Greek mythology, and *helio-* came to appear in a number of sun-related English words. The genus known as the heliotropes consists of about 250 species; many are thought of as weeds, but the best-known species, garden heliotrope, is a popular and fragrant perennial that resembles the forget-me-not. The heliotrope tends to follow the sun—that is, turn its blossoms toward the sun as it travels from East to West every day. But the fact is, *heliotropism*—turning toward the sun—is common among flowers (and even leaves), and some, like the sunflower, are more dramatically *heliotropic* than the heliotrope. Those in the far North actually use their petals to reflect the sun's heat onto the flower's central ovary during the short growing season.

psychotropic \\ˌsī-kə-'trō-pik\\ Acting on the mind.

- My mother is taking two drugs that may produce psychotropic side effects, and I'm worried that they might be interacting.

Psychotropic is used almost always to describe substances that we consume. Such substances are more numerous than you might think, and some have been known for thousands of years. Native American religions, for example, have used psychotropic substances derived from certain cactuses and mushrooms for centuries. Caffeine and nicotine can be called psychotropic. Psychotropic prescription drugs include antidepressants (such as Prozac) and tranquilizers (such as Valium). Any medication that blocks pain, from aspirin to the anesthetics used during surgery, can be considered a psychotropic drug. Even children are now prescribed psychotropic drugs, often to treat attention deficit disorder. And all recreational drugs are psychotropic. *Psychoactive* is a common synonym of *psychotropic*.

Quizzes

A. Indicate whether the following pairs of words have the same or different meanings:

1. psychotropic / mind-altering   same ___ / different ___
2. encyclopedic / important   same ___ / different ___
3. entropy / disorder   same ___ / different ___
4. heliotrope / sunflower   same ___ / different ___
5. pediatrician / foot doctor   same ___ / different ___
6. tropism / growth   same ___ / different ___
7. pedagogy / teaching   same ___ / different ___
8. pedant / know-it-all   same ___ / different ___

B. Match the definition on the left to the correct word on the right:

1. thorough   a. entropy
2. decay   b. pediatrician
3. boring teacher   c. heliotrope
4. fragrant flower   d. encyclopedic
5. automatic motion   e. tropism
6. education   f. pedant
7. affecting the mind   g. psychotropic
8. children's doctor   h. pedagogy

NEO comes from the Greek *neos*, meaning "new." *Neo-* has become a part of many English words. Some are easy to understand; for example, *neo-Nazi*. Some are less so; you might not immediately guess that *neotropical* means "from the tropics of the New World," or that a *neophyte* is a "newcomer." When William Ramsay discovered four new gases, he named them all using Greek roots that at first glance might sound slightly mysterious: *argon* ("idle"), *krypton* ("hidden"), *xenon* ("strange")—and *neon* ("new").

neoclassic \ˌnē-ō-ˈkla-sik\ Relating to a revival or adaptation of the styles of ancient Greece and Roman, especially in music, art, or architecture.

• He had always admired the paintings of the French neoclassical masters, especially Poussin and Ingres.

In the arts and architecture, a style that has existed for a long time usually produces a reaction against it. So after the showy style of Europe's so-called baroque era (from about 1600 to the early 1700s), the reaction came in the form of the neoclassical movement, bringing order, restraint, and simpler and more conservative structures, whether in plays, sonatas, sculptures, or public buildings. Its inspiration was the art of ancient Greece and Rome—that is, of *classical* antiquity. Why *classical*? In Latin *classicus* meant "of the highest *class*," so in English *classic* and *classical* originally described the best ancient Greek and Latin literature, but soon came to mean simply "of ancient Greek and Rome," since these were already seen as the highest and best cultures. *Neoclassic* generally describes artworks from the 1700s or early 1800s (by the painter David, the composer Mozart, the sculptor Canova, etc.), but also works from the 20th century that seem to have been inspired by the ideals of Greece and Rome.

Neolithic \ˌnē-ə-ˈlith-ik\ Of or relating to the latest period of the Stone Age, when polished stone tools were used.

* Around the Mediterranean, the Neolithic period was a time of trade, of stock breeding, and of the first use of pottery.

Since *lithos* in Greek means "stone," the Neolithic period is the "new" or "late" period of the Stone Age, in contrast to the Paleolithic period ("old" or "early" period—see PALEO, p. 646) and the Mesolithic period ("middle" period) of the Stone Age. The use of polished stone tools came to different parts of the world at different times, but the Neolithic Age is usually said to begin around 9000 B.C. and to end around 3000 B.C., when the Bronze Age begins. The Neolithic is the era when the farming of plants and animals begins, and when, as a result, humans first begin to create permanent settlements.

neoconservative \ˌnē-ō-kən-ˈsər-və-tiv\ A conservative who favors strongly encouraging democracy and the U.S. national interest in world affairs, including through military means.

* Many believed that foreign policy in those years had fallen into the hands of the neoconservatives, and that the war in Iraq was one result.

In the 1960s several well-known socialist intellectuals, including Norman Podhoretz and Irving Kristol, alarmed by growing political extremism on the left, began to move in the other direction. Soon the term *neoconservative* (or *neocon* for short) was being attached to them. Rather than simply drifting toward the political center, Podhoretz and Kristol actually moved far to the right, especially on the issue of maintaining a strong military stance toward the rest of the world. The main magazine of *neoconservatism* became Podhoretz's *Commentary*; it was later joined by the *Weekly Standard*, edited by Kristol's son William. Not everyone agrees on how to define these terms; still, it's clear that today you don't have to be a former liberal in order to be a neoconservative.

neonatal \ˌnē-ō-ˈnā-t°l\ Of or relating to babies in the first month after their birth.

• The hospital's newest addition is a neonatal intensive-care unit, and newborns in critical condition are already being sent there from considerable distances.

Partly based on the Latin *natus*, "born," *neonatal* means "newly born." Neonatal babies themselves are called *neonates*. Most hospitals now offer neonatal screening, which is used to detect diseases that are treatable only if identified during the first days of life, and specialized neonatal nursing as well. But despite spending much money on neonatal care, the U.S. still ranks lower than some much less wealthy countries (such as the Czech Republic, Portugal, and Cuba) in infant mortality (infant deaths).

NOV comes from the Latin word *novus*, meaning "new." To *renovate* an old house is to "make it new again"—that is, put it back in tip-top shape. The long-running PBS show *Nova* keeps its large audience up to date on what's new in the world of science. And when the British king sent Scottish settlers to a large island off Canada's Atlantic coast in the 17th century, he named it *Nova Scotia*, or "New Scotland."

---

novice \ˈnä-vəs\ (1) One who has no previous training or experience in a specific field or activity; beginner. (2) A new member of a religious order who is preparing to become a nun or monk.

• It's hard to believe that a year ago she was a complete novice as a gardener, who couldn't identify a cornstalk.

Among the ancient Romans, a novice (*novicius*) was usually a newly imported slave, who had to be trained in his or her duties. Among

Catholics and Buddhists, if you desire to become a priest, monk, or nun, you must serve as a novice for a period of time, often a year (called your *novitiate*), before being ordained or fully professing your vows. No matter what kind of novice you are—at computers, at writing, at politics, etc.—you've got a lot to learn.

novel \\'nä-vəl\ (1) New and not resembling something formerly known or used. (2) Original and striking, especially in conception or style.

* His techniques for dealing with these disturbed young people were novel, and they caught the attention of the institute's director.

If someone tells you that you've come up with a novel idea or a novel interpretation of something, it's probably a compliment: not everyone is capable of original thinking. But not everything new is terribly worthwhile; a *novelty,* for example, is often a cute (or maybe just silly) little object that you might put on a display shelf in your house. It may seem surprising that the familiar noun *novel* is related as well. In the 14th century, Italian writers began writing collections of short tales, each of which they called a *novella* because it represented a new literary form; from this word, three centuries later, the English coined the noun *novel.*

innovation \\,i-nə-'vā-shən\ (1) A new idea, device, or method. (2) The introduction of new ideas, devices, or methods.

* "Smooshing" bits of candy into ice cream while the customer watched was just one of his innovations that later got copied by chains of ice-cream outlets.

Innovation is a word that's almost always connected with business. In business today, it's almost a rule that a company that doesn't *innovate* is destined for failure. The most important and successful businesses were usually started by *innovators.* And company managers should always at least listen to the *innovative* ideas of their employees.

supernova \\,sü-pər-'nō-və\ (1) The explosion of a star that causes it to become extremely bright. (2) Something that explodes into prominence or popularity.

* After exploding, a nova leaves a "white dwarf" which may explode again in the future, but a supernova destroys the entire star.

A *nova*, despite its name, isn't actually a "new" star, but rather one that wasn't noticed until it exploded, when it may increase in brightness by a million times before returning to its previous state a few days later. A supernova is far larger; a star in its supernova state may emit a billion times as much light as previously. After a few weeks it begins to dim, until it eventually ceases to exist; it's often replaced by a black hole. (Though remains that were shot out into space may survive; those of a great supernova seen in A.D. 1054 are now known as the Crab Nebula.) All this may serve as a warning to those human stars whose fame explodes too rapidly; supernovas of this kind have sometimes vanished by the following year.

Quizzes

A. Fill in each blank with the correct letter:

a. Neolithic   e. supernova
b. novice   f. neoconservative
c. novel   g. neoclassic
d. neonatal   h. innovation

1. My father subscribes to the _____ magazines and still thinks we had no choice but to invade Iraq.
2. The building's style is _____, with Roman columns and with white statues on either side of the entrance.
3. In his youth he had intended to join the priesthood, and he even served as a _____ for six months before giving it up.
4. They're now working at a _____ site in Syria, where they've found evidence of goat, pig, and sheep farming.
5. The baby might not have survived if the hospital hadn't had an excellent _____ ward.
6. The _____ seen by Asian astronomers in 1054 was four times as bright as the brightest planet.
7. The company had a history of _____ that had earned it immense respect and attracted many of the brightest young engineers.
8. She often comes up with _____ interpretations of the evidence in cases like this, and she's sometimes proven correct.

B. Match the word on the left to the correct definition on the right:

1. novice
2. innovation
3. neoclassic
4. neoconservative
5. neonatal
6. novel
7. supernova
8. Neolithic

a. star explosion
b. new invention or method
c. beginner
d. newborn
e. ancient
f. cleverly new
g. favoring aggressive foreign policy
h. resembling Greek and Roman style

POS comes from the Latin verb *ponere,* meaning "to put" or "to place." You *expose* film by "placing it out" in the light. You *compose* a song by "putting together" a series of notes. And you *oppose* locating a new prison in your town by "putting yourself against" it.

---

impose \im-ˈpōz\ (1) To establish or apply as a charge or penalty or in a forceful or harmful way. (2) To take unfair advantage.

• After seeing her latest grades, her parents imposed new rules about how much time she had to spend on homework every night.

The Latin *imposui* meant "put upon," and that meaning carried over into English in *impose.* A CEO may impose a new manager on one of the company's plants. A state may impose new taxes on luxury items or cigarettes, and the federal government sometimes imposes trade restrictions on another country to punish it. A polite apology might begin with "I hope I'm not imposing on you" (that is, "forcing my presence on you"). And a *self-imposed* deadline is one that you decide to hold yourself to.

juxtapose \ˈjək-stə-ˌpōz\ To place side by side.

• You won't notice the difference between the original and the copy unless you juxtapose them.

Since *juxta* means "near" in Latin, it's easy to see how *juxtapose* was formed. Juxtaposing is generally done for examination or effect. Interior designers constantly make decisions about juxtaposing objects and colors for the best effect. Juxtaposing two video clips showing the different things that a politician said about the same subject at two different times can be an effective means of criticizing. The *juxtaposition* of two similar X-rays can help medical students distinguish between two conditions that may be hard to tell apart. And advertisements frequently juxtapose "before" and "after" images to show a thrilling transformation.

transpose \trans-'pōz\ (1) To change the position or order of (two things). (2) To move from one place or period to another.

* She rechecked the phone number and discovered that two digits had been transposed.

Though transposing two digits can be disastrous, transposing two letters in a word often doesn't matter too much. (You can prboalby raed tihs setnence witohut too mcuh toruble.) Transposing two words or sounds—as in "Can I sew you to another sheet?"—has been a good source of humor over the years. Doctors sometimes discover that something in the body—a nerve, an organ, etc.—has been transposed, or moved away from its proper place. For musicians, transposing means changing the key of a piece; if you can do this at a moment's notice, you've been well trained.

superimpose \ˌsü-pər-im-'pōz\ To put or place one thing over something else.

* Using transparent sheets, she superimposes territory boundaries on an outline of Africa, showing us how these changed in the late 19th and early 20th century.

Superimposition was one of the magical effects employed by early filmmakers. Using "mirror shots," with semitransparent mirrors set at 45° angles to the scene, they would superimpose shadowy images of ghosts or scenes from a character's past onto scenes from the present. Superimposing your own ideas on something, such as a historical event, has to be done carefully, since your ideas may change whenever you learn something new about the event.

TEN, from the Latin verb *tenere*, basically means "hold" or "hold on to." A *tenant* is the "holder" of an apartment, house, or land, but not necessarily the owner. A *lieutenant* governor may "hold the position" ("serve in lieu") of the governor when necessary.

---

tenure \\'ten-yər\ (1) The amount of time that a person holds a job, office, or title. (2) The right to keep a job, especially the job of teacher or professor.

• I know two assistant professors who are so worried about being denied tenure this year that they can't sleep.

Tenure is about holding on to something, almost always a job or position. So you can speak of someone's 30-year tenure as chairman, or someone's brief tenure in the sales manager's office. But *tenure* means something slightly different in the academic world. In American colleges and universities, the best (or luckiest) teachers have traditionally been granted a lifetime appointment known as tenure after about six years of teaching. Almost nobody has as secure a job as a *tenured* professor, but getting tenure can be difficult, and most of them have earned it.

tenacious \tə-'nā-shəs\ Stubborn or determined in clinging to something.

• He was known as a tenacious reporter who would stay with a story for months, risking his health and sometimes even his life.

Success in most fields requires a tenacious spirit and a drive to achieve. Nowhere is this more apparent than in the entertainment business. Thousands of actors and actresses work *tenaciously* to build a TV or film career. But without talent or beauty, *tenacity* is rarely rewarded, and only a few become stars.

tenable \\'te-nə-bəl\ Capable of being held or defended; reasonable.

• She was depressed for weeks after her professor said that her theory wasn't tenable.

Tenable means "holdable." In the past it was often used in a physical sense—for example, to refer to a city that an army was trying to "hold" militarily against an enemy force. But nowadays it's almost always used when speaking of "held" ideas and theories. If you hold an opinion but evidence appears that completely contradicts it, your opinion is no longer tenable. So, for example, the old ideas that cancer is infectious or that being bled by leeches can cure your whooping cough now seem *untenable*.

tenet \\'te-nət\ A widely held principle or belief, especially one held in common by members of a group or profession.

- It was soon obvious that the new owners didn't share the tenets that the company's founders had held to all those years.

A *tenet* is something we hold, but not with our hands. Tenets are often ideals, but also often statements of faith. Thus, we may speak of the tenets of Islam or Hinduism, the tenets of Western democracy, or the tenets of the scientific method, and in each case these tenets may combine elements of both faith and ideals.

Quizzes

A. Choose the closest definition:

1. impose   a. force b. request c. seek d. hint
2. tenacious   a. stubborn b. intelligent c. loving d. helping
3. superimpose   a. surpass b. put into c. place over d. amaze
4. juxtapose   a. place on top of b. put away c. place side by side d. put into storage
5. transpose   a. emerge b. change into c. cross d. switch
6. tenable   a. decent b. tough c. reasonable d. controllable
7. tenet   a. claw b. belief c. renter d. shelter
8. tenure   a. strong hold b. permanent appointment c. lengthy period d. male voice

B. Indicate whether the following pairs have the same or different meanings:

1. impose / remove   same __ / different __
2. tenet / principle   same __ / different __
3. transpose / exchange   same __ / different __
4. tenure / absence   same __ / different __
5. superimpose / offend deeply same __ / different __
6. tenacious / sensible   same __ / different __
7. juxtapose / switch   same __ / different __
8. tenable / reasonable   same __ / different __

Number Words

MONO comes from the Greek *monos*, meaning "alone" or "single." So a *monorail* is a railroad that has only one rail; a *monocle* is an old-fashioned eyeglass that a gentleman used to squeeze into his eye socket; a *monotonous* voice seems to have only one tone; and a *monopoly* puts all ownership of a type of product or service in the hands of a single company.

---

monogamous \mə-ˈnä-gə-məs\ Being married to one person or having one mate at a time.

• Geese, swans, and most other birds are monogamous and mate for life.

American marriage is by law monogamous; people are permitted to have only one spouse at a time. There are cultures with laws that permit marriage to more than one person at a time, or *polygamy*. Although the term *polygamy* may refer to *polyandry* (marriage to more than one man), it is more often used as a synonym for *polygyny* (marriage to more than one woman), which appears to have once been common in most of the world and is still found widely in some cultures.

monoculture \ˈmä-nə-ˌkəl-chər\ (1) The cultivation of a single crop to the exclusion of other uses of land. (2) A culture dominated by a single element.

• Monoculture is practiced on a vast scale in the American Midwest, where nothing but corn can be seen in the fields for hundreds of square miles.

The Irish Potato Famine of 1845–49, which led to the deaths of over a million people, resulted from the monoculture of potatoes, which were destroyed by a terrible blight, leaving farmers nothing else to eat. Almost every traditional farming society has practiced crop rotation, the planting of different crops on a given piece of land from year to year, so as to keep the soil from losing its quality. But in the modern world, monoculture has become the rule on the largest commercial farms, where the same crop can be planted year after year by means of the intensive use of fertilizers. Modern monoculture has produced huge crops; on a large scale, it permits great efficiency in planting, pest control, and harvesting. But many experts believe this all comes at a huge cost to the environment.

monolithic \ˌmä-nə-ˈli-thik\ (1) Appearing to be a huge, feature-less, often rigid whole. (2) Made up of material with no joints or seams.

- The sheer monolithic rock face of Yosemite's El Capitan looks impossible to climb, but its cracks and seams are enough for experienced rock climbers.

The -*lith* in *monolith* comes from the Greek *lithos*, "stone," so *monolith* in its original sense means a huge stone like those at Stonehenge. What's so impressive about monoliths is that they have no separate parts or pieces. To the lone individual, any huge institution or government bureaucracy can seem monolithic. But the truth may be different: The former U.S.S.R. once seemed monolithic and indestructible to the West, but in the 1990s it crumbled into a number of independent republics.

monotheism \ˈmä-nō-thē-ˌi-zəm\ The doctrine or belief that there is a single god.

- The earliest known instance of monotheism dates to the reign of Akhenaton of Egypt in the 14th century B.C.

Monotheism, which is characteristic of Judaism, Islam, and Christianity, is distinguished from *polytheism*, belief in or worship of more than one god. The monotheism that characterizes Judaism began in ancient Israel with the adoption of Yahweh as the single object of worship and the rejection of the gods of other tribes and nations without, initially, denying their existence. Islam is clear in acknowledging one, eternal, unbegotten, unequaled God, while Christianity holds that a single God is reflected in the three persons of the Holy Trinity.

UNI comes from the Latin word for "one." A *uniform* is a single design worn by everyone. A *united* group has one single opinion, or forms a single *unit*. A *unitard* is a one-piece combination leotard and tights, very good for skating, skiing, dancing—or riding a one-wheeled *unicycle*.

---

unicameral \ˌyü-ni-ˈka-mə-rəl\ Having only one lawmaking chamber.

- In China, with its unicameral system of government, a single group of legislators meets to make the laws.

Unicameral means "one-chambered," and the term almost always describes a governing body. Our federal legislature, like those of most democracies, is *bicameral,* with two legislative (lawmaking) bodies—the Senate and the House of Representatives. And except for Nebraska, all the state legislatures are also bicameral. So why did the nation decide on a bicameral system? Partly in order to keep some power out of the hands of ordinary voters, who the Founding Fathers didn't completely trust. For that reason, the original Constitution states that senators are to be elected by the state legislatures; not until 1914, after passage of a Constitutional amendment, did we first cast direct votes for our senators.

unilateral \ˌyü-ni-ˈla-tə-rəl\ (1) Done by one person or party; one-sided. (2) Affecting one side of the body.

• The Japanese Constitution of 1947 includes a unilateral rejection of warfare as an option for their country.

The world is a smaller place than it used to be, and we get uncomfortable when a single nation adopts a policy of *unilateralism*—that is, acting independently with little regard for what the rest of the world thinks. A unilateral invasion of another country, for instance, usually looks like a grab for power and resources. But occasionally the world welcomes a unilateral action, as when the U.S. announced unilateral nuclear-arms reductions in the early 1990s. Previously, such reductions had only happened as part of *bilateral* ("two-sided") agreements with the old Soviet Union. *Multilateral* agreements, on issues such as climate change, often involve most of the world's nations.

unison \ˈyü-nə-sən\ (1) Perfect agreement. (2) Sameness of musical pitch.

• Unable to read music well enough to harmonize, the village choir sang only in unison.

This word usually appears in the phrase "in unison," which means "together, at the same time" or "at the same musical pitch." So an excited crowd responding to a speaker may shout in unison, and a group of demonstrators may chant in unison. The old church music called Gregorian chant was written to be sung in unison, with no harmonizing voices, and kindergarten kids always sing in unison (at least when they can all find the same pitch). In a similar way, an aerobics class moves in unison following the instructor, and a group or even a whole town may work in unison when everyone agrees on a common goal.

unitarian \ˌyü-nə-'ter-ē-ən\ Relating or belonging to a religious group that believes that God exists only in one person and stresses individual freedom of belief.

• With his unitarian tendencies, he wasn't likely to get into fights over religious beliefs.

Unitarianism, originally a sect of Christianity believing in a single or *unitary* God, grew up in 18th-century England and developed in America in the early 19th century. Though they believe in Christ's teaching, they reject the idea of the three-part Trinity—God as father, son, and holy spirit—and thus deny that Christ was divine, so some people don't consider them truly Christian. In this century the Unitarians joined with the *Universalist* Church, a movement founded on a belief in *universal* salvation—that is, the saving of every soul from damnation after death. Both have always been liberal and fairly small; today they count about half a million members. Without a capital letter, *unitarian* refers simply to belief in a *unitary* God, or in *unity* within some nonreligious system.

Quiz

Fill in each blank with the correct letter:

a. monotheism
b. unilateral
c. monolithic
d. unison

e. unitarian
f. monoculture
g. unicameral
h. monogamous

1. The president is allowed to make some ＿＿ decisions without asking Congress's permission.
2. The relationship was unbalanced: she was perfectly ＿＿, while he had two other women in his life.
3. In rejecting a ＿＿ legislature, America seemed to follow Britain's lead.
4. The sheer mountain face, ＿＿ and forbidding, loomed over the town.

5. As a strict Catholic, she found _____ beliefs unacceptable.
6. Most religious groups in this country practice one or another form of _____.
7. Corn was a _____ in the village, and the farmers would simply move to a new field each year to keep the soil from wearing out.
8. At Halloween and Thanksgiving assemblies, the children would recite holiday poems in _____.

Review Quizzes

A. Choose the correct synonym:

1. unilateral   a. one-sided b. sideways c. complete d. multiple
2. cryptography   a. gravestone writing b. physics writing c. code writing d. mathematical writing
3. monotheism   a. nature worship b. worship of one god c. worship of pleasure d. sun worship
4. abscond   a. steal b. discover c. retire d. flee
5. transpose   a. send out b. take place c. overcome d. switch
6. tenet   a. shelter b. principle c. choice d. landlord
7. pedagogy   a. study b. teaching c. research d. child abuse
8. unison   a. solitude b. melody c. collection d. agreement
9. crypt   a. code b. granite c. tomb d. church
10. superimpose   a. increase b. lay over c. improve d. excel
11. monogamous   a. with one spouse b. without a spouse c. with several spouses d. with someone else's spouse
12. tenable   a. available b. unbearable c. agreeable d. reasonable

B. Fill in each blank with the correct letter:

a. tenure
b. pediatrician
c. pedant
d. unitarian
e. impose

f. abstraction
g. tenacious
h. cryptic
i. encyclopedic
j. abstruse

1. Their son had just called to tell them that the university had decided to grant him _____.
2. Tuesday the baby sees the _____ for her immunizations and checkups.
3. The only clues for the treasure hunt were in a _____ poem that his father had written.
4. By the time she was 25 she had an _____ knowledge of her state's history.
5. The notion of a savior was foreign to his _____ beliefs.
6. The legislature is threatening to _____ strict limits on this kind of borrowing.
7. The speech contained one _____ after another, but never a specific example.
8. At the age of 72 he was regarded by most of the students as a boring _____.
9. The sick child's _____ grip on life was their only hope now.
10. The researcher's writing was _____ but it was worth the effort to read it.

C. Indicate whether the following pairs of words have the same or different meanings:

1. monotheism / growing of one crop   same ___ / different ___
2. unison / unitedness   same ___ / different ___
3. cryptic / gravelike   same ___ / different ___
4. monolithic / boring   same ___ / different ___
5. abstemious / self-controlled   same ___ / different ___
6. tenet / ideal   same ___ / different ___
7. crypt / tomb   same ___ / different ___
8. tenable / reasonable   same ___ / different ___
9. unicameral / one-chambered   same ___ / different ___
10. abstruse / difficult   same ___ / different ___

ANSWERS

UNIT 1

p. 4
A 1. c 2. c 3. a 4. b 5. c 6. a
   7. a 8. b
B 1. d 2. c 3. b 4. b 5. d 6. d
   7. d 8. a

p. 8
A 1. d 2. g 3. f 4. c 5. h 6. e
   7. b 8. a
B 1. e 2. a 3. f 4. d 5. c 6. h
   7. b 8. g

p. 12
A 1. S 2. D 3. D 4. D 5. D 6. S
   7. S 8. D
B 1. e 2. a 3. b 4. f 5. d 6, h
   7. g 8. c

p. 16
A 1. d 2. f 3. c 4. h 5. b 6. a
   7. e 8. g
B 1. f 2. a 3. g 4. b 5. c 6. h
   7. d 8. e

p. 19
1. d 2. b 3. a 4. c 5. b 6. d
   7. a 8. c

p. 20
A 1. e 2. d 3. k 4. b 5. h 6. l
   7. f 8. j 9. a 10. c 11. n 12. g
   13. m 14. i
B 1. d 2. a 3. c 4. c 5. b 6. b
   7. d 8. b 9. c 10. c 11. c 12. a

C 1. f 2. c 3. e 4. d 5. h 6. g
   7. j 8. a 9. b 10. i

UNIT 2

p. 26
A 1. d 2. a 3. e 4. f 5. b 6. c
   7. g 8. h
B 1. f 2. g 3. h 4. b 5. a 6. c
   7. e 8. d

p. 30
A 1. h 2. g 3. d 4. a 5. b 6. f
   7. e 8. c
B 1. f 2. d 3. b 4. g 5. h 6. c
   7. e 8. a

p. 34
A 1. d 2. c 3. d 4. d 5. d 6. c
   7. b 8. a
B 1. d 2. e 3, h 4. f 5. g 6. a
   7. c 8. b

p. 38
A 1. b 2. c 3. e 4. a 5. g 6. h
   7. d 8. f
B 1. h 2. d 3. a 4. f 5. e 6. b
   7. g 8. c

p. 42
1. a, c 2. d, b 3. b, a 4. c, b
   5. c, a 6. a, b 7. c, a 8. d, a

p. 42
A 1. b 2. b 3. b 4. d 5. d 6. c
   7. c 8. c 9. a 10. d

B 1. c 2. f 3. e 4. a 5. i 6. d 7. b
   8. g 9. j 10. h
C 1. f 2. h 3. c 4. i 5. d 6. e 7. j
   8. b 9. g 10. a

UNIT 3

p. 48
A 1. b 2. c 3. f 4. d 5. e 6. a
   7. g 8. h
B 1. c 2. f 3. e 4. h 5. a 6. d
   7. b 8. g

p. 53
A 1. b 2. d 3. b 4. b 5. d 6. c
   7. b 8. a
B 1. D 2. D 3. S 4. D 5. D 6. S
   7. D 8. D

p. 57
A 1. a 2. g 3. f 4. d 5. c 6. b 7.
   h 8. e
B 1. D 2. S 3. S 4. D 5. S 6. D
   7. S 8. S

p. 62
A 1. d 2. b 3. b 4. d 5. c 6. d
   7. a 8. d
B 1. d 2. g 3. h 4. a 5. f 6. e
   7. b 8. c

p. 65
1. c 2. b 3. a 4. c 5. a 6. a
   7. b 8. d

p. 66
A 1. b 2. b 3. a 4. d 5. d 6. d
   7. b 8. d
B 1. m 2. j 3. c 4. l 5. f 6. i 7. e
   8. g 9. d 10. k 11. b 12. n 13. h
   14. a 15. o
C 1. S 2. D 3. S 4. S 5. D 6. S
   7. S 8. D 9. D 10. D 11. D
   12. D 13. D 14. S 15. D

UNIT 4

p. 72
A 1. S 2. D 3. S 4. S 5. D 6. S
   7. D 8. S
B 1. f 2. g 3. b 4. h 5. e 6. c
   7. d 8. a

p. 76
A 1. h 2. b 3. a 4. c 5. g 6. e
   7. f 8. d
B 1. a 2. c 3. h 4. g 5. f 6. b
   7. e 8. d

p. 80
A 1. c 2. b 3. e 4. f 5. g 6. h
   7. a 8. d
B 1. h 2. a 3. c 4. b 5. g 6. f
   7. d 8. e

p. 84
A 1. c 2. b 3. b 4. c 5. d 6. b
   7. a 8. a
B 1. b 2. d 3. c 4. a 5. d 6. d
   7. a 8. d

p. 88
1. b 2. c 3. f 4. a 5. d 6. e 7. h
   8. g
p. 89
A 1. b 2. b 3. d 4. d 5. b 6. a
   7. c 8. b 9. b 10. c
B 1. D 2. D 3. S 4. S 5. S 6. D
   7. S 8. D 9. S 10. S
C 1. b 2. d 3. d 4. a 5. a 6. c
   7. c 8. b

UNIT 5

p. 94
A 1. a 2. c 3. c 4. b 5. d 6. c
   7. b 8. d
B 1. D 2. D 3. S 4. S 5. S 6. D
   7. S 8. D

p. 98
A 1. d 2. g 3. c 4. b 5. a 6. e
   7. h 8. f

B 1. f 2. e 3. d 4. a 5. h 6. g
7. b 8. c

p. 102
A 1. c 2. b 3. d 4. c 5. d 6. b 7.
c 8. a
B 1. D 2. S 3. D 4. D 5. D 6. S
7. S 8. D

p. 106
A 1. a 2. g 3. c 4. e 5. f 6. d
7. h 8. b
B 1. c 2. e 3. f 4. g 5. a 6. h
7. b 8. d

p. 110
1. h 2. f 3. d 4. e 5. b 6. g 7. a
8. c

p. 110
A 1. d 2. b 3. c 4. b 5. c 6. d
7. b 8. a 9. a 10. d
B 1. g 2. i 3. a 4. o 5. b 6. n
7. m 8. k 9. c 10. c 11. f 12. d
13. h 14. j 15. l
C 1. S 2. S 3. S 4. S 5. D 6. D
7. D 8. S 9. D 10. D 11. D
12. D 13. S 14. D 15. D

UNIT 6

p. 116
A 1. D 2. D 3. S 4. D 5. D 6. S
7. D 8. D
B 1. g 2. b 3. c 4. a 5. e 6. f
7. d 8. h

p. 120
A 1. d 2. f 3. h 4. b 5. e 6. a
7. g 8. c
B 1. b 2. c 3. d 4. a 5. b 6. a
7. d 8. b

p. 124
A 1. S 2. D 3. S 4. S 5. D 6. D
7. D 8. S
B 1. b 2. e 3. c 4. h 5. g 6. a
7. f 8. d

p. 127
A 1. c 2. b 3. d 4. c 5. d 6. a
7. c 8. b
B 1. f 2. c 3. e 4. b 5. d 6. a
7. h 8. g

p. 131
1. c 2. c 3. b 4. a 5. a 6. b 7. c
8. a

p. 132
A 1. g 2. a 3. j 4. c 5. i 6. b
7. d 8. e 9. h 10. f
B 1. a 2. b 3. b 4. c 5. a 6. d
7. d 8. e 9. h 10. f
C 1. e 2. j 3. a 4. i 5. f 6. h 7. c
8. b 9. d 10. g

UNIT 7

p. 137
A 1. b 2. d 3. g 4. f 5. c 6. h
7. a 8. e
B 1. c 2. e 3. f 4. b 5. a 6. g
7. d 8. h

p. 141
A 1. c 2. a 3. a 4. b 5. a 6. a
7. d 8. b
B 1. D 2. D 3. D 4. S 5. D 6. S
7. D 8. D

p. 145
A 1. a 2. e 3. b 4. f 5. c 6. g
7. d 8. h
B 1. d 2. c 3. c 4. a 5. b 6. b
7. d 8. a

p. 150
A 1. S 2. D 3. D 4. D 5. D 6. S
7. D 8. D
B 1. c 2. f 3. d 4. a 5. e 6. g
7. h 8. b

p. 153
1. a 2. d 3. c 4. h 5. f 6. g 7. b
8. e

p. 154
A 1. d, a 2. d, b 3. a, b 4. b, c
5. c, a 6. a, b 7. d, c 8. c, a 9. d,
a 10. a, c 11. c, d 12. b, c
B 1. c 2. a 3. b 4. b 5. c 6. a
7. c 8. a 9. d 10. a 11. b 12. b
13. c 14. a 15. c
C 1. i 2. f 3. c 4. h 5. e 6. j 7. g
8. a 9. b 10. d

UNIT 8

p. 161
A 1. d 2. b 3. d 4. a 5. c 6. d
7. b 8. c
B 1. f 2. b 3. e 4. a 5. g 6. c
7. h 8. d

p. 165
A 1. a 2. g 3. b 4. h 5. e 6. c
7. d 8. f
B 1. D 2. S 3. D 4. S 5. S 6. D
7. S 8. D

p. 169
A 1. d 2. a 3. c 4. f 5. g 6. b
7. e 8. h
B 1. b 2. f 3. d 4. c 5. g 6. h
7. a 8. e

p. 174
A 1. d 2. a 3. b 4. d 5. c 6. b
7. d 8. b
B 1. e 2. d 3. g 4. h 5. c 6. f
7. a 8. b

p. 178
1. g 2. f 3. e 4. d 5. a 6. h 7. b
8. c

p. 179
A 1. j 2. e 3. c 4. f 5. h 6. b
7. a 8. d 9. g 10. i
B. 1. D 2. S 3. S 4. D 5. S 6. S
7. D 8. S 9. S 10. D 11. D
12. D 13. S 14. S 15. D 16. D
17. D 18. S 19. D 20. S
C 1. h 2. g 3. i 4. b 5. a 6. f
7. d 8. j 9. c 10. e

UNIT 9

p. 184
A 1. a 2. g 3. f 4. b 5. c 6. e
7. h 8. d
B 1. a 2. b 3. c 4. d 5. d 6. b
7. d 8. b

p. 188
A 1. b 2. b 3. b 4. a 5. b 6. b
7. a 8. d
B 1. d 2. c 3. e 4. f 5. g 6. h
7. a 8. b

p. 192
A 1. b 2. a 3. b 4. a 5. a 6. c
7. b 8. c
B 1. S 2. D 3. S 4. D 5. S 6. D
7. S 8. D

p. 196
A 1. h 2. c 3. g 4. d 5. e 6. b
7. f 8. a
B 1. g 2. f 3. b 4. c 5. h 6. a
7. e 8. d

p. 200
1. c 2. b 3. b 4. b 5. c 6. d 7. b
8. c

p. 200
A 1. a 2. d 3. c 4. b 5. a 6. d
7. c 8. a 9. a 10. c
B 1. d 2. g 3. a 4. b 5. j 6. e
7. c 8. i 9. h 10. f
C 1. a 2. h 3. i 4. b 5. e 6. d
7. g 8. c 9. j 10. f

UNIT 10

p. 205
A 1. S 2. S 3. D 4. D 5. S 6. D
7. D 8. D
B 1. d 2. c 3. d 4. b 5. a 6. b
7. d 8. d

p. 209
A 1. c 2. c 3. d 4. c 5. b 6. a
7. b 8. d

B 1. f 2. h 3. g 4. e 5. d 6. a
7. c 8. b

p. 213
A 1. a 2. g 3. c 4. f 5. b 6. h
7. e 8. d
B 1. c 2. a 3. d 4. c 5. b 6. c
7. a 8. b

p. 217
A 1. d 2. d 3. a 4. a 5. d 6. b
7. a 8. d
B 1. c 2. d 3. h 4. a 5. b 6. e
7. g 8. f

p. 221
1. e 2. b 3. d 4. c 5. g 6. f 7. a
8. h

p. 222
A 1. D 2. S 3. D 4. S 5. D 6. D
7. S 8. D 9. S 10. D 11. S 12. D
13. S 14. S 15. D 16. D 17. S
18. D 19. D 20. S
B 1. d 2. a 3. d 4. b 5. a 6. a
7. d 8. a 9. d 10. a
C 1. c 2. e 3. a 4. d 5. f 6. b
7. h 8. g

UNIT 11

p. 227
A 1. b 2. a 3. a 4. b 5. c 6. b
7. a 8. d
B 1. D 2. D 3. D 4. D 5. D
6. D 7. D 8. D

p. 231
A 1. a 2. g 3. b 4. h 5. e 6. c
7. d 8. f
B 1. c 2. d 3. b 4. c 5. a 6. a
7. b 8. d

p. 235
A 1. d 2. b 3. a 4. d 5. c 6. a
7. c 8. a
B 1. b 2. e 3. h 4. a 5. f 6. g
7. d 8. c

p. 238
A 1. a 2. d 3. e 4. b 5. h 6. c
7. f 8. g
B 1. S 2. D 3. S 4. S 5. D 6. S
7. D 8. D

p. 242
1. a 2. g 3. f 4. d 5. c 6. e 7. b
8. h

p. 243
A 1. d 2. a 3. c 4. d 5. d 6. b
7. d 8. d 9. a 10. b 11. c 12. c
13. a 14. c 15. d
B 1. D 2. D 3. D 4. S 5. D 6. S
7. S 8. S 9. D 10. S
C 1. f 2. b 3. e 4. g 5. i 6. j 7. l
8. h 9. a 10. d 11. k 12. c

UNIT 12

p. 248
A 1. f 2. c 3. g 4. d 5. e 6. a
7. b 8. h
B 1. f 2. h 3. g 4. c 5. b 6. e
7. a 8. d

p. 253
A 1. a 2. g 3. c 4. b 5. f 6. d
7. e 8. h
B 1. c 2. f 3. h 4. e 5. d 6. g
7. a 8. b

p. 258
A 1. b 2. b 3. c 4. b 5. c 6. d
7. a 8. d
B 1. a 2. f 3. d 4. b 5. g 6. c
7. h 8. e

p. 262
A 1. b 2. c 3. a 4. b 5. c 6. b
7. d 8. c
B 1. S 2. D 3. S 4. D 5. D 6. S
7. D 8. D

p. 266
1. a 2. f 3. b 4. g 5. e 6. h 7. d
8. c

p. 266
A 1. b 2. b 3. d 4. a 5. c 6. a
7. d 8. a 9. d 10. c 11. b 12. d 13.
b 14. d 15. a 16. b
B 1. f 2. b 3. g 4. j 5. d 6. e 7. i
8. a 9. h 10. c
C 1. h 2. j 3. g 4. a 5. i 6. c 7. d
8. f 9. e 10. b

UNIT 13

p. 272
A 1. b 2. d 3. c 4. b 5. c 6. c
7. b 8. a
B 1. g 2. h 3. b 4. f 5. a 6. e
7. d 8. c

p. 276
A 1. c 2. b 3. f 4. g 5. a 6. h
7. e 8. d
B 1. D 2. D 3. D 4. S 5. D 6. S
7. S 8. S

p. 280
A 1. g 2. b 3. a 4. c 5. e 6. h
7. d 8. f
B 1. e 2. f 3. a 4. c 5. b 6. g
7. h 8. d

p. 284
A 1. e 2. a 3. b 4. g 5. c 6. h
7. f 8. d
B 1. a 2. b 3. d 4. d 5. b 6. c
7. a 8. b

p. 288
1. D 2. S 3. D 4. D 5. D 6. S
7. D 8. S

p. 288
A 1. g 2. h 3. c 4. m 5. j 6. e
7. k 8. i 9. a 10. b 11. n 12. f 13.
d 14. l 15. o

B 1. c 2. a 3. d 4. a 5. b 6. c
7. d 8. a 9. d 10. b
C 1. c 2. b 3. d 4. d 5. a 6. c
7. b 8. c 9. b 10. d

UNIT 14

p. 294
A 1. d 2. g 3. a 4. e 5. f 6. b
7. h 8. c
B 1. g 2. a 3. d 4. c 5. h 6. f
7. e 8. b

p. 299
A 1. S 2. D 3. S 4. D 5. D 6. D
7. S 8. S
B 1. d 2. a 3. f 4. c 5. e 6. h
7. g 8. b

p. 303
A 1. f 2. g 3. b 4. a 5. d 6. e
7. h 8. c
B 1. c 2. b 3. h 4. g 5. d 6. f
7. a 8. e

p. 307
A 1. a 2. a 3. c 4. c 5. d 6. c
7. b 8. b
B 1. D 2. S 3. S 4. D 5. D 6. D
7. D 8. S

p. 311
1. b 2. h 3. g 4. c 5. e 6. a 7. f 8. d

p. 312
A 1. a 2. c 3. b 4. d 5. d 6. b
7. b 8. d 9. c 10. b 11. a 12. d
B 1. a 2. b 3. h 4. i 5. d 6. e
7. f 8. c 9. g 10. j
C 1. D 2. S 3. D 4. D 5. S 6. S 7.
S 8. S 9. S 10. S

INDEX